BATTLESTAR GALACTICA

INVESTIGATING CULT TV

Series Editor: Stacey Abbott

The **Investigating Cult TV** series is a fresh forum for discussion and debate about the changing nature of cult television. It reconsiders cult television and its intricate networks of fandom by inviting authors to rethink how cult TV is conceived, produced, programmed and consumed. It also challenges traditional distinctions between cult and quality television.

Offering an accessible path through the intricacies and pleasures of cult TV, these books are for scholars, students, fans and TV watchers worldwide. They include close studies of individual contemporary television shows. They also reconsider genres at the heart of cult programming, such as science fiction, horror and fantasy, as well as genres like teen TV, animation and reality TV when these have strong claims to cult status. Books also examine themes or trends that are key to the past, present and future of cult television.

Ideas and submissions for **Investigating Cult TV** to
s.abbott@roehampton.ac.uk
p.brewster@blueyonder.co.uk

BATTLESTAR GALACTICA

Investigating Flesh, Spirit and Steel

EDITED BY
ROZ KAVENEY AND
JENNIFER STOY

I.B. TAURIS

LONDON · NEW YORK

Published in 2010 by I.B.Tauris & Co Ltd
6 Salem Road, London W2 4BU
175 Fifth Avenue, New York NY 10010
www.ibtauris.com

Distributed in the United States and Canada Exclusively by
Palgrave Macmillan,
175 Fifth Avenue, New York NY 10010

ISBN 978 1 84885 373 7

A full CIP record for this book is available from the British Library
A full CIP record is available from the Library of Congress

Library of Congress Catalog Card Number: available

Typeset by JCS Publishing Services Ltd, www.jcs-publishing.co.uk
Printed and bound in India by Replika Press Pvt. Ltd.

Contents

Contributors

Sérgio Dias Branco is Researcher in Film and Philosophy at the New University of Lisbon. He has taught film and television at the University of Kent, where he is completing a PhD in Film Studies on the aesthetics of television fiction series. His research has been presented at Yale University and the Universities of Nottingham and Glasgow, among others. Sérgio is the author of 'The Mosaic-Screen: Exploration and Definition', *Refractory* 14 (2008), and an invited member of the film analysis research group the Magnifying Class of the University of Oxford.

Karen K. Burrows is a Canadian prairie girl living on the British seaside, where she watches television for fun and profit. She is currently working on her DPhil in Media and Cultural Studies at the University of Sussex, exploring the political implications of the representation of the female spy on television.

Benjamin Halligan completed his MPhil and PhD in the Department of Theatre, Film and Television Studies at Aberystwyth University and is Senior Lecturer in the School of Media, Music and Performance at the University of Salford. His critical biography *Michael Reeves* (Manchester University Press) was published in 2003 and the co-edited collection *Messing Up the Paintwork: The Aesthetics and Politics of Mark E. Smith and The Fall* (Ashgate) in 2010. Other areas of recent publication include Andrei Tarkovsky's aesthetics, Socialist Realism, New Hollywood and underground cinema, questions of theatre etiquette and the Sarajevo Documentary School.

Matthew Jones is a PhD candidate at the University of Manchester's Centre for Screen Studies. His current research investigates the British interpretation of US science fiction cinema from the 1950s. He also has an MA in Screen Studies and a BA(Hons) in Drama, both also from the University of Manchester.

Lorna Jowett is a Senior Lecturer in Media at the University of Northampton, where she teaches some of her favourite things, including science fiction, horror and television. Her research interests focus on genre and gender across film, television, and literature

Roz Kaveney is a well-known writer, reviewer and activist. Her books include *Superheroes!* (I.B.Tauris, 2007), *Teen Dreams* (I.B.Tauris, 2006) and *Reading the Vampire Slayer* (I.B.Tauris, 2003).

Steven Rawle is a Lecturer in Film Studies at York St John University. He is the co-author of *Basics Film-Making: The Language of Film* (AVA, 2010) and has published work on *Eternal Sunshine of the Spotless Mind* and transnational cinema, particularly Japanese cult genres. He has a particular interest in cinematic memory and repetition and how all of this has happened before and will happen again.

Geoff Ryman is an award-winning writer of science fiction, fantasy and less classifiable fiction. His novels include *Was* (Gollancz, 1992), *253* (Flamingo, 1998), *Air* (Gollancz, 2006), *The Child Garden* (Gollancz, 2005) and *The King's Last Song* (Harper, 2007).

Jennifer Stoy is an independent writer and editor whose works have appeared in other volumes of the Investigating Cult TV series, including *Reading the Vampire Slayer*. She has an MA in English from the University of California, Santa Barbara.

Of Great Zeitgeist and Bad Faith

An Introduction to *Battlestar Galactica*

JENNIFER STOY

Introducing a television series as critically influential as the reimagined *Battlestar Galactica* (*BSG*) in the space of ten thousand words is a troublesome undertaking. What, after all, does one focus on? The typical accolades given to a quality television series – stories, acting, production values, directing? Does one move away from the textual to focus instead on the media-historical moment that turned *Battlestar Galactica* into a science fiction television series that transcended the usual mainstream critics' supercilious disregard for science fiction, or its place in television as a watershed series that presaged a dramatic rise in standards for American basic cable drama? And to add yet another layer to the enterprise, what if the series' second half went dramatically quite wrong in the eyes of only *some* critics but not others?

This last problem is my own particular one; when I agreed to co-edit this volume, *BSG* was in its third season and, despite occasional troublesome wobbles (the interminable romantic quadrangle between Lee Adama, Kara 'Starbuck' Thrace, Anastasia 'Dee' Dualla, and Samuel Anders), the show appeared to remain close to its strong base as an allegory of the bleak sociopolitical moment following 9/11. Flashing forward two years, rather like in 'Lay Down Your Burdens (Part Two)' (2.20), and I find myself evaluating a Peabody Award-winning television series, a series with such cachet that the United Nations asked members of the production team to speak with them on a panel[1] – and ultimately finding it lacking in critical ways.

I do not even deny that the first two seasons of *Battlestar Galactica* were a relevation during a period when genre television was otherwise at a nadir; they brought the art of political commentary back to television science fiction in a way that had been missing for years. In particular, Ronald D. Moore and David Eick's choice to pay higher-quality actors – namely Edward James Olmos and Mary McDonnell – to play their leads, rather than spending their limited budget on special effects, and their insistence on aiming to be part of a 'quality' television tradition like *The West Wing* or *The Shield* rather than the science fiction tradition that their remake of a corny 1970s *Star Wars* knock-off fitted into more naturally, had a powerful effect on the media landscape, especially in the realm of American basic cable television. Suddenly, Oscar-calibre actresses over forty, such as Holly Hunter and Glenn Close, populate the basic cable landscape and are awarded for their choices with Emmy nominations, and Matthew Weiner's low-rated high-concept series (*Mad Men*) about advertising executives in the 1960s on channels that no one inside or outside the United States have ever heard of win Best Drama Emmys, partially because Moore and Eick refused to conform to what a *Battlestar Galactica* remake *should* look like.

As an example of what Moore and Eick's *BSG* does look like, consider the episode 'Downloaded' (2.18), my favourite episode of the series. 'Downloaded' reintroduces us to the Number Six we last saw in the miniseries, seducing Baltar for information on Colonial defences, betraying him and protecting him at the cost of her life. While her image and many of her mannerism are preserved in the Head Six[2] throughout the show's narrative, in 'Downloaded' we learn that the physical Six, now known as Caprica Six, is resurrected after the original attacks on the Twelve Colonies, and that she is now a haunted robot femme fatale. Her previous zeal for the Cylon genocides has dissolved and, like Baltar, she is constantly visited by a version of her lost love, whom she believes to be dead. Similar to Head Six, Head Baltar is constantly manipulating and reassuring Caprica Six for reasons that are unclear. Far from being the cliché of the sexy yet deadly female robot shown in so many of the show's promotional material, Caprica Six gains a pathos and humanity far beyond her origins, as a fully realized character.

Later in the episode, Caprica Six meets another Cylon who has grown disillusioned with genocide – the Eight the viewer knows as Boomer/Sharon Valerii. After a traumatic conflict between the two human-sympathizing Cylons, the terrorist human resistance still on Caprica, and the genocidal representative of Cylon leadership, D'Anna Biers/Three, the two women decide to create a political countermovement to end the war between human and Cylon – a rare note of hope in a series that is known for its grim darkness. Even in lighting, where the alliance between Boomer and Caprica is marked by clasped hands and the sudden influx of bright sunshine,[3] 'Downloaded' ends on a bright note and gives even partial critics like myself much to cheer about.

First, the narrative focus in the episode is on female characters, a well-known rarity in all science fiction and an especial rarity in televisual sci-fi. In this case, even the secondary plot of 'Downloaded' is focused on women; the Eight we later come to know as Athena gives birth to her hybrid child, Hera. Hera is promptly kidnapped and given to another woman to raise by Laura Roslin, who chooses not to involve Bill Adama in this transaction at all, instead relying on her female aide, Tory Foster, for the occasion; further, she asserts her power over the male doctor involved by ordering him to tell Athena that the child has died. While Roslin is usually more subtle in her machinations, her use of power is not unusual in her character arc and is presented in an ambivalent, complicated manner that is usually reserved for male leaders.

Another point in the episode's favour is the way the women's concerns are broad, rather than narrow. Motherhood and relationships to men are certainly a concern in the episode.

However, the primary focus is on the relationships between the various women – particularly Boomer and Caprica Six and their disenchantment with Cylon eliminationist ideology, as well as their dislike of the bullying D'Anna Biers – and the ethical dilemmas engendered by these interactions. The episode is not undermined by the weaknesses of later seasons, where female interest in anything besides various forms of motherhood and men is a rarity.

Writing and acting are also first rate; the actresses, especially the excellent Tricia Helfer, are given free rein to showcase their characters' depth. Mary McDonnell gets a rare chance to show off Roslin without Adama about, though – as always – Roslin is almost never permitted to be the primary character that many of the other female characters are allowed to be. 'Downloaded' also has strong writing that takes a standard tactic of science fiction television – the point of view shift episode – and applies it with remarkable strength. Rather than break away from the Cylons when a human – in this case, Sam Anders – enters the narrative, the primary action stays with Boomer and Caprica Six. Their ethical choices and relationship remain what the audience is supposed to focus upon, even when a more typical protagonist enters the scene. Cylon motivation becomes more complex, and is somewhat poignant in light of the showrunners' decision to make the Cavil-model responsible for duping the Cylons into genocide in Season Four.

Episodes such as 'Downloaded' also crystallize why so many critics adored *Battlestar Galactica*. When you compare it to the two episodes of *Grey's Anatomy* nominated for Best Writing in a Dramatic Series in 2006 by the Emmy Awards, 'Downloaded' was robbed of the mainstream acclaim it deserved. One should note, though, that *BSG* did garner two Emmy writing nominations during its run, one in 2007 for 'Occupation/Precipice' (3.01/02) and 'Six of One' (4.02), so it would be inaccurate to say that the show completely missed mainstream attention.

However, I cannot pretend that 'Downloaded' is what the series always was; in rewatching the entire series, I counted at least eight episodes where drunken actions were a plot driver, and the occasional plot hole from early seasons reminds us that Moore and Eick perhaps did not plot the full arc of their series meticulously – or even with the occasional backward glance to avoid embarrassing themselves. For example, Baltar tests the final Cylon, Ellen Tigh, with his working Cylon detector in 'Tigh Me Up, Tigh Me Down' (1.09). He informs the audience via a conversation with Head Six that he'll never tell anyone the true results of the test, but his later wild scrambling to discover if he is a Cylon and the identities of the Final Five then become incomprehensible and lead one to assume that the test was negative. We know the Cylon detector works: it has previously identified Boomer as a Cylon. How are we then to explain Baltar's actions? If he was aware that Ellen Tigh was a Cylon – which he should have been – why didn't the man seek her out during the Cylon occupation of New Caprica? Or mention to D'Anna that he knew at least one of the Final Five during their frantic search for the Five in Season Three when he was so desperate to discover if he himself were Cylon?

The most likely answer is that the writers forgot the episode, and anyway the ambiguous results allowed them to retcon an explanation – for example, that the Final Five had genetic makeups different from the other seven models that would not be detectable. Still, it is a useful example of the writerly sloppiness that marks so much of the later *BSG* and will have a significant impact upon the show's legacy.

But, putting various episodes against each other and pointing out the increased carelessness in later seasons is not precisely the introduction that should be written, either. As with many other television shows since the mainstream popularity of the internet, critical comment from professional critics *and* from everyday viewers have become increasingly part of the creative process for television. Among genre television shows in particular, this dialogue can literally make or break a show. In 2009, for example, two shows with 'louder' fanbases – NBC's *Chuck* and Fox's *Dollhouse* – were renewed by their respective networks, as compared to similar low-rated niche shows such as *Terminator: The Sarah Connor Chronicles*, or *Life*. Both network presidents claimed that these fanbases were important to their decisions, with NBC's Ben Silverman saying of *Chuck*, 'the demand for Chuck that came out of the online community, the critical press and our advertising base made us have to pick up that show' (Sepinwall); to ignore the audience and the critics in the case of *Battlestar Galactica* is to ignore information crucial to understanding the show as it unfolded.

Hence, I feel that three most important things to cover in this introduction to *Battlestar Galactica* are: the genuine accomplishments of the series, the increasingly large failings of the series in its second half, and also how the critics and the audience shaped the perception of the series in a way that contributed to the troubles that the show had in its second half. In making such serious charges against a series widely (and rightly) viewed as a watershed for television science fiction, spending a lengthy section of my introduction overviewing the series would be unhelpful; my overview to the series' plots can thus be found in the appendix Episode Guide.

Battlestar Galactica: Its Triumphs

A typical moment of triumph for *Battlestar Galactica* in the press happened in 2006, when fellow Peabody Award recipient Matt Stone of *South Park* spent his part of the acceptance speech 'praising' the creative team of *BSG*, saying, 'I think Trey and I will always be grateful to the Peabody Awards for introducing us to *Battlestar Galactica*' (Woodson). Indeed, coming after the second season as it did, Stone's praises were the icing on two creatively strong seasons of science fiction television that had earned the title of Best Television Show of 2005 from *Time* magazine, with critic James Poniewozik saying, 'Most of you probably think this entry has got to be a joke. The rest of you have actually watched the show.'

What was it about the series' run through 2005 that earned such plaudits from mainstream television critics, whose phobia of science fiction is such that even Poniewozik must deem the original *Battlestar Galactica* as 'a cheesy '70s *Star Wars* clone' and apologize for 'the basic-cable budget' of the show? The strengths of the series were never so visible as they were during the first two seasons, and the praise of 2005 came during the initial arc that worked as a single story and ended with the cliffhanger of 'Pegasus' (2.10). Using that time frame, it is not difficult to isolate the strengths of *BSG*.

First, there is the strong allegorical exploration of the American political moment surrounding the fallout from George W. Bush's disputed election in 2000, the Al Qaeda attacks of 9/11 and the invasion and occupation of Iraq in 2003. While using the events of the original 1970s *Battlestar Galactica* as a rough base, where the citizens of the Twelve Colonies of Kobol are escaping towards Earth after the Cylons destroy their civilization and kill all but a few of their people, the tone and allegorical connections are inextricable from 9/11 and the American sociopolitical zeitgeist of the time – and nobody on television did it better. The reimagined Cylons become indistinguishable biological robots whose religious fervour inspires them, strongly opposed to the 'false' religion of the Colonial humans as well as the decadence of Colonial civilization. Meanwhile, the ostensibly secular Colonial society has a strong fundamentalist minority that the new president, Laura Roslin, ends up manipulating for political gain that she feels necessary to save her people. Roslin's place in the succession – forty-three – is an oblique reference to George W. Bush's presidential number, and her fundamentalist ties are most certainly meant to evoke the former American president.

Nor is this the only parallel the series draws between the historical moment and itself. Issues of torture, electoral democratic values in a crisis and the relationship between the military and democratic in a 'long emergency' such as the one faced in *BSG* and the United States after 9/11 are all used as part of *Galactica*'s plots. Not coincidentally, many of these integrative, allegorical episodes are among the strongest of the series.

An example of an early episode that uses American political topics to create a fully realized episode within the *BSG* universe, and that still intelligently addresses the topic at hand is 'Flesh and Bone' (1.08), which deals with torture. In this episode, a Cylon known as Leoben Conroy is found in the fleet, and when captured, claimed that a nuclear warhead was within the fleet and shortly due to go off. Roslin, upon hearing this news, assigns Starbuck to interrogate the prisoner. In the same ticking time bomb scenario as in most seasons of *24*, *BSG* also has the protagonist Starbuck resort to torture. Starbuck has Marines hold Leoben underwater, presaging the debate over the American use of waterboarding and 'enhanced interrogation techniques'. However, unlike *24* and its glorification of torture,[4] the psychological effects of using torture are immediately apparent upon Starbuck, and Leoben uses those effects against her, telling her that their destinies are intertwined, and getting under her skin. Further, the torture is useless: Leoben is lying about the existence of a nuclear warhead and the entire sequence appears to be a sort of test of moral character, one that the Colonials fail. For them, the threat of danger outweighs the ethics that suggest that democracies do not torture.

Toni Graphia, writer of the episode, adds another layer to this examination of torture and prisoner ethics in war by the actions of President Roslin. Roslin is suffering her own trials; already dying of cancer, she is now having strange dreams that have all concerned Leoben Conroy in some way, but their meaning is unclear. Her actions are as ambiguous as Starbuck's: when she arrives at the interrogation scene to find Starbuck torturing Leoben, she immediately puts a stop to the torture with a strong air of disapproval. However, she then orders the execution of Leoben, much to Starbuck's dismay.

Leoben, however, has one last card to play, and when he explosively embraces Roslin, he whispers 'Adama is a Cylon', sowing a seed of paranoia in the president's mind that plays out in the next episode, 'Tigh Me Up, Tigh Me Down', where – ironically – Adama may be surrounded by Cylons in the form of Saul and Ellen Tigh, but is most certainly not one himself. Overall, the episode is a standout in a strong sequence of episodes, utilizing the talents of Katee Sackhoff and Mary McDonnell to their utmost and examining with nuance the idea of prisoner treatment during war while at the same time being able to innovate to some extent with this narrative, by making it about women.

Indeed, one of the triumphs *Battlestar Galactica* manages as science fiction television in its early seasons is its ability to create complex female characters, give them plots, and when using classic sexist science fiction clichés – such as sexy blonde robot Number Six – to subvert the power dynamics within those clichés. To avoid going over territory that many of the contributors to this volume so ably cover, and to give credit where credit is due in the weaker second half of the series, Ellen Tigh is a particular example of *BSG's* gender experiments. While she fits into a certain stereotype – the outspoken boozy blonde who would probably be dubbed a 'cougar' in the media landscape of the late 2000s – Ellen Tigh is an able politician for her own needs, and there is something potentially revolutionary to the idea that Moore and Eick make the ultimate Cylon a middle-aged woman whose previous talents seemed to be causing trouble among the leadership of the fleet, sexual prowess and alcoholism. Turning the grand narrative of the Cylons from a Miltonian 'evil, be thou my good' or even sheer belief in Nietschzean *ubermenschen* gone wrong into a family narrative where the slightly socially outré Tigh pairing had the technical know-how to create biological resurrection as well as marry Cylon technology with organic flesh has a certain flair. Of course, this flair has a lot to do with *BSG's* unwavering ability to give the best character revelations to the older characters, which includes the Tighs as well as Adama and Roslin, which is not executed well, leading to more writing failures. Had Ellen Tigh's creation of the Cylons led to more than the kidnapping of Hera, a squabble-filled reunion with her husband and their unconventional but not ground-shaking eternal love, and a rather typical search narrative to end the series, it might have been a far stronger move than it turned out to be, but in those late episodes the writers seemed incapable of making moves that had more than a single-episode 'wow' factor to them.

In general, it seems the series was more willing to challenge gender stereotypes in the first half of the show – Roslin is a consummate politician and was formerly the uncowed mistress of the former president, as revealed in 'Epiphanies' (2.13) and has no problem calling for Admiral Cain's execution in 'Resurrection Ship (Part One)' (2.11); Head Six is far stronger than Baltar in their relationship and regularly dominates him; Starbuck, not Lee, is the unconventional-thinking military genius; even the Cylons appeared dominated by the strong-willed, fast-talking D'Anna Biers instead of the nihilistic Brother Cavil who takes the reins during the second half of the show. While many of these characters are interested in species survival, none of them are mothers, nor is there a fetishistic concern about motherhood that is so typical in media representation of women and in many science fiction programmes.

The final 'triumph' of *Battlestar Galactica* is the series' uncanny ability to influence the media landscape around it, despite its modest viewership and genre counting against it in mainstream television – a realm where viewer numbers and location on the dial count for so much. When the show began its run in 2004, the idea of resurrecting mediocre or worse media properties was even more of a joke than in the 1990s, when every nostalgia-inducing American television show was being made into a bad movie – *Wild Wild West*, *The Brady Bunch Movie*, and so on.

Given the general disregard of the source material, the idea that *Battlestar Galactica* could 'reimagine' itself – even under the care of a moderately accomplished sci-fi television creator such as Ronald D. Moore[5] – was of interest to no one except true science fiction fans. Yet now, reimagining old properties (especially ones with dubious pasts) for wild commercial success[6] is a mainstream Hollywood technique and one that has resurrected more than one classic science fiction franchise. In near-parallel to Moore and Eick's *BSG*, Russell T. Davies brought back the venerable British science fiction classic *Doctor Who* with many of the same tactics as Moore and Eick. The Ninth Doctor is haunted, thanks to a 'Time War' that has rendered his species, the Time Lords, extinct at the hands of the Whovian nemeses, the Daleks, who are now supposedly equally extinct. That neither the Time Lords nor the Daleks are quite as extinct as first claimed should surprise no science fiction enthusiast, but the initial bleakness of the reimagined *Who* as well as the long plots shares some significant DNA with the reimagined *BSG*.

One even sees a trace of *Battlestar Galactica*'s long shadow in Christopher Nolan's *The Dark Knight*, the most commercially successful movie of the last decade. While the Batman comics have always had some of the darkest writing in the medium, the Batman films had slipped into comic irrelevance following *Batman and Robin*. Nolan's remake of the series has other progenitors, of course, but when looking at these three together, the pattern of how dark remakes of classic genre media translated into commercial and critical success is quite clear.

Yet, for every *Dark Knight*, there is a 'reimagined' *Transformers* to account for; having discussed the triumphs of *Battlestar Galactica*, it is now time to discuss its shortcomings.

Battlestar Galactica: Its Mistakes

Nitpicking science fiction shows and their plot inconsistencies and failures in coherent science is a stereotypical fan pastime. My issues with *BSG* fall at a somewhat higher level. The three main areas where *Battlestar Galactica* became increasingly, even damagingly, weak as a series are in its blindness to typical representational issues endemic to science fiction, sloppy theology and world building, and pacing issues.

The representational issue is particularly unfortunate because, as I pointed out earlier in this chapter, in the first two seasons,

BSG's portrayal of women and its willingness to interrogate stereotypes was one of its great strengths. Succumbing to the sloppiness that is permitted to a television production under stresses like the WGA writers' strike of 2006/7 and the Sci-Fi Network's whimsies in programming is more of a disappointment, given the higher standards to which *BSG* is held by critics. Further, if Ronald D. Moore's public statements at San Diego Comic-Con 2005[7] are to be taken at face value, many missteps, such as making the religious fundamentalist Gemenese largely black, are a case of laziness, not malice – but this is not a reason to excuse them.

So why is there little doubt that hegemonic values of homophobia, sexism and racism exist in the series, despite Jane Espenson's shock that 'anyone' could call the show woman-hating?[8] One need only look at the body count, where the female bodies outweigh the male bodies, bodies of colour are less regarded than white bodies, and the closeted gay characters with audience sympathy both died horrible, violent deaths compared to the normal (and usually violent) *BSG* death.

While *every* male character in the credit sequence survived, as well as the overwhelming majority of high-profile male characters such as Tyrol and Tigh, not a *single* credited female character made it to the end of *Battlestar Galactica* without dying once – and most of them didn't have the Cylon trick of resurrection to fall back on. Caprica Six and Athena may survive and thrive on prehistoric Earth, but their deaths are unpleasant and their resurrections and thriving tied to their relationships with human men such as Baltar and Helo.

Meanwhile Boomer is dead without hope of resurrection. Roslin is dead; Starbuck has been dead for a long time without the audience or the character realizing it and, worse yet, all of the secondary female characters that the audience cares about are dead: Dee, Kat, Cally, Racetrack and, perhaps most objectionably of all, there is Tory's death in the finale. Tory's death is perhaps a long time coming – she murdered her fellow Cylon Tyrol's wife Cally in 'The Ties That Bind' (4.03) and concealed it ruthlessly.

However, unlike many deaths in the series, Tory's death at the hands of a man is literal – Tyrol throttles her to death in a frankly idiotic move that leads to a bloodbath and destroys a chance at peace. Also, while Tory's sins are grave, they are not beyond the pale on a show where the (female) president tells her (male) military leader to murder his (female) superior in a burst of *realpolitik*, or where Tory's counterpart Saul Tigh has murdered his wife for treachery. But, unlike Saul Tigh, the woman of colour is unforgiven and unforgivable; instead, her white male murderer is allowed to go free with murmurings of sympathy from the major characters of the show.

One might point out that another woman of colour – Boomer – is murdered in 'Daybreak (Part Two)' (4.20); there is equally little censure when Athena murders her for kidnapping Hera, even though Boomer is returning Hera at the time. What this says about the moral universe of *Battlestar Galactica*, where characters can apparently get away with murder if they are an audience or writer favourite, I leave to the imagination of my readers. The point I will make is that the reactions to these murders is sloppy for a show that prides itself on ambiguity and thoughtfulness. Perhaps some negative judgement on Tyrol for murdering someone . . . or at least, for causing a nearly life-extinguishing bloodbath because he couldn't control his bloodlust for ten minutes . . . might have been a better choice.

It is also disappointing in general that after the interesting and genre-refuting narratives that the female characters have in the first half of the series, the writers seem unable to be creative any further and lapse back into the same sexist clichés. Roslin, the politician, dies tragically. But first she must first understand love – classic heterosexual coupled love – before she can be a great leader, we're informed in 'The Hub' (4.09), and so pairs off with Adama before her death from cancer. Caprica Six, leader of an insurgent political movement among her people, suffers a miscarriage of Tigh's child and is given another man – Baltar – as a dubious consolation prize once the writers reunite their eternal 'meant-to-be' couple in the form of Saul and Ellen Tigh.

Even the female characters who survive and thrive, Athena and Hera Agathon, are a disappointment, as the writers turn to the domestic – a mother who will even commit murder for her child, and a special child whose 'special' fate is to be the mother of an entire species – as reward. That it did not occur to the writers that, among the fascinating array of female characters that *BSG* created, it was a dubious choice to allow the only two to end up happy to be the two that most strictly hew to acceptable, traditional gender roles demonstrates those slapdash writing choices that continually mar the later *BSG*.

Nor do queer characters – such as they are – fare any better. *None* of the four gay-identified characters on the show[9] is actually identified as such during aired episodes of the show. During 'Razor' (4.00), we may infer the nature of the relationship between Cain and Gina, but it is never explicit, and the relationship between Gaeta and Hoshi is only mentioned during the webisodes of 'The Face of the Enemy'. In a television era where mainstream darling *Grey's Anatomy* continues to make fumbling attempts to include queer characters as regulars with storylines, the supposedly more avant-garde *BSG* erases and closets them – an odd choice, given that sexuality in the military and the American policy of 'Don't Ask, Don't Tell' remains an extremely hot political topic of the sort that the series usually embraced.

Worse still are the deaths, which play into typical queer death stereotypes. Gaeta, Cain and Gina all die extremely violent deaths on a show that kills characters with gusto. Cain is murdered by Gina, whom she has condemned to torture and rape. Gina commits suicide with a nuclear warhead. Gaeta is executed for treason after committing a mutiny. The sop of letting Hoshi, the most obscure of the four characters, live and temporarily act as admiral of the fleet while Adama and his crew rescue Hera Agathon does not particularly ameliorate this situation. Once again, these representational choices are conservative and typical and do not live up to the mythos of *Battlestar Galactica* being uniquely high-quality science fiction.

Race is another battlefield for *BSG* where the series does not show well. The death of Tory Foster is charged, not simply because of the character's gender, but because of her race and the way that her narrative fits into that of the 'tragic mulatta'.[10] Even as someone who never liked the character, the fact that she was twice as ruthless as her white male predecessor and narratively set up to take the fall for some of Roslin's more heinous decisions – attempting to rig the election and kidnapping Hera Agathon – raises alarms for me. Why is the woman of colour among the Final Five Cylons the xenophobe who believes in Cylon superiority? Why isn't it Anders?

These objections might have narrative reasons, but the treatment of the other Cylon who is not white – Number Four, Simon – is also suspect. Simon is a non-character; apart from in 'The Farm' (2.05), he exists as a henchman background character who never makes a particular impression compared to the other bad guy Cylons, even the deliberately Milquetoast Five, Aaron Doral. It did not have to be this way. 'The Farm' established a bond between Four and Starbuck before his dubious medical rape of her, but the series made the creative choice to have Starbuck's true Cylon bond to be with blond, white Leoben Conroy (equally guilty of sexual misconduct with Starbuck), which does not build confidence that the writers made attempts to stretch their characters of colour beyond stereotype.

The Eights are a little more complicated; time and again, Grace Park's character(s) get the most consistent writing on the show, but once again appearances make it trickier. For example, in 'Kobol's Last Gleaming (Part Two)' (1.13), Boomer is confronted by a group of naked, naive versions of herself who declare love for her and seem unable to realize that Boomer has delivered a nuclear bomb to destroy their basestar. The Eight model's interest in nudity becomes a childish joke; she, the beautiful small Asian woman, is the only Cylon to run about nude. This destroys the idea that Ronald D. Moore floated about this,[11] that Cylons do not care about modesty. Instead, it appears that only beautiful Cylon women who fit stereotypes about Asian women do not care about modesty.

In summation, like Joss Whedon before them, Ronald D. Moore and David Eick take some pleasure and critical acclaim for representational progress, while the typical representational prejudices of genre television remain. As my co-editor Roz Kaveney points out, fanboy creators are often prone to this error, though at least – unlike Whedon – Moore and Eick do not spend an inordinate amount of time declaiming themselves as feminists. There is a certain level of disappointment in realizing that 'the best show on television' contains few or no characters of colour, kills all the women and erases the gay characters, when turgid, conventional network soap operas such as *Grey's Anatomy* can focus on a female character, have a large number of prominent characters of colour and attempt to have regular out gay characters.

This sloppy conventionality also infects several other areas of the show that are perhaps less controversial for audiences and critics to debate. Chief among them is the incredible ignorance and carelessness of the theology and mythology within the show. This is extraordinarily problematic, given that religious concerns are a prominent and recurring theme on the show, starting with the genocidal attacks that set off the entire plot of the reimagined *BSG*.

One of the constant actions of the series is to examine a culture clash of religions that has parallels with the clash between American Christianity and Islamic fundamentalism. Nor do Moore and Eick shy away from religion in the series; many, if not most of the characters are devout believers in some religion or other, and the battle for Gaius Baltar's soul between his atheistic materialist philosophy and the Cylon monotheism preached by Head Six is a major storyline that ripples out into most plots. Further, the difference between the more religious, monotheistic Cylons and the less religious, polytheistic Colonials is a key theme of the entire series. In short, the theology and mythology is not a minor theme that only concerns a few characters: it colours and motivates the entire show, which is why it is that much worse that Moore and Eick so bungled things.

The key way things became problematic is in the choice that Moore and Eick made for the 'correct' theological force in their mythic universe. Ignoring the fact that devotion to the Cylon God and that his (of course the Cylon God is male and obsessed with female reproduction, as apparently are the gods of the Colonial people, according to their fundamentalists) exploitation led directly to the original genocide in the miniseries, Moore and Eick choose to make the mysterious Head Six and Head Baltar to be true emissaries of the actually existing and correct Cylon God. This deity has morphed into a wishy-washy liberal type that seems far too close to a non-denominational Christian/theist interpretation of God by an American raised in a Protestant tradition, rather than anything that organically arises from the series or from the original allegory that links Cylons to Muslims and Colonials to American Christians. There is also an extremely troubling anti-scepticism, pro-religion turn that shows up in the clunky final scene of 'Daybreak (Part Two)', where Head Six and Head Baltar follow Ron Moore around Manhattan, discussing how current humanity is doomed because of humankind's interest in gadgetry and robots. Excessive religious devotion and how it can be manipulated to do evil, the way that Cavil used religion to convince the other Cylons to kill billions of people, is conveniently off the table.

I think I speak for anyone with any training in Christianity or general religious or mythology studies when I suggest that perhaps the reason we are doomed is because Lee Adama and the other humans decided to die of cholera and tuberculosis by sending their spaceships into the sun instead of using their superior technology to maintain a history of why Colonial civilization and the previous Cylon civilization annihilated itself in nuclear war. Wrapping it in gauzy mystic theism does not impress, especially when one considers that the final ten episodes of *BSG* had the bad luck to air against the third season of *Big Love*, a television series that is also about religion (and in a much more primary way than *BSG*), but, unlike *BSG*, takes the ambiguities and irrationalities of religion seriously and does not assume a cheery pluralistic way out.

One example of this is how the polytheism of the Colonial Fleet is allowed to lapse almost completely as a serious plot force by the third season. Roslin, the supposed true believer in polytheism, simply seems anti-monotheist because the Colonial monotheist sect is run by a man she personally dislikes by 'Faith' (4.06). Indeed, the cosmology preached by Baltar seems to comfort her greatly. This contrasts with *Big Love*, where the idea of being excommunicated from the LDS church causes the lead female character Barb (who is also over forty and a cancer survivor with intense personal conflicts) personal agony, even though she has been inactive in her church for nearly a decade and believes in polygamy, in strong opposition to the mainstream church. Perhaps Roslin is never a strong believer in her polytheistic gods . . . but from someone who believes in Pythia to such an extent that she is willing to send Starbuck to her death in 'Kobol's Last Gleaming (Part One)' (1.12) for that faith, the lack of conflict jars.

As with so many failures in the show, it is 'Daybreak (Part Two)' that is the most problematic. In the previously mentioned final scene, Ronald D. Moore walks through Manhattan, with Head Baltar and Head Six commenting on the actions of the series, which is revealed to have taken place 150,000 years before the present day. The mysteries of who or what these characters are is revealed – Moore and Eick go with the simple choice. They are divine emissaries of the one god of the Cylons, and their point of view of events has always been the most correct. Apparently, the genocide of billions of both biological Cylons and Colonial humans came to pass and was acceptable in order that Hera Agathon, the half-human, half-Cylon hybrid, can become Eve[12] and perhaps end 'the cycle', a mysterious set of events that sentient humans apparently always repeat. Yet, as Baltar begins preaching, the one god of the Cylons is a good god, and his will and actions have been shaping things since the beginning . . . and this is, overall, a good thing.

The implications are troubling. First, the audience must accept that the Cylon God is the one true god and that, via not-sobenign neglect, he allowed Cavil to kill billions of human beings in his name, but cares enough about the two or more species in his care to have a plan, which primarily consists of getting *one* human and *one* Cylon to fall in love and have a child in an elaborate scheme that comes uncomfortably close to a Bond villain parody. When one considers that Karl 'Helo' Agathon was already in unrequited love with the Boomer version of Sharon Valerii, it raises the question of why an omniscient, all-powerful god with an obsession with reproduction could not simply arrange a *Robinson Crusoe*-style situation where Helo and Athena were lost in space together and the obvious came to pass. Further, the usual dodge of free will is even more unsatisfying than usual – if the one true god can spend his time breaking down Gaius Baltar to become his tool, could he not have sent his representatives to manipulate the birth of Hera Agathon and send a battlestar full of castaways to our planet, à la *Lost*, if that is the most important thing? Moreover, why does the existence of Hera Agathon somehow justify the tens of billions of deaths that Moore and Eick's theology brushes away as 'the cycle' and blames on technology rather than religion, neglectful gods and the manipulation of both by cynics such Brother Cavil and, to a lesser extent, Laura Roslin? The standard complaints of Job apply more than usual to the situation that the Colonial Fleet suffers in *Battlestar Galactica*; the writers provide an answer that leaves open the question of whether the one god of the Cylons is anything other than a sadist and a bully.

Admittedly, *Battlestar Galactica* is neither the first nor last science fiction series to include a sadistic all-powerful bully as a deity. Moore and Eick, though, out of the same misguided mysticism that moves most of the finale, try to convince the audience that this deity is actually a good guy, which is much harder to swallow, especially when it's placed in the last scenes of a show that was initially about the perils of blind religious belief. If Roslin's faith that the gods have chosen her to lead the people is meant to raise questions about George W. Bush's religious fervour and the suffering that zeal caused for people around the world, what conclusions are we to draw? Roslin, after all, was right. Her life and death met the prophetic conditions that Pythia set, and all of her actions – including ending resurrection for the Cylons – were apparently quite right and divinely ordered.

It seems that the main trouble is that *Battlestar Galactica* blithely contradicted the grand allegorical points of earlier in the series, rendering the end message – and one cannot argue that a show that ends with 'Daybreak (Part Two)' isn't trying to communicate a grand social message – incoherent. How, precisely, are the viewers of *Battlestar Galactica* supposed to end the cycle? By shunning technology and giving up their Roombas and believing in a benevolently neglectful twelve-step god? The weakness of the theology renders Moore and Eick's grand ethical lesson trite, ambiguous and without the courage of its own convictions.

There are further mythological/theological failures within *BSG*, such as the odd and ultimately pointless use of Greek and Roman deities to stand in for the Colonial ones, and the ignorance of the Mormon mythology that flavoured the original *BSG*. But instead, I would rather turn to another area of weakness that is purely televisual – the pacing failures of the show.

Like many other major weaknesses of *Battlestar Galactica*, the pacing ills are so objectionable because they contrast badly against earlier seasons of the show. The miniseries and the first twenty episodes of the series have phenomenal pacing; one critic declares 'it makes the original look downright ludicrous by comparison – and even for those of us who grew up when Starbuck was a man, there's just no getting around that' (Casamassina). From the original attack on the Twelve Colonies in the miniseries to Boomer's shocking attack on Adama in 'Kobol's Last Gleaming (Part Two)', the narrative moved organically towards its conclusions. Even in supposedly weaker episodes such as 'Colonial Day' (1.11) and 'Tigh Me Up, Tigh Me Down', the plot and character concerns of the show moved along at a good clip, building suspense, building and finishing stories. That narrative streak continued until its original conclusion – 'Home (Part Two)' (2.07). When Adama and Roslin are reconciled, with the map to Earth as given to them in the Tomb of Athena in their possession, a very distinct story is completed. Had the show been ended at that point, it would have felt like a finished story, even though there was clearly much more to *BSG's* universe to explore and more to the story. As allegory, as a story about flawed, fully realized and human characters (even the robot ones) and as a narrative, the miniseries and the twenty episodes that follow are a triumph – eighteen hours of nearly flawless television.

After the initial narrative vision, the series never recovers the same overarching narrative, nimbleness or suspense in pacing. This is not to say that every narrative arc after 'Home (Part Two)' is bad; but, beginning with the episodes between 'Epiphanies' (2.13) and 'Downloaded', Moore and Eick demonstrate that when they don't have a contained story to work with, they are prone to far more conventional science fiction stories with little or no narrative heft and that fail to engage with the character complexities they have as a baseline. These episodes are bookended with three to five arc-like episodes within the season that demonstrate a mastery of suspense and story, but the writers do little to maintain that tension or – curiously for writers who have been in Hollywood for so long – to create standalone episodes.

The second season is the one that best handles the weaknesses of Moore and Eick as show-runners. Episodes such as 'Pegasus' and 'Resurrection Ship (Part One/Two)' (2.11/12) work well as brief dramatic arcs that use plots from the original series. Further, most of the best standalone episodes are from Season Two: 'Flight of the Phoenix' (2.09), 'Scar' (2.15) and 'Downloaded' are all strong works that allow secondary characters such as Tyrol, Cally, Kat and Anders to gain more of the depth of the credited cast. Even the finale, 'Lay Down Your Burdens (Part Two)', with its gimmicky time jump, works by cutting out most of the inevitable dullness of waiting for a Cylon attack that the audience knows must happen on New Caprica.

Unfortunately, that same time jump chokes off any possibility of the New Caprica arc having dramatic suspense in and of itself.

We as viewers know that the Colonials will not be able to live under the occupation of the Cylon forces that appear on New Caprica, nor will the Cylons leave the Colonials alone, so while the individual episodes of the early third season are quite good · and have some effective dramatic tension, the viewer knows that main characters will survive – particularly the male ones. Add in the grim violence and squalid conditions, and pondering the small breaches in continuity becomes a way to get through the arc.

Further trouble with these short arcs is that they are, first, better than the standalone episodes and, second, placed towards the beginning or end of a season. Standalones in Season Three focus heavily on character territory already covered – namely, Starbuck's alienation from the fleet and descent into nihilistic aimlessness. We already watched Starbuck's drunken Anders-missing antics kill a nameless pilot in 'Scar'; in Season Three, Starbuck's callow immaturity costs us Kat in 'The Passage' (3.10). Even the previous tactic of focusing on secondary characters that worked better in Season Two is hit or miss here – 'Dirty Hands' (3.16) is a good look at the marriage between Tyrol and Cally and the vast parts of the fleet we don't see, but it is counterbalanced by the terrible, heavy-handed anti-racist episode 'The Woman King' (3.14) that only reinforces Helo's priggish moral superiority. Despite the acknowledged skill of the *Battlestar Galactica* writers in discussing politically sensitive topics, in Season Three they could not turn that skill into strong standalone episodes with consistency, which leaves long stretches between the more compelling arcs.

Further, one cannot even make the argument that a lack of character material is to blame for this dearth of compelling standalones; instead of incorporating material organically throughout the series, the writers showcased the leftovers of their writers' bible in 'Daybreak (Part One)' (3.19). This episode serves to highlight the disproportionate focus on Starbuck, the Adamas and even Tyrol and Tigh: vast and rather compelling portions of Roslin and Baltar's past are left untouched until the penultimate episode so viewers could ... see another episode where Lee Adama ponders his place in the fleet, or Starbuck hates the world and wants to die, or Adama feels the weight of the world and his yearning for Roslin on his shoulders.

One of the reasons for this is clearly a bias towards the military characters. When non-military characters receive a standalone episode spotlight, the focus is usually split with a military-based plot, as in 'Epiphanies' and 'Taking a Break From All Your Worries' (3.13). In the latter, an episode about the chemical torture of Gaius Baltar is split with an inane domestic plot where Lee and Tyrol drink and hide from their women troubles at a semi-secret bar on Galactica. The contrast between the two storylines is jarring, but not in an illuminating way. Baltar's agonized guilt under torture, the sheer fury Roslin communicates when dealing with him and their confrontations are high drama and suspense – putting it alongside petty domestic drama doesn't really work. Mixing humour and high suspense is not a strong point of the *BSG* writing team – unlike Joss Whedon or even Chris Carter of *The X-Files* – and neither are standalone plots.

In short, while the first two seasons of *Battlestar Galactica* are certainly among the strongest in television history, something went increasingly wrong as the series progressed. Why was this weakness never strongly criticized? How did a show prone to so many typical science fiction errors continue to be deified by the critical establishment at large? For the final section of this introduction, the mainstream media's expectations of *BSG*, as well as their attitudes towards science fiction, need to be brought into consideration to see how, in part, the best show on television became something much more problematic.

The Monsters and the Critics

If *Battlestar Galactica* was never quite a hit with audiences – and it never was, not even for basic cable[13] – the critics had no such qualms. The writer/comedian John Hodgman,[14] in his feature about the series, declared in a way not uncommon to *BSG* critics, 'It is sometimes jarring to watch *Battlestar Galactica*, for it is not like any science fiction show on television today'. *Time*, *Rolling Stone* and *New York Newsday* declared it the best show of 2005, and even that grande dame of highbrow criticism, *The New Yorker*, said of the show: 'what interests people who normally don't care about science fiction is how timely and resonant the show is, bringing into play religion and religious fanaticism, global politics, terrorism, and questions about what it means to be human' (Franklin). The common thread of mainstream criticism focused on how *Battlestar Galactica* was unlike other science fiction, and further, to belittle 'its fans' awestruck romance with the idea that God is in the details of equipment and uniforms and security codes' (Franklin).

Ironically, Hodgman is correct about another key point of science fiction that, as I've demonstrated in the previous section, undoes some of the rapturous praise for the series. 'Science fiction is a genre that, for all its imaginative expansiveness, tends also to be very conservative', he tells us – quite correctly for the tradition of science fiction that he places *BSG* in.[15] And he points out a further truth: 'its fans sometimes defend its clichés fiercely'. In 2005 Hodgman simply had no way of knowing that those fans would not be the stereotypical basement-dweller of the critic's anxiety dreams, but the middlebrow and highbrow cultural critic. When we look at these early raves about the series – and most of the highest praise of the series comes from the second season that aired in 2005 when *Battlestar Galactica* was at its creative peak – a troubling critical trend comes across. For Hodgman and Franklin and Poniewozik, the show must be walled away from the tradition of television science fiction and, even more importantly, its dubious, pointy-headed fans who cheerfully ignore sexism and politics and other Important Things to focus on weird details that clearly don't matter compared to allegories about torture and terrorism.

Ignoring those traditions and the effect they had upon the production staff of *Battlestar Galactica*,[16] the critics actually become the very fan they feel obligated to denigrate. Indeed, most of the decay of *BSG* is because the writers and producers disregarded the science fiction tradition; one cannot upend clichés if one has lost a grip on them, and if one dismisses world-building and mythology in a science fiction series, it becomes that much harder to make a trenchant point. It may not matter how many moons New Caprica had or the names of the Colonial gods, but it certainly does matter why Laura Roslin has to die of cancer when Hera Agathon's blood was enough to restore her health the first time, or how the Cylons differ from humans while calling themselves the machines they are clearly not. Nuance about religious devotion disintegrates when one is too busy making ham-fisted points about theism that do not even have the courage of a coherent theological framework about them.

To return to the Franklin *New Yorker* piece, where the contempt for science fiction fans is at its strongest, she talks about a famous staged event: 'Making fun of science fiction became even easier after William Shatner, in a 1986 *Saturday Night Live* sketch set at a *Star Trek* convention, exploded at fans who asked him insanely pointless questions, "Get a life!"' (Franklin), and how it led science fiction fans to become more contemplative. Sadly, while science fiction fans need to get a life in Franklin's world, middlebrow critics are allowed to let their contempt run free because, well . . . science fiction fans are geeks.

'Don't feel bad', she declares, 'if you don't like watching shows filled with characters who have disturbingly shaped heads and faces. I myself am of the school that believes that frontal lobes belong inside the skull.' With that airy line, Franklin dismisses vast swaths of the television science fiction genre, though she has already indicated her anti-science fiction leanings by saying, 'If you switch to the term "speculative fiction," which many sci-fi writers prefer, the genre seems more interesting'. While rolling one's eyes at the *New Yorker* critic for predictable condescension,[17] one also notes that for critics like Nancy Franklin, it's all a question of branding, like using 'magical fiction' in place of fantasy, or avoiding visibly different aliens because our imaginings may strike civilians as laughable.

Given these prejudices, it's hard not to recognize why *BSG* so strenuously tried to be speculative fiction, not science fiction. The path to mainstream critical regard and Emmy nominations is not via wallowing in the science fiction tradition. Yet Ronald D. Moore is at least to some extent a fanboy creator, one of the generation of writer-producers who began work in the 1990s, having grown up immersed in a tradition of the original *Star Trek*, *Doctor Who* and yes, the original *Battlestar Galactica*. The creators are self-aware – as are the fans. Franklin's greatest crime in her breezy write-up of *BSG* is to assume that fans have remained the caricature that Shatner lampooned on *Saturday Night Live* some twenty-plus years ago. Fan sophistication and self-awareness has grown over the decades (as has its gender diversity) and, given the prominence of fan-critic sites such as Television Without Pity, the lines between fan and professional grow increasingly hazy.

Truly, the critics did *Battlestar Galactica* no favours by incessantly focusing on why *BSG* was not typical science fiction. Another show that was prone to this critical de-genrefication was J. J. Abrams' *Lost*, a show that has also suffered from its creator's whims and weaknesses. It is equally unsurprising that, as *Lost* and *BSG*'s quality veered, numerous viewers declared them the only science fiction television they were willing to watch, because of their differentness from regular science fiction. That fact leads me to wonder whether *Battlestar Galactica* was really that different from 'regular' science fiction (no), or if any of them would deign to watch *BSG*'s spiritual predecessor, the overlooked and underrated *Star Trek: Deep Space Nine*, where Ronald D. Moore got a great many of the ideas he used to such great effect in *BSG*.

After all, political allegory in television science fiction is nothing new: the original *Star Trek* and its spin-offs did more than their share of issue-type episodes, which in part led to the cheesy reputation the show suffers from. *Doctor Who* hit a zenith of vaguely anti-Thatcher sentiment with the Seventh Doctor, and so on. Nor is bleakness in visual science fiction terribly novel: few would dispute that *BSG* owes a debt to *Blade Runner* in its stylistics (and use of Edward James Olmos to great effect). One could even argue that Hodgman is partially wrong: *BSG*'s early triumphs were a function of doing science fiction tropes and visual styles extremely well – *Trek*-style issue episodes without the squeaky-clean preachiness, *Who*-style short arcs without the low production values, *Blade Runner* and Ridley Scott's claustrophobic sci-fi-horror visions brought into the post-9/11 world where they were newly relevant. While certain aspects, particularly the role of women in the first two seasons, were departures from the norm in science fiction television, just as much came from doing the norm well.

What makes the critical involvement a bit more interesting is that as the later seasons came along, some critics were more likely to recognize the blemishes on *BSG*'s pristine image, but they were rarely the mainstream critics such as *Variety*, *Entertainment Weekly*, and so on. Instead, they came from critics looking from a feminist perspective, and from science fiction fans themselves. Apparently, the key factor in recognizing the failures of *Battlestar Galactica* seems to be some familiarity with science fiction and a lack of the need to declaim one's antipathy for science fiction.

For example, Slate, that middlebrow web production of the *Washington Post/Newsweek* Interactive corporation, dutifully praised *Battlestar Galactica* during its high period, though it did so about six months later than the early raves of the *New York Times* and *Time*. 'Sullen, complex, and eager to obsess over grand conspiracies and intimate betrayals alike, it is TV noir', Troy Patterson said of the series, adding, '*Battlestar Galactica* – like the movie version of *The Big Sleep* – is not especially eager to make any sense'. Indeed, Patterson's review, coming at the beginning of the third season, is surprisingly cognizant of what would become increasing flaws in *BSG*'s façade, including its lack of interest in making sense for fear of being dubbed too science fiction-y. A key insight is this:

It's all very groovy that you can read *Battlestar Galactica* as a political parable, but the program doesn't seem to have a complete confidence in its goals – in its ability to work as both a piece of art engaged with life during wartime and as a slip of entertainment about robot hotties.   (Patterson)

This is a slight departure from the critics who spent so much time constructing *BSG's* image as '*The West Wing* in space' ('Man of Duty'), and as neat a way as any to point out that – no matter how much critics refuse to take science fiction seriously as art – *Battlestar Galactica* does remain the most serious show ever made that involves robot women whose spines glow during orgasm who were created by a jealous drunk and her hapless husband. Patterson also sees that the refusal of the show to accept its heritage is itself a flaw, suggesting that it causes trouble with the series tone. As a long-time genre television watcher and amateur scholar, I would second that sentiment and add that if one is making pop art, one cannot divorce the pop because the critic from the *New Yorker* doesn't grok it.

Yet the 2006 Slate review is largely complimentary. Juliet Lapidos' piece, 'Chauvinist Pigs in Space', is far less polite about the show . . . and its critics. Lapidos starts by listing publications that have given *BSG* feminist praise, including *Elle*, *Wired* and the scholarly collection *Cylons in America*. Then she courteously but textually debunks them, revealing just how wrong these critics have become. She does a shorter version of the analysis I did of the female characters' fates and comes to a similar conclusion: 'taken together [the fates of the women in *BSG*] suggest a troubling, if unintentional message: Women – the human ones, anyway – just can't hack it when the going gets rough' (Lapidos).

Lapidos takes it one step further and points out that the seeds of *BSG's* increased misogyny have always been present, by tracking the narrative storyline of Cally. She demonstrates that 'the strange circumstances surrounding Cally's marriage are less offensive than her death scene', by pointing out that, despite creating a society with 'divorce and . . . plentiful free day care', the writers can think of no other way for Cally to handle her depression than with suicide. Had this article been written after Tory was duly punished for Cally's murder while Tyrol got away with murder scot-free, one suspects that Lapidos would point out that this is par for the course for the later *BSG*, whose laziness truly grew criminally sexist by the fourth season. She even comes to the same conclusion as me: that 'the writers don't sit around inventing new, technologically advanced ways to denigrate women'. But for the best science fiction show ever, *BSG* had some truly retrograde science fiction clichés, and its raving fan critics bought into them fully, from disparaging the fanbase to turning a blind eye to the actual flaws of the show. Apparently, science fiction that appeals to middlebrow genre-distrusting critics is forgiven any number of ludicrous sins.

This is never so evident as in Amanda Marcotte's reaction to the series. Chief blogger at the popular feminist blog Pandagon and author of *It's a Jungle Out There*, Marcotte is a well-known online feminist voice also recognized for indie tastes, including a distrust for television. Upon discovering *Battlestar Galactica* very late in the series' broadcast run, her enjoyment of the show, and her distrust in science fiction and its fans, outweighed the misogyny in the series for her. As she says in her post that addresses Lapidos' article: 'I think the show is very feminist, with a few blindspots that stem from the writers being mostly male and mostly stuck in sci-fi conventions' (Marcotte, 'Saturday Battlestar Galactica Blogging'). Lest anyone mistake Marcotte's negative views of science fiction and clichéd view of science fiction fan culture, she reiterates: 'the abundance of sexualized women without sexualized men in sci-fi . . . isn't a mere result of a male audience, but a way of signaling to a male audience that this is for them, and they are not, in any way, going to run into threats to their heterosexual manhood by watching it'. Decades of women fans who are both aware of the sexism in science fiction and utterly unwilling to render themselves as not part of the audience, women who have genuine interest in science fiction television, are rendered wrong in their concepts and dismissed by Marcotte, a very occasional television watcher. She seems unaware of the idea of 'women in refrigerators' or any other science fiction television tropes that Lapidos does seem conscious of, and is occasionally quite dense about the facts of the show: 'minor characters that don't get Cylon'd or killed all seem to be men', Marcotte claims, ignoring the fact that Lapidos is not mourning the death of say, Jean Barolay, or the Six who sacrifices herself in the middle of the fourth season for a prejudiced crewmate on Galactica. The characters Lapidos lists are first- and second-rank characters at least on the level of Anders, Tyrol and Tigh, and by the end of the series, most of them are dead or otherwise marginalized.

Oddly, Marcotte gets it much more correct about the primal pull of *Lost*, suggesting, 'the question of whether or not you could hack it if you had to survive under these conditions has a powerful pull on people, and so does the fantasy of really leaving the modern world and going back to some kind of basics', which is a point that could have been more critically applied to the *Battlestar Galactica* finale and its damaging elements. But Marcotte, like so many critics who dislike science fiction, stays loyal to *BSG* and seems unwilling to recognize logistical criticism as convincing, saying:

> I do think some folks exaggerated the implications of the ending – they divided supplies up, so it's not like people had no technology, and Lee makes a speech about bringing the best of their world to this new one, including cultural innovations that surely involved agriculture and some kinds of technology.
> (Marcotte, '"Some Way Out of Here"')

But at the same time she ignores the fact that, if the Colonial Fleet are our fictional ancestors, they failed in their idealized mission for future generations, even if those few survivors managed to live a pleasant existence for themselves in their very own Luddite fantasyland. There is also the ignored fact that many viewers – including this author – think that the idea that technology rather than religious belief is the villain in *BSG* is fatally flawed and destabilizes the entire heft of the series.

Overall, Marcotte's *Battlestar Galactica* criticism, while not all bad, demonstrates that there remains a wide range of opinion on the series and that this range is as much influenced by the critics' opinions on television, science fiction and sci-fi television as much as any other factor. To bring this section to a close, I am pleased to point out that science fiction fan critics seem the most accepting of this range of opinion. The Gawker-owned sci-fi blog, io9, had perhaps the most honest and amusing view of the *BSG* finale, stating, 'opinions are wildly divided about *Battlestar Galactica*'s final episode, with some comparing it to "explosive diarrhea" and others calling it "near-perfect." What we need is an objective scale of awesomeness . . . like the *Star Trek* finales' (Anders).

Indeed, it's true. Critical reaction varied immensely in regards to *Battlestar Galactica* after its second season, though most of that range was not found in mainstream publications about *BSG* because, once it was dubbed the greatest sci-fi show of all time, few mainstream outlets wanted to question that pronouncement, to their discredit.

While I dispute the idea that *Battlestar Galactica* is the best science fiction television series, I admit that it is a watershed show, rather like *Twin Peaks* for both American basic cable television and science fiction television, primarily through its relationship with critics. *Battlestar Galactica*, especially when considered in conjunction with *Lost*, began a mid-decade trend of critical regard for genre fiction that I suspect hit its peak with the Oscar for Heath Ledger's performance as The Joker. Dark *GI Joe* remakes and the advent of a second *Transformers* film that makes $200 million in its first week suggest that eventually, taking science fiction seriously as mythmaking and political allegory will recede until the next *Battlestar Galactica* reminds critics that genre fiction can be art.

However, the effects of the series on basic cable television are more likely to be long lasting as there have been more variations on the formula *Battlestar Galactica* used in its critical success to produce commercial and critical successes in the basic cable realm. For example, the network TNT has taken a cue from *BSG*'s use of Mary McDonnell, a former Oscar nominee and film star, and regularly imported film actresses of a certain age to star in cookie-cutter crime procedurals to critical acclaim: indeed, McDonnell has a guest appearance on *The Closer*, the first of these series, in the summer of 2009. These star vehicles have been quite successful and led to more actresses over forty appearing in prominent roles on television, which may indeed be the most revolutionary effect of *Battlestar Galactica*, despite its other failings when it comes to women.

The watershed effect of *BSG* also gave viewers *Mad Men*, the first American basic cable show to win a Best Drama Series Emmy. *Mad Men*, as the brainchild of a writer for HBO's *The Sopranos*, is not directly an offspring of *BSG*, as the idea of gritty realistic series with historical sheen is primarily descended from HBO and its high-quality television series tradition. However, Matthew Weiner's decision to take *Mad Men* to the basic cable channel AMC once HBO and other pay-cable channels chose not to produce the series shows what a post-*BSG* cable landscape is capable of. *Mad Men*'s critical triumph – indeed, the 2008 Emmys featured a dramatic writing category that only included basic cable dramas, including an entry from *Battlestar Galactica* itself – demonstrates the long tail of using basic cable for 'quality' television product. A show need not have twenty million viewers – or two million, for that matter – to be acknowledged to be good television.

In summation, *Battlestar Galactica* did indeed change the face of television, but despite its failings and weaknesses, rather than because of its strengths. It is perhaps the most influential show that nobody in particular watched since *Twin Peaks*, and most certainly the most influential genre television since David Lynch's oddball masterpiece. Its first two seasons, by quite nearly living up to the hype that the series built up from the miniseries onwards, created a critical echo chamber that focused rather too much upon *Battlestar Galactica*'s differences from other science fiction without recognizing how many of its strengths came from that source. This led to a pair of far more erratic seasons, ending in the dubious choice of Ellen Tigh as final Cylon and a final set of episodes that do not hold up well when they are given any scrutiny. While multiple factors, including a lack of network money, Sci-Fi's choice to continually break seasons in half and the WGA strike of 2007 play their part in this decline, Moore and Eick and their lazy narrative choices cannot escape censure. If a show with this many flaws is as influential and valuable as *Battlestar Galactica* was to the American media landscape, it is left to its critics to ponder what might have been had its promise been fully met.

Notes

1 The United Nations and several key players for *Galactica*, including lead actors Edward James Olmos and Mary McDonnell, co-hosted a panel discussion about 'human rights and armed conflict' as summarized at: http://www.un.org/apps/news/story. asp?NewsID=30217&Cr=television&Cr1

2 There is no agreed way to refer to these characters; I choose to use the internet-ism 'Head Six' to refer to the supernatural being who advises Baltar throughout the series, as portrayed by Tricia Helfer, and to use 'Head Baltar' to refer to her equivalent, played by James Callis.

3 As my colleague Roz Kaveney will note in her chapter 'On the End, Decline and Fall of Television Shows', sunlit shots are a rarity on *Battlestar Galactica*.

4 Joel Surnow, co-creator of 24, 'has jokingly called himself a "right-wing nut job"' and is quite conservative, as chronicled in Jane Mayer's piece for *The New Yorker*.

5 Moore, of course, worked for *Star Trek: Deep Space Nine* (the darkest of the *Treks*) as well as the HBO series *Carnivale*, making it ironic that in the end *Trek* itself would be reimagined à la *Battlestar Galactica*.

6   One should point out that the reimagined *Battlestar Galactica* was never a ratings hit; it got high ratings for the Sci-Fi Channel at first, but compared to even *Doctor Who* – or other basic cable series like *Nip/Tuck* – it was not a blockbuster ratings success.

7   The author was at this event, where Ronald D. Moore admitted that the producers of *Battlestar Galactica* had not realized that the most religiously ardent Gemenese were all black until seeing the episodes. At this point, Lucy Lawless jumped in and gave the usual 'best person for the job' explanation that many media producers give at conventions when asked about representation issues.

8   See Interview with Jane Espenson in this volume.

9   Admiral Cain, the Six called Gina, Felix Gaeta and Lt. Hoshi. One might want to add Caprica Six and D'Anna Biers in this, as both were involved with a bisexual polyamorous relationship with Gaius Baltar, but that seemed to play into male fantasy rather than being a genuine polyamorous relationship.

10   David Pilgrim of Ferris State University says of the stereotype, 'A century later, literary and cinematic portrayals of the tragic mulatto emphasized her personal pathologies: self-hatred, depression, alcoholism, sexual perversion, and suicide attempts being the most common,' all of which are sadly true of the character of Tory.

11   On his blog, Moore says, 'First and foremost, the naked Boomers were just a neat idea and that's really why we wanted to do them. But beyond that, the idea was that on the Baseships, the Cylons live closer to their true nature as machines and that certain concepts and social conventions of human society would be less relevant to them than when they were interacting in an inherently human setting like on Caprica.'

12   Mitochondrial Eve, that is. Mitochondrial Eve is an evolutionary concept and entity covered in many locations, including Richard Dawkins' *River Out of Eden*. Moore's failure in the usage of this concept will be covered by Geoff Ryman in his chapter in this volume.

13   The miniseries did have the highest ratings Sci-Fi Channel had ever seen until that point, but not only was that title stolen by the series premiere of *Eureka* in 2006 (http://www.thefutoncritic. com/news.aspx?id=20060719scifi01), it looks small compared to say, the average new episode of *Spongebob Squarepants*, a more consistent number one on American basic cable.

14   Hodgman, best known as 'PC' in the Macintosh 'I'm a Mac/I'm a PC' advertisements, guest starred in the episode 'No Exit' (4.15).

15   One could of course point out that feminist and liberal science fiction have always been a part of the genre, but the mainstream, most well-known strain of science fiction does have a conservative bent.

16   Which seems myopic of them, considering the polished science fiction pedigree of the producers. Ronald D. Moore was a staff writer and/or producer for three *Star Trek* series, as well as executive producer for teen sci-fi drama *Roswell* and speculative fiction/fantasy series *Carnivale*; Eick has ties to *Xena: Warrior Princess* and *American Gothic* and went on to produce a short-lived remake of *Bionic Woman*, and the series imported fan favourite writer Jane Espenson from *Buffy the Vampire Slayer*, who not only was gracious enough to grant us an interview, but also wrote many episodes of the series.

17   While browsing the web-archived version of Franklin's article, I noted that no less a luminary than Hendrick Hertzberg was comparing Kirk to McCain in a classic fan rhetorical amusement.

Works Cited

Anders, Charlie Jane. 'How Did Battlestar Galactica's Ending Rank Among the Star Trek Finales?' io9. 25 Mar 2009. <http://io9.com/5184249/how-did-battlestar-galacticas-ending-rank-among-the-star-trek-finales>

Casamassina, Matt. 'Battlestar Galactica – Season One.' ign.com. 22 Sept 2005. <http://dvd.ign.com/articles/652/652996p1.html>

Franklin, Nancy. 'Across the Universe.' *The New Yorker*. 26 Jan 2006. <http://www.newyorker.com/archive/2006/01/23/060123crte_television>

Hodgman, John. 'Ron Moore's Deep Space Journey.' *New York Times*. 17 July 2005.

Lapidos, Juliet. 'Chauvinist Pigs in Space.' Slate. 15 Mar 2009. <http://www.slate.com/id/2213006/>.

'Man of Duty: GateWorld Talks with Jamie Bamber.' Online article. GateWorld. 22 June 2009. <http://www.gateworld.net/galactica/articles/bamber02.shtml>

Marcotte, Amanda. 'Saturday Battlestar Galactica Blogging: Is "BSG" Sexist? Edition.' Pandagon. 13 Mar 2009. <http://pandagon.net/ index.php/site/saturday_battlestar_galactica_blogging_at_your_ service_edition/>

———."Some Way Out of Here" Has Real Appeal in 2009.' Pandagon. 24 Mar 2009. <http://pandagon.net/index.php/site/some_way_ out_of_here_ has_real_appeal_in_2009/>

Mayer, Jane. 'Whatever It Takes.' *The New Yorker.* 19 Feb 2007. <http:// www.newyorker.com/reporting/2007/02/19/070219fa_fact_ mayer>

Moore, Ronald D. 'News and Q & A.' SciFi.com. 27 July 2006. <http:// blogs.scifi.com/battlestar/archives/2006/07/>

Patterson, Troy. 'Apocalypse Noir.' Slate. 13 Oct 2006. <http://www. slate.com/id/2151426/>.

Pilgrim, David. 'The Tragic Mulatto Myth.' Online article. Jim Crow Museum of Racist Memorabilia, Ferris State University. Nov 2000. <http://www.ferris.edu/jimcrow/mulatto/>

Poniewozik, James. 'Best of 2005: Television.' *Time.* 16 Dec 2005. <http://www.time.com/time/arts/article/0,8599,1141640,00. html>

Sepinwall, Alan. 'Chuck: Talking Renewal with Ben Silverman and Chris Fedak.' *The Star-Ledger.* 19 May 2009. <http://www.nj.com/ entertainment/tv/index.ssf/2009/05/chuck_talking_renewal_ with_ben.html>

Stone, Matt and Trey Parker. 'Matt and Trey Acceptance Speech.' YouTube video. YouTube. 24 Jun 2008. <http://www.youtube. com/watch?v=9tdog65eraw>

Woodson, Alex. 'South Park Wins Coveted Peabody Award.' *Hollywood Reporter.* 5 Jun 2006. <http://www.msnbc.msn. com/id/13155092/>

Adama and (Mitochondrial) Eve
A Foundation Myth for White Folks

GEOFF RYMAN

I was commissioned to write an essay about the science of *Battlestar Galactica*. That's easily done. There is none.

Battlestar Galactica is not science fiction. It is an historical, religious fantasy. It uses two familiar science fiction elements to make its storytelling easy to create, and easy to understand.

Element One: Faster-Than-Light Travel

Faster-than-light travel (FTL) is not a piece of speculation. It is more like a bad habit inherited from the original version of *Battlestar Galactica* (BSG1) and from fantasy and science fiction.

Relativity tells us that for all kinds of reasons faster-than-light travel is impossible. If Galactica does travel faster than the speed of light, then special and general relativity (or perhaps key parts of them) do not describe the universe.

Galactica is able to jump limited distances of light years in an instant. Wormholes are never mentioned, nor is a warp drive; the show calls it an FTL drive that moves them without rockets into FTL speeds and that somehow makes travel effectively instantaneous. According to some show participants it's actually a dimensional leap. Why not say so? Why so muddled?

If it is anything like FTL, instant acceleration should result in the crew being slammed against the rear wall at more than the speed of light. For *BSG* to work, not only relativity but Newton's Laws of Motion and their description of inertia might have to be different, or an 'inertia dampener' invented. Just how much science has to be tweaked or just plain ignored for this fantasy to have its magic wands?

Why Not Fast Sub-Light Speeds?

There is such a simple alternative: very fast sub-light speeds. Special relativity is able to describe them. Travellers would have to accelerate slowly up to those speeds but, once attained, the effects described by special relativity would give interstellar travel the most enormous boost.

As you approach the speed of light, time dilates, that is to say, expands. From someone watching Galactica from another frame of reference, the clocks on the battlestar would appear to slow down. But from the point of view of the crew in Galactica's frame of reference, the voyage would last for significantly less time. How much less?

Say that Galactica is able to get almost to the speed of light, very precisely 0.999 of that speed. A voyage of five light years at that constant speed would take them 81.6 days. If they got faster, up to 0.999999, then a voyage of five light years would only take 2.5 days (in their time frame). At 0.999999999999999 of the speed of light, it would take seven seconds. Seven seconds to go five light years would surely qualify as something like a jump.[1]

However, outside Galactica's frame of reference, five years will have passed. Crewmembers will leave Galactica's frame of reference if they turn around and go back to Caprica.

So, to take an example from the first season 'Kobol's Last Gleaming (Part One/Two)' (1.12/13): Kara Thrace goes back to Caprica to find the Arrow of Apollo. Say that her first voyage after acceleration is five light years. Depending on how fast she goes, in her time frame the voyage might take 81.6 days or even only seven seconds.

Outside her time frame during that part of her voyage, five years will have passed on Caprica and on Galactica. She would find the arrow and then accelerate towards Kobol and the Temple of Athena. Say that she again travels five light years at maximum speed. During that part of the voyage, another five years will have passed in Kobol's time frame. (Plus however long it took to accelerate and decelerate from such a colossal speed. We have to leave to one side issues of what would power such acceleratation and deceleration and the time it would take.)

As far as Adama is concerned, more than ten years have passed since he last saw Kara. This defies common sense, and our experience of life.

It would also make nonsense of the traditional military structures shown in *BSG*. You can't have a chain of command with no communications and ten-year gaps between debriefings. Unless, of course, you create FTL communications as well – radio that somehow goes faster than light.

One benefit of having no special relativity, no inertia and no idea how you create the massive energy needed to jump to FTL speed is this: the show's creators did not have to imagine new military strategies and social relationships. They got to keep crusty old admirals, military hierarchies and spaceships that act like aircraft carriers. They got to keep the band-of-brothers storylines[2] that people expect from military science fiction.

Bad or non-science frequently function this way in space fantasies. Non-science frees the creators from the need to reimagine society. Familiar social relationships, customs, structures and experiences can be copied onto that future or indeed past time. It's no accident that an available alternative that fitted with special relativity was not used. To work with it would have meant that the show's creators would need to imagine a completely different society.

Element Two: The Cylons

Along with space travel, rebellious human-created intelligence must be the most familiar idea in fantasy and science fiction. It dates back to the Golem legend and *Frankenstein* (1818). The term robot goes back to the 1921 play *R.U.R.* by Karel Čapek. Skin jobs, machines that look like beautiful women were shown on the screen as early as *Metropolis* (Fritz Lang, 1926).

The idea is so familiar now that there is no need to make it credible, and the show doesn't waste time explaining the robotic Centurions. Skin jobs seem to be made entirely of flesh and blood, so it's not clear in what sense they are machines, or quite why their personalities and memories are downloadable. But they too fit with a long tradition of androids and other invaders who look like us – not least the Terminator series. Cylons are inherited from *BSG1* and fantasy and science fiction as a whole, rather than ideas based on speculation from science.

And That Is About It

Otherwise the inhabitants of Caprica are not one jot more scientifically advanced than Americans in 2003.

Guns fire bullets; the cars look like ours. Amputations and treatments for cancer are no different or more effective. Hospitals have those devices that bleep and flatline dramatically. Existing communications media seem to be television and radio.

A new physics of instant acceleration to FTL brings with it no other technological changes?

Genuine AI did not affect any other aspects of culture? No intelligent prosthetics, or new kinds of intelligent military hardware? No new forms of mass media?

In fantasy and science fiction, bad science often travels with a lack of speculation about culture and social change.

Caprica, a human but alien culture existing 150,000 years ago, has baby showers, bars, shot glasses and boxing. It has elections, presidents, military hierarchies that duplicate ours, models of sailing frigates and sushi. Its race relations, styles of funerals; its attitudes to sex, marriage, birth and death; and its system of family relations all duplicate America's in 2003. They wear the same clothes.

The few concessions to setting are inexpensive substitutes: 'frak' for 'fuck', books with cut corners, 'gods' used instead of 'God' in otherwise identical expressions. These fool no one; and are readable as jokes. Even signs and book titles are often in English, not Caprican.

This is not America of the 1960s – the military integrates fighting men and women, as did America by the start of the Iraq war.

This is not America of 2009 – this America does not have a black candidate for president. This is America in 2003, after the catastrophe of 9/11. And with the exception of the small corner of the Colonies with a British accent, it certainly resembles no other country.

In storytelling terms, this Xeroxing of America onto Caprica is brilliant.

It's Cheap

Not only is it less expensive to film on real locales with real cars. The writers don't have to spend any time speculating. They don't need to invent new family structures, ways of saying hello, or doors that iris. All of that work has been saved.

It's Tasteful and Credible

No tinfoil shoulder pads or bizarre hairdos. You can eliminate the cheesy by relying on current good taste. And since we see them every day, we find cars, guns and baby showers credible.

It Makes Characterization Richer and More Efficient

You can show that Doc Cottle is a crusty leftover from an earlier age by having him smoke cigarettes. Kara Thrace's tattoos place her as an edgy, contemporary character. You don't need to imagine what a devastating tragedy might be in this alien world; you simply have a drunk driver ram Laura Roslin's sisters and father. The writers can draw on their own memories and imaginations to create easily understood and moving human stories.

Topicality

The cultural and technological fit between contemporary America and Caprica means that recent history can be copied as well. The moral dilemmas of the last ten or so years can be explored. The show gains topical relevance. Since there are elections, Laura Roslin (however admirable she may be) can try to rig one. As president, Gaius Baltar can have sex with interns. Aspects of Bush and Clinton can be dramatized or satirized. Tables can be turned to show us what it might be like to be ruled by an alien's puppet regime: New Caprica is Iraq with us as the Iraqis.

Credible characters and a morally complex view of current events are, of course, the show's major virtues. Praise is due.

The frankly impossible fit between Caprica and America gives the writers an everyday life to work with. *BSG* ends with a series of vignettes from everyday life that no other space opera could have managed. Spaceships are easy. It's convincing lives that are hard to imagine. *BSG* filled seventy-three broadcast episodes with wonderful, three-dimensional characters and relevant moralizing, not to mention spectacular action and equally spectacular acting. No small achievement.

The *BSG* Gods

The major difference between Caprica and modern America
are those Greek gods. Well, sort of Greek, as they are muddled
with Roman gods (Hera is Greek, Jupiter is Roman). Though the
original series featured some classical names, the *BSG1* Capricans
referred to god, not gods. From the spoken introduction onwards,
it was made clear that Earthmen and Capricans had common
ancestors. However, *BSG1* was most probably set in the future.
The Capricans in *BSG1* see footage of the Apollo moon landing
(which would in any case have had to cross many light years to
get there).[3]

Capricans clearly worshipping Athena or Jupiter was an
innovation of the revised series. At first glance, this Caprica could
only have been settled by modern Americans, yet Americans are
not going to start worshipping Greek gods in the future. If the
series could not be set in the future then it might well be set in
the past. From my earliest viewings of Season Two, I was worried
that the twist in the tale would be that these Capricans founded
our Earth (rather than sharing a common history with us in the
past).

Since *Star Wars* there's been a tendency to set science fiction
material in the past. This seems to free up a mix of magical and
sci-fi elements, a sense of fairy tale and the mythic mixed with
hyperdrives. *BSG* was so plainly about America that it's tempting
to soundbite this. America doesn't see a future for itself, so it's
looking for an important new job in the past.

Second, I was worried that Galactica would land on Earth in
the past and establish the Greek gods. In other words, Galactica
would be a source of Greek civilization, and thus of the Western
tradition. And since in this series the Capricans were so obviously
Americans – down to the sushi – that would make Western
culture American in origin.

This would have the effect of cutting the ancient Greeks and
the Classical tradition free from their debt to other religions. No
longer would the Greek gods have been inherited from Hittite,

Sumerian and Egyptian deities. Classical Greece would owe less to Africa and the Middle East.

The Western tradition would have been founded by Americans from outer space. Like I said, an important new job in the past.

How the West was Won

The show went even further than I at first feared.

The Cylons are monotheists. Gaius Baltar is the unlikely prophet who has founded a thriving monotheist religion among the Caprican colonists.

So Americans from outer space brought monotheism to Earth as well as well as the Greek gods.

This is a substantial rewrite of Earth's history. The Pharaoh Akhenaten (d. c.1336 BC) is often credited with anticipating or even originating monotheism. He was preceded by Apophis, of the Hyksos dynasty, who took Set to be his sole god.

In the universe of *BSG*, neither Africa nor the Middle East gave the world monotheism. The worship of one god also arrived with the Caprican settlers.

It's possible that monotheism was forgotten and re-established, but it's unlikely that the very names of Hera and Athena survived 150,000 years. It's far more likely that Baltar's cult and the gods spread across the planet with the migration of the Colonists shown in the last episode.

So Caprica/America is the source of both the Classical tradition and the worship of the one true god.

It goes further than that. Baltar to Adama, as they observe primitive humans on Earth II:

> There you have it, Admiral. The most advanced civilization we could locate on this planet. I can't see them talking to each other so either they communicate in a different way or they're preverbal. Judging by the look of their tools that are rudimentary to say the least, I'd suggest that we've found an early ritualistic tribal society.
> ('Daybreak (Part Two)' 4.20)

Language came from America as well.

Not to mention tools that are more than rudimentary.

And, by the way, how do you get 'a ritualistic tribal society' without language?

Rituals embody symbols. If your ritual is to dance with an ostrich egg, how do you communicate the symbolic significance of the egg? How do you preserve the external forms of the ritual if you can't communicate how it is to be performed or why?

The characters come back to that lack of language, so it's plainly a key element in the BSG story. These people have rituals, tools and burial of the dead, but they can't talk and are 'preverbal'? As recently as 150,000 years ago? Without language, these brown humans are very undeveloped indeed. One is tempted to say, very much closer to the animal than we would expect.

America (or rather something so like it as to be indistinguishable from it) is the source of civilization. Not Sumer, the Indus Valley, the kingdom of Chin, nor Catal Huyuk in Turkey. And most especially not Africa.

But, more than that, Americans are the source of what may be a defining aspect of what it means to be human. And those Americans were overwhelmingly white.

A Foundation Myth for White Folks

To put it bluntly, white folks came from outer space.

The line of savages being observed as if they were wildlife are unambiguously brown.

The Caprican settlers fan out in groups across the planet, settling different lands. Galen Tyrol describes his choice. 'Last raptor out tomorrow is going to drop me off on this island I found off one of the northern continents. It's cold, it's up in the highlands, there's no people.'

Island? Northern continent? Highlands? Is this an origin myth about *Scotland*?

Galen Tyrol is going alone and is unlikely to reproduce, but it does sound as though *BSG* is explaining how white folks ended up in Europe, the source of America. We don't need to have Cro-Magnon man migrating from Africa. This is an origin myth of the white homelands.

Manifest Destiny

The Colonists pioneer settlements in a New World with minimal technology. Adama plans to build a rough cabin. Gaius and Caprica Six will become farmers. It's clear that Capricans interbreed with the indigenes, and in some cases take their land, make them sick or shoot some of them. Maybe that's what happened to the European Neanderthals.

Sound familiar?

It's a repeat of American history, in which values of independence, blindness to other kinds of property rights and the ability to shoot come in handy. America has been copied back onto the past. That history and those virtues have been made timeless.

They could have called the show *Battlestar Manifest Destiny*. There is another article to be written on the resonances between television fantasy and science fiction and Westerns, how *Star Trek* mimicked *Wagon Train*, and how *Firefly* copied the Old West onto the future.

It would be unfair to nickname the show *Battlestar Aryan*. Fascists believe in racial purity, and the show's heroes, from the rebel Cylons to Roslin and Adama, all see good in miscegenation.

They believe in the melting pot.

The Quota System

In the universe of *BSG*, white people run everything.

Tot them up, even among the Cylons. The only black male skin job is a background character. Tory, who may be South Asian, is the exception, being a presidential aide and one of the Final Five.

Otherwise, white folk are in power. Yet *BSG* does show a diverse civilian fleet with people of all races showing up as Capricans or Cylons.

Battlestar Galactica is treading very familiar ground. This kind of diversity has been seen in shows like *Star Trek* or *Firefly*. Like them, it resembles a Second World War propaganda film.

In those old movies, the bomber has an ethnically diverse crew. There is a Hernandez, and a Luigi and a Sheldon. In the Second World War this seemed to say: look, America welcomes all. Also it said, look, you all have something to fight for.

Fantasy and science fiction seems to say: in the future all our racial differences will be solved. There is one of everybody, but united within a power structure that is white.[4]

What you won't see in these diverse crews are three Latinos talking Spanish to each other. You don't see ten black people sitting together in the crew canteen, enjoying their own culture. They don't have a culture to enjoy.

Take Sharon Valerii before she realizes she's a Cylon. Does she woo Helo by wearing a traditional dress? Does she have a sisterly chat with another Asian woman about the difficulties of living in a mostly white Caprica? Can she find a nice Asian man to have children with?

There is no Asian-like culture for Sharon to draw on or to come from. It has been assimilated completely. Not only has it been assimilated, but in terms of numbers, there don't seem to be many Asian people left. This begins to look like diversity through cultural genocide.

It is no accident that the only coherent non-white culture we are shown in *BSG* is that line of preverbal savages on Earth II.

The melting pot is great so long as you're not the one being melted. It's wonderful if it's your culture that runs things.

Did Dee Kill Herself Because She Ran Out of Hair Straightener?

The great undissolved lump in America's melting pot is black people. If you talk about race in American culture, sooner or later your examples will be drawn from African-American history.

It's an explosive topic. Race makes people feel anxious and sometimes angry. Everyone recognizes the need to show black people in key roles. But for some reason there is a very limited palette of roles for black people, even in fantasy and science fiction television.

The same kinds of characters repeat. That different shows come up with similar characters suggests that similar priorities and perhaps pressures are resulting in similar choices.

There is the Uhura character, a comely and college-educated black girl, on the bridge, most often in something like communications. She's Dee in *BSG*, she's Zoe in *Firefly*. This character has a tendency to marry Lee or Wash. Not surprising, as there seem to be no young, commanding black males around. For Nalo Hopkinson the show began to go wrong when she saw 'a black female character who apparently had unlimited access to hair straightener in a community in which even food is severely rationed.'[5]

There are black preachers: Shepherd Book in *Firefly*, or the female priestess in *BSG*. They end up dead.

There are heroic black males in media fantasy and science fiction: Lando Calrissian in *Star Wars*, Benjamin Sisko in *Deep Space Nine*, but again, they are isolated from other black people. There is only one commanding black male in *BSG*: Bulldog. Despite his big build-up, he is only in one episode, clearly named after him: 'Hero' (3.08). Why didn't he come back?

Other black characters in *BSG* are congruent with the most readily available images of African Americans: the gangster in the sensitively titled episode 'Black Market' (2.14) or the background grunts who are like draftees to Vietnam or the economically motivated recruits who bulk up the forces in Iraq.

Structural racism is difficult to see. You get a sense of it by imagining what is *not* there, what options are ignored, not available or rejected because they are too disruptive. Why isn't Hera's father a black fighter pilot?

Structural racism is beyond the power of an individual's beliefs, intentions or decency. This is something that Americans, with their emphasis on individual responsibility, find particularly difficult to accept. Structural racism is an inherited social structure that sets roles for different kinds of people, roles that are immensely difficult to break out of, even with good will and legislation.

This is partly because society has baked into layers that resist change. It is also because structural racism makes it very much easier to imagine certain people in some roles rather than in others. When you're tired or stressed – perhaps when you have a script to deliver to a deadline – these immediately available images take over. You imagine a gangster to be black. *BSG* follows the norm for the portrayal of black people in most fantasy and science fiction. I don't for a moment think that its creators are racists themselves. And, as for validating even those inherited images and social structure, it probably depends on who is watching.

Target Africa

As I was writing this essay, the summer 2009 issue of a British lifestyle magazine, *Intelligent Life*, ran a cover story: 'We Are All Africans Now'.

It was a not-particularly-scientific article about the evidence that humankind first appeared in Africa and that we are all descended from Africans. This sense of African origins is having a popular impact.

The element of *BSG* that made my chin hit the carpet was making Hera Mitochondrial Eve.

The show plainly doesn't get what Mitochondrial Eve is. She is *not*, as Head Six's voiceover tells us, the most recent ancestor of all human beings.

Mitochondria are structures inside human cells with DNA of their own. They are passed only through the female line. So Eve is the most recent common ancestor as traced through the female line using mitochondrial DNA. It means that everyone on the planet has mitochondrial DNA that can be traced back to her. There are many more common ancestors of all mankind and for various reasons, not least harems, they are likely to be male. The most recent common ancestor is now calculated to have lived about 3,000 years ago.

One of the nonsenses of the show is the discovery of 'fossilized remains of a young woman who they might [sic] actually be Mitochondrial Eve'.

The existence of a Mitochondrial Eve has been constructed by postulating how long it would have taken for the different branches of the mitochondrial family tree to branch off from an original source. A fossil could not be identified as remains of Eve. Fossils, except in the rarest cases, do not preserve proteins, so no DNA. Even if the fossil could be shown to have the right mitochondria, it could have been Eve's great-great granddaughter.

(Hey! *BSG* could be an origin myth for mitochondria. Mitochondria are evidently something the Cylons decided to include in the Eight model.)

The show intends Hera to be the most recent ancestor of us all, not just the earlier common ancestor following back mitochondrial DNA. In terms of the show's imagery, Hera is source of all humankind.

This would mean, incidentally, that none of the progeny of the Caprica colonists has survived. I'm not sure that the show's creators are aware of that. The only Caprican ancestor we would have is Hera's father. This is a complication I frankly find too geeky for even me to explore further.

Hera is one of the drivers of the plot; half the cast seem to have prophetic visions of the Opera House and her centrality. The final battle takes place to rescue her from the evil Cylon Cavil. It is a battle for the creation of humankind.

To make again one very obvious point: she is the daughter of a white Viper pilot and an engineered life form who resembles an Asian. The source of humankind in *BSG* is not African. Her children would have interbred with Africans, yes. But all people on Earth II have a white man as their common ancestor too.

If you were a closet racist uncomfortable with the fact that you may be descended from Africans, no doubt that would offer some comfort. If you wish to think of the Caprican settlers as founding the white homelands, perhaps without any interbreeding with blacks at all, you are perhaps more comfortable still.

So Africa via Egypt did not contribute monotheism to Western culture, nor are Africans the ancestors of us all. White people have their origin among the stars.

Certainly not in primates. If Hera is the source of humankind, then we all carry Cylon blood. That part of our genome is not inherited or shared with higher mammals. Part of us shares no common ancestry with apes.

We can only assume that white Capricans evolved from Kobolian primates, but who is to say? What we do know is that the Earth II part of human genetic inheritance does share genes with gorillas. It's possible in the world of the show that modern Africans share more of this inheritance than other races. For example, Asians may carry more of Athena's Cylon genes, whites more Caprican genes. This association of blacks and our animal inheritance is mild, no doubt unintentional on the part of the show's creators, and probably invisible to them. But it's there. Blacks in the world of *Battlestar Galactica* are to a greater degree evolved from primates, and our African ancestors needed whites to give them language.

They Evolved

The show's grasp on reality is weakest whenever it uses the term 'evolution'.

Crazily, the show appears unable to distinguish evolution from intelligent design.

To give one example of the use of the term. The Final Five have decided to set the Centurions free. Lampkin objects: 'And what if they evolve again on their own and decide to come back in a few hundred years and wipe us all out?'

The Centurions are metal robots with perhaps some organic components. They are the product of intelligent design.

If they 'evolve on their own', it can only mean that they have redesigned and rebuilt themselves. They are their own intelligent designers. This has nothing to do with the process of genetic change over eons.

Perhaps Lampkin is just loosely talking, using 'evolution' in a popular sense. Is this the voice of a character, rather than the show itself?

In the early seasons, the show's titles repeatedly show a skin job with the slogan 'They evolved'. That is not a character talking loosely about evolution. That's the show's own words. Plainly, skin jobs did not evolve. They were intelligently designed by Ellen. The title is nonsense.

To take another example. Doc, Adama, Baltar and others observe the dark-skinned indigenes.

> *Adama:* How is that possible . . . human beings naturally evolved on another planet one million light years away? The odds against that are . . .
>
> *Baltar:* Astronomical, yes . . . One might even say that there was a divine hand at work.
>
> *Adama:* Whoever is responsible, we're here to stay . . .
>
> ('Daybreak (Part Two)' 4.20)

Note that expression 'naturally evolved'. The term 'natural evolution' is needed to make it clear that Adama is *not* talking about that other kind of evolution, intelligent design. He means human beings evolving out of mammals.

Adama doesn't want to pander to Baltar's religiosity, but he doesn't say something like 'Whatever happened, we're here to stay.' Evolution, even of human beings from primates, must still be the responsibility of someone – God or Ellen or 'whoever'.

In the real world, evolution is no one's responsibility. It happens because no system of copying is perfect. Genes change over time. Populations separated by distance change in different ways and eventually are no longer able to interbreed.

Our Cylon inheritance is clearly the result of intelligent design.

But so is the natural evolution of our African ancestors. How are two alien races able to interbreed? Gaius' explanation is the only one available. The whole cycle is, as Head Six keeps telling us, part of God's plan.

Religion

Religion is a plot function in BSG.

The show has a deus-ex-machina plot. Aristotle hated deus ex machina, but then he didn't write for television.

A deus ex machina is when a god descends (onstage in a machine) to sort out the characters' problems and to bring a just end to the conflict.

Deus-ex-machina plots take the solution out of the hands of your characters, which can be disappointing for readers or viewers. Also, a deus-ex-machina plot could end at any point in the story. Why didn't God intervene at once? Why go through all those battles, trips back to Caprica, on to Kobol and on to the Temple of Jupiter? Kara could have been killed in episode two, come back as an angel in episode three and led us to Earth II in episode four.

That's why a deus-ex-machina plot is perfect for television.

A deus ex machina can happen as soon as the ratings drop or networks lose commitment to a project.

(You also can keep extending the story, in the case of *BSG*, by using devices from gaming, such as a series of quests for mystical objects.)

Deus-ex-machina plots also establish and clarify moral schemes. If a god tells you what is just, and who is good, then there is moral certainty. At least in your universe, unless you portray your fictional god as being mischievous.

Which is why, students of writing, when you introduce God, you'd better make darn sure of what you're validating.

A Plot Excused by Mysticism

God and magic drive this story.

Prophecies come true. A magic book prophecies that a dying leader shall appear turns out to be right. Leoben accurately says that when he looks at Kara he sees an angel. Her mother forecasts a great destiny.

Prophecy is another bad habit of fantasy and science fiction. To quote author Nalo Hopkinson, 'But the story went completely off the rails when they introduced into a supposed science fiction story the tired old fantasy trope of The Prophecy that explains everything and points the way to salvation. It doesn't even work in fantasy. It's a way to save yourself the effort of plot.'[6]

In storytelling terms, prophecies save work because they accustom your audience to the totally unlikely. You keep telling people it will happen until it seems inevitable. This means you are saved having to work out how things might actually happen through cause and effect.

Instead of, for example, Caprican scientists spending years scanning the heavens for spectroscopic and infra-red evidence of Earth-type planets, you can have Kara Thrace mystically intuit jump coordinates to a beautiful new Earth. The audience will accept it.

It's easy, it's fast and it works. It's untruthful.

'Commercialism, Decadence, Technology Run Amok. Remind You of Anything?'

That's a quote from the last scene in the show, its capstone, Head Six to Head Baltar. They are immortal virtual beings, with access to truth, and that's us they're describing, now.

What do you mean, 'corruption and decadence'?

Corrupt politicians perhaps? Decadence: maybe the bonuses paid to big bankers? Our greed and need for comfort generating human-made climate change? I'm not sure.

It's left up to the viewer to decide. Any good story gives the reader room to make up her own mind.

But you will forgive me for worrying if your angels don't mean me, a gay man who is legally married to another man.

Why isn't Kara Thrace a dyke? She'd make great dyke, tattoo and all. Not one moment of curiosity about same-sex lovemaking? Why is Admiral Cain (and Abel?) the only visible lesbian on the show and also *BSG*'s equivalent of Pol Pot, a mass murderer? Is it because images of untrustworthiness surface faster if you're imagining lesbians?

Is it an accident that Kara seems to feminize as the show progresses, growing her hair long, and getting more involved in stories about her marital status and love affairs?

For someone like me, this last scene takes the tone of a traditional, prophetic jeremiad. It backwashes over the rest of the series. It makes Roslin's election fixing, Baltar's conniving with Cylons and sleeping with interns, Lee's use of prostitutes or Adama's drunkenness look less like moral complexity and much more like a judgemental rant against modern life.

What do you mean by 'technology run amok'?

Do you mean cures for cancer? Carbon filament limbs that allow amputees to run? Do you mean the very system of communications through which *BSG* is distributed? The computers that generate its spectacular special effects?

Do you mean cars, planes, air-traffic control, weather forecasts, the internet, the weapons technology that allows modern armed forces to bomb installations in complete safety, the sat-nav that tell you where to drive? The technology that chills your designer water and transports it round the globe, and which means you can buy cheap toys from China and go there for the Olympics?

That kind of science and technology?

Or are you a prisoner of your own tropes? We created Frankenstein's monster, *there are things mankind is not meant to know?*

Battlestar Galactica mirrors America's current confusion about technology. It loves toys and comforts, prays for a colour television, but distrusts science.

That distrust has existed for a long time and not just in America, because science changes its mind. God-given holy writ does not. Science forces change on authority and on ordinary people. Science brings you evolution, a universe billions of year old, dinosaurs without human beings, and the idea that climate change is our fault. And it's technology that pumps out greenhouse gases.

For *BSG*, the main problem with human beings is their science.

'No, No City, Not This Time'

That's Lee, at the moment of deciding to destroy technology.

All the fleet, with its labs, cameras, hair-dryers and medical equipment is to be driven into the sun.

At first I thought that was just a piece of hasty plotting. The creators needed to explain why the Caprican colonists left no archaeological remains.

It is also, I'm afraid, an expression of a fundamental view that the show has about science and technology.

Adama protests at how vulnerable the colonists will be without technology. Part of the threat are the natives who are, he says, 'Tribal. Without language even.'

Lee replies:

> But we can give them that. I mean we can give them the best part
> of ourselves, and not the baggage, not the ships, the equipment,
> the technology, the weapons. If there's one thing we should have
> learned it's that, you know, our brains have always outraced our
> hearts. Our science charges ahead, our souls lag behind. Let's
> start anew. ('Daybreak (Part Two)' 4.20)

If only science would let itself be guided by some wiser
moral authority? Something that makes sure it keeps pace with
something called our soul?

Religion? Especially in this fictional universe that definitely
has an intervening god?

In this myth, technology and science are wrong. They have
locked us into a repetitive cycle of destruction, described by
Head Baltar in that last scene. He lists Kobol, old Earth, Caprica,
all part of a cycle of history driven by science.

Eternal America

In this myth something like America will always develop, and
– to be fair to the show – that is not a good thing.

But that still makes America primal, original, central and
special. *BSG* rewrites history to explain why white folks are
privileged and different. It can't tell evolution from a shoelace
and fuels itself with magic and God and stale genre tropes and
compromises over race.

No Wonder There's No Science in It

Genuine scientific speculation would have blown apart the
central image of Caprica-as-America. It would have refined the
concept of Mitochondrial Eve down to a much smaller issue.

Evolution would not have been so muddled. Time dilation would have altered how the fleet fought and travelled together. Bad science allowed old social relations to go unchallenged; aspects of American life could seem inevitable, eternal if not actually ordained by God.

Science would also have blown away the wonderful characters to whom we can so easily relate and the topicality of the storylines. *BSG*'s new myth of an inevitable America founding and re-founding technical civilization would go.

Science in *BSG*? They couldn't have afforded it.

Notes

1 I am indebted to Tim O'Brien of the University of Manchester for this ready-reckoner.
2 I am indebted to David Kirby of the University of Manchester for pointing out in conversation how *BSG* drew on expectations of non-sf military television shows and movies.
3 See Battlestar Wiki. 'Religion in the Twelve Colonies.'
4 For a more detailed discussion of how this works in *Star Trek*, see Bernardi 1998.
5 Email to author dated 30 April 2009.
6 Email to author dated 30 April 2009.

Works Cited

Battlestar Wiki. 'Religion in the Twelve Colonies (TOS)'. Battlestar Wiki. <http:en.battlestarwiki.org/wiki/Religion_in_the_Twelve_Coloniesthe_Twelve_Colonies_(TOS)>.
Bernardi, Daniel. *Star Trek and History: Race-ing Towards a White Future.* New Brunswick: Rutgers University Press, 1998.
'We Are All Africans Now'. *Intelligent Life* (summer 2009).

Frak Me

Reproduction, Gender, Sexuality

LORNA JOWETT

Reproduction is often a major concern of science fiction, and images of it have at times been remarkable, from an alien 'born' from the stomach of a man (*Alien*, 1979) to the birth of a gunship from a cybernetic space vessel (*Farscape*, 1999–2003). Reproduction is certainly a key concern and a source of iconic images in the reimagined *Battlestar Galactica*, where it becomes an overtly public issue because of two underlying premises. The existence of the Cylons, artificial life forms, and especially the humanoid or bio-Cylons, poses questions about how we reproduce and what we classify as human. The Cylon attacks on the Twelve Colonies that begin the narrative reduce the human population to a fragment forced into a quest for survival where replenishing the population is imperative. The opening of each episode reinforces these two ideas, reminding us of the Cylons' genesis and their ability to reproduce and 'evolve', while the ever-changing number of human 'survivors' appears on screen at the start of most episodes. With reproduction such a key issue, what effect does this have on how the show deals with birth, pregnancy and reproductive technology? And how does it negotiate related issues like gender and sexuality?

In science fictions such as the *Alien* films, difference is partially located in reproduction: aliens are alien because they do not reproduce like us (as the first violent alien birth implies, 'the Alien is not only a killing machine but also a relentless reproductive machine', Gallardo C. and Smith 7). Reproduction functions to denote difference in *Battlestar Galactica* too and several dynamics and contradictions are at work in its treatment and representation. The mode of reproduction/replication that allowed the Cylons to evolve is represented as unnatural and apparently opposed to the human because of its relation to technology – they are literally 'reproductive machines'. However, this difference is consistently undermined. The Cylons attempt a more human form of reproduction and, while the Cylon-human hybrid might seem a step towards the post-human, Matthew Gumpert suggests it is a step back to the notion of unified identity – 'a fantasy of wholeness retrieved' (151). Once the Cylons adopt human reproductive methods, they also potentially adopt social structures of heteronormativity, which serve to further erase (one form of) difference. The Cylons who become the most 'human' are those who adopt recognizable gender and sex roles.

While other science fictions at times destabilize connections between sex, gender and reproduction, *Battlestar Galactica* feminizes reproduction for Cylons and humans alike within a context of compulsory heterosexuality. At least one scholar has suggested that '*Battlestar Galactica* is set in a nonpatriarchal world. On gender issues the show is utopian, despite its overall dystopian tone' (Moore 110), but, although it has strong female characters, their representation is inflected by the feminization of reproduction. Just as Judith Newton argues that in *Alien*, 'the alien becomes the site of all anxieties which the feminist gestures of the film evoke' (85), here the Cylons, especially the female Cylons, become the site of our own anxieties about reproduction and its relation to traditional roles for women.

Reproduction as Public

Since the show makes population a public issue for Cylons and humans, reproduction becomes both political and social. Kathleen Woodward notes that in the USA medicine 'has generally been thought to be a more "private" or "personal" matter, not one that requires "public" debate or policy' (285). Yet, in science fiction, 'special' or alien reproduction may become, by its very nature, 'a public event that requires complex monitoring and regulation', as Jes Battis notes of cybernetic spaceship Moya's pregnancy in *Farscape* (43). Something similar occurs in *Battlestar Galactica* with the birth of Hera, as discussed below, but early in the show *any* reproduction is shown to be of public note when President Laura Roslin starts to track the changing population. This is then foregrounded in the show's opening sequence, as the number of 'survivors' is shown onscreen (the population soon also includes children born since the attack – technically these are not survivors). In 'The Captain's Hand' (2.17) Admiral Adama tells Roslin, 'I'm just remembering what you said. Right after the Cylon attack. That if we really want to save the human race, we'd better start having babies.' This stands in contrast to 1970s science fiction films, such as *Soylent Green* (1973) or *Logan's Run* (1976), which dealt with overpopulation and the politics of reproduction in relation to limiting the human race, but is in keeping with post-apocalyptic scenarios where 'civilized' behaviour, especially about sexuality and reproduction, might be viewed as outmoded (see, for example, the British series *Survivors*, 1975, remade 2008).

The relation of population to reproduction is made clear in 'The Captain's Hand', which presents abortion as a political, religious and gendered matter. Dr Cottle has been performing terminations requested by young women who sometimes have to be smuggled onto Galactica for fear of religious reprisals, with obvious allusions to how various interest groups argue the right to life or the right to choose. Specific reference is made to President Roslin's record on upholding 'a woman's right to control her own body' when she reneges on her principles for the sake of her political career and the survival of the fleet, apparently a prioritization of the public over the personal. Roslin must 'betray' her gender, her belief in freedom for women and, in contrast to Robert W. Moore's reading of the show's utopian gender roles, actor Mary McDonnell sees Roslin as having to operate 'in a man's world' (in Bassom, *The Official Companion Season Three*, 114). The decision to 'criminalize' terminations could undermine the maintenance of a democratic society, and later struggles about class are framed in a wider context of social inequality ('Dirty Hands' 3.16), something not made clear about gender here. This treatment of reproduction as a public issue is consistently revisited, though the show sometimes displaces it onto individual characters (as with Athena, Helo and Hera Agathon), regularly switching between political drama and melodrama in negotiating it. In this way, as Tama Leaver observes, 'the Cylons and humans appear both, at times, to regard women as reproductive systems first, and citizens second' (139). The short-lived *Dark Angel* (2000–2) offered a variant on this: its 'transgenics' are products of genetic experimentation by the military (supersoldiers), whose barcodes stamp them literally as commodities. The alignment of disenfranchisement and femininity is highlighted by a breeding programme that forces female transgenics to mate with assigned males; any children are valuable objects for scientific study (as Cylon-human Hera potentially is here).

Scholars such as Woodward speculate that science associated with reproduction, such as biotechnology, does 'not receive the sustained scholarly interest it deserves because many of its most spectacular results, as well as its more mundane concerns, were associated with women – with motherhood, children, and caregiving' (285). Yet, although reproduction (real and fictional) may be seen as largely personal and mostly concerning women, men are in charge of reproductive science (here, Cottle, Baltar, even Cylon Simon). This is complexly negotiated in a show such as *The X-Files* (1993–2002), which features the character of Dana Scully – who is sometimes a passive object of study as well as an active scientific investigator – in addition to many mad scientist figures, including Nazis given immunity by the US government. Some of these scientists are female, and alien abductees or victims of scientific experimentation are sometimes male, indicating that biological sex is immaterial to the gendered power structure of masculinized subject/feminized object. As Lisa Parks argues, 'monsters are feminized by processes such as reproduction and demonic possession', but the 'feminization of monstrosity . . . is symptomatic of the failure of historically masculinized and institutionalized scientific rationality' (129–30).

In *Battlestar Galactica* this masculinized science is typically invasive or downright hostile to female subjects, as seen in 'The Farm' (2.05), arguably again in 'Downloaded' (2.18) when Athena gives birth to Hera, and in 'Daybreak (Part One)' (4.19) when Cylon leader Cavil insists that the child Hera is simply 'a half-human, half-machine object of curiosity that holds the key to our continued existence somewhere in her genetic code' and tells Simon to 'put a tube in her and get her ready' for investigation. In this last instance, both the controlling power and the scientist who carries out his orders are male, in direct contrast to Hera herself – the object of intense scientific (as well as political and religious) scrutiny – and female characters who seek to protect her, such as her mother Athena, Caprica Six and even Boomer, who becomes visibly concerned about Cavil's treatment of Hera. Such representations epitomize Zoe Sofia's observation that, with 'the onset of obstetrics and gynaecology, women's bodies have been increasingly subject to technological penetration and manipulation', but she goes on to describe how science fiction might disrupt this dynamic. 'Cyberpunk is one of the places where the femininity latent in the masculine dream of reason becomes manifest: male bodies now become vulnerable to the technological penetration, leaky boundaries, and pregnancy-like states that have long been part of women's history and ontological condition' (61). Other texts play out this potential and Ximena Gallardo C. and Jason Smith observe that in the *Alien* films 'all humanity is female (a womb) in the face of the Alien' (42) since 'men can suffer the same abuse and bodily violation as women' (180). While *Alien*, at least, presents this as horrific, other science fictions play it for laughs, as in an episode of *Star Trek: Enterprise* (2001–5) where male engineer Trip gets pregnant after contact with an alien race ('Unexpected' 1.05). The use of horror or comedy helps manage anxieties inherent in blurring biological distinctions between men and women. Such reproductive role reversal is not highlighted in *Battlestar Galactica*. Instead, reproduction and Cylon technology are feminized.

'The Farm' was considered potentially offensive, with the production team wondering if it would 'scare off female viewers, because of the issues it explores about female reproductive organs' (Ronald D. Moore in Bassom, *The Official Companion Season Two*, 40–1). Kara Thrace has been injured on Cylon-occupied Caprica and finds herself in hospital undergoing medical procedures. She is not sure whether she is among friends (the Resistance) or has been captured by the Cylons. Eventually she escapes, discovering that the Cylons are using human women like her in reproductive experiments. While it might be easy to align the invasive medical science shown in this episode with the Cylons, Simon's conversations with Kara serve as a reminder that human policy on reproduction is not dissimilar. 'Gotta keep that reproductive system in great shape. It's your most valuable asset these days,' he tells her, pretending to be a human doctor. 'You do realize that you're one of the handful of women left on the planet actually capable of having children', he continues. The Cylons' primary motivation is ascribed to religion: 'Procreation, it's one of God's commandments, be fruitful. We can't fulfil it, we tried,' Athena reveals, and one way to continue their efforts is to effectively rape human women. The episode thus simultaneously draws parallels between Cylon and human desperation to reproduce, and uses reproduction to demonstrate difference.

Birth, Technology, Feminization

Reproduction as represented on *Battlestar Galactica* is aligned with the female: it is also consistently seen in relation to technology and hybridity. While medical/reproductive science tends to be masculinized in fictional representations, rendering the female subject a passive object of study, Cylon technology and technological reproduction is feminized in *Battlestar Galactica*. Allecquere Rosanne Stone suggests that we often 'attempt to *keep technology visible* as something separate from our "natural" selves and our everyday lives' (85, emphasis in original), and the desire to do this is apparent in films such as *Blade Runner* (1982) and, less ambivalently, the *Terminator* movies. Thus *Battlestar Galactica's* oscillating contrast/conflation of Cylon and human reproduction is a particularly interesting strategy. The humanoid Cylons blur boundaries between technology and biology, natural and artificial, and female Cylons play a significant role in this. Mary Ann Doane argues that in the first two *Alien* films 'the technological is insistently linked to the maternal' (25), with visual images combining organic and technological; she concludes that the 'confusion of the semes of sexual difference indicates the fears attendant upon the development of technologies of reproduction that debiologize the maternal' (26). The same could be argued of *Battlestar Galactica's* Cylons, though often the show seems rather to biologize the technological, gendering it female. In science fiction, 'anxieties about technology are frequently displaced onto the figure of the woman' (Wolmark, 13) so that 'unresolvable contradictions about both technology and the maternal . . . are endlessly re-enacted in the figure of the artificial woman' (14). This is demonstrated by the female transgenics of *Dark Angel*; the female Cylons operate in the same fashion.

Cylon reproduction is not strictly seen as reproduction in the diegesis, which privileges/valorizes procreation. Because of this, both humans and Cylons seem to operate under compulsory heterosexuality. While fleeting moments of alternative sexualities have been admitted (Baltar, Six and Three sharing a bed on the Cylon baseship in 'A Measure of Salvation' (3.07) and Cain's liaison with Gina in 'Razor' (4.00), as well as Gaeta and Hoshi's relationship in 'The Face of the Enemy' webisodes), these have – perhaps necessarily, given the nature of television – been unspecified and lacking in explicit detail compared to representations of heterosex. Heterosexuality is not, apparently, enforced but, while recreational sex is part of everyday life, normality equates to heterosexuality and the reproductive imperative affords little divergence. Two instances of alternatives to heterosexuality are associated with Cylons and with characters of dubious moral standing among the humans (arguably the latter also becomes true of Gaeta, who is eventually executed for mutiny). Paradoxically, in both cases the relationship is imbued with emotion as well as desire, and therefore serves to humanize Baltar (though his 'true' emotion is reserved for Six), Cain and even Three – all otherwise potentially cold and unsympathetic characters. 'Love' seems to be another correlate of compulsory heterosexuality and one that fulfils the demands of serial television: it allows for negotiation of heterosexual romance, not only furthering character development but also contributing to the debate about the nature of the Cylons as people, if not humans.

Replenishing the population may be a top priority for humans in *Battlestar Galactica* yet Hera is the only child seen regularly. For a brief time, Cally's son Nicky also features, but he fades from view once he is revealed to be Hot Dog's son, not Tyrol's and therefore not another Cylon-human hybrid; other children feature only briefly to further the narrative. Instead, reproduction is most insistently visualized as Cylon reproduction, technological and feminized. The Cylons are an image of reproduction: since all Centurions look the same, and there are a limited number of humanoid Cylon models, multiple versions of Cylons co-exist at the same time and often in the same place. Actors and production teams work to construct differences in numerous versions of any one Cylon model, but they are genetically identical, a constant reminder Cylon reproduction is 'unnatural' since numerous identical copies would not be found in nature. While Torsten

Caeners argues that the Cylons suffer from Oedipal anxiety, just as humans might, this replication signals a further difference: the Cylons are not human because they are not born; they never grow up but are downloaded into fully adult bodies. A comment on the fact that Adama has seen Tigh ageing occurs in 'Revelations' (4.10) but this is never explained coherently. Alison Peirse has explored how the Cylons operate as a version of the uncanny double (124), identifying ways in which Cylon reproduction/ replication is presented as disturbing and potentially horrific. Again, this is not unusual in science fiction, as seen in several episodes of *The X-Files* involving clones, or, more reflectively, the two Crichtons in Season Three of *Farscape*.

Battlestar Galactica retains elements of the uncanny and this, too, tends to be aligned with the female, especially with the abject female body. One of the first scenes featuring multiple identical Cylon models, in 'Kobol's Last Gleaming (Part Two)' (1.13) shows Boomer literally faced with her Cylon identity as an Eight, surrounded by versions of herself. Both the nakedness of the Eights and the design of the baseship work to feminize and sexualize this uncanny replication. The effect aimed for is 'womb-like', and visual effects supervisor Gary Hutzel relates how the scene was treated to look 'more bloody and meaty' (in Bassom, *The Official Companion*, 94). While later views of baseships appear to contradict this feminized bio-tech with a more traditional genre approach – bright light and colour generating an 'unworldly' look (Bassom, *The Official Companion Season Three*, 49) – the same concern is apparent. The outside of the ship is made 'more flesh-like', with attacks causing 'a ripping-of-the-skin effect' (152), sustaining the fusion of technological and organic elements. Nicola Nixon suggests that in some cyberpunk fiction the feminine hybridizes biology and technology, that it 'is essentially the "soft" ware, the fantasy (and world) that exists beyond the "hard" ware of the actual technological achievements realized in the silicon chip' (199). Applying this theorization, the female humanoid Cylons operate as 'soft' Cylon technology (in contrast with the robotic-looking Centurions) and, rather than maintaining a distinction between natural and artificial, they are used to blur it: the feminine operating as a signifier of the organic and biological. This sits in direct contrast to cinematic cyborg hardbodies of the 1980s, such as the Terminator, *RoboCop* (1987), or even the Marines from *Aliens* (1986), whose bodies are 'the product of technique or technology (bodybuilding), that can be enhanced by formfitting machines . . . resulting in cyborg soldiers' (Gallardo C. and Smith, 85). Gallardo C. and Smith point out, however, that the Marines' 'firmness of body is clearly a constructed state acquired through discipline, and their belief in the hard body's ability to protect them from harm and delusion' (85). Cylons are equally penetrable and penetrating. They can 'jack in' to computer systems in the traditional cyberpunk sense (as seen in the *Matrix* films or, with more self-consciousness about penetration, in *eXistenZ*, 1999), as Athena does by inserting a 'fibre-optic com link' into her arm during 'Flight of the Phoenix' (2.09). The use of liquids as an interface on the baseship could also be read as a more feminized mode and becomes increasingly dominant. Tigh 'remembers' Ellen, the last of the Final Five Cylons, as he stands in the sea on the now-desolate Earth ('Revelations' 4.10) and he even places his hands in the water in a version of Cylon interfacing. In 'Daybreak (Part Two)' (4.20), when the Final Five offer resurrection technology to the other Cylons in return for Hera, they literally pool their information by placing their hands into the Hybrid tank liquid, interfacing with each other and then passing the data to the other Cylons.

As Anne Balsamo notes, 'Female cyborgs embody cultural contradictions which strain the technological imagination. Technology isn't feminine, and femininity isn't rational' (149). Every female Cylon model demonstrates this contradiction, whether in relation to religion and mysticism (D'Anna/Three) or to reproduction. As the object of scientific investigation and the site of reproduction, the female body is presented as abject in terms familiar from both science fiction and horror (as Peirse also notes). The image of women hooked up to machines for reproduction appears in *Dark Angel* and *Alien Resurrection* (1997), as well as 'The Farm'. Until 'The Ties That Bind' (4.03) (with the exception of Baltar's hallucination in 'Taking a Break From All Your Worries' 3.13), we have only seen female Cylons being re/born in the resurrection tanks, an important choice that keeps birth feminized. As Peirse points out, a shot of Six in the tank is used in the opening sequence of Season Three, becoming a repeated image under the words 'They evolved' (122). Given that Battis describes the notion of abjection as 'the unconditional (if forever partial, deferred, and frustrated) disavowal of anything relating to the maternal body, but specifically those bodily functions and fluids that render the body violable and dependent – an open text rather than a closed system' (48), this conjunction is integral to their representation.

The revelation that Ellen is the last of the Final Five is followed in 'No Exit' (4.15) by lingering images of her naked resurrected body recovering from the trauma of death/birth. Furthermore, her antagonism with Cavil is inflected with sexual tension and jealousy despite, or because of, the fact that she is his 'mother'. Making Ellen the creator of the humanoid Cylons balances talk of a (male) God with a female creator, as well as making another link between the female and technology/science. It is notable that Cavil attempts to keep Ellen subordinate (leaving her in the resurrection chamber with no clothes, for instance), while she tries to retain agency by verbally resisting and reminding him of their shared past. Cavil sees his human body as abject in and of itself; she embraces the abjection (if such it is) of humanity, as her alcoholism and hypersexuality demonstrate. Ellen's body is consistently presented as abject, in contrast to Hera, who is only rarely seen in this way (though her added vulnerability as a child intensifies the physical dangers and abuses she faces, similar to those faced, and endured, by other female Cylons such as Ellen, Athena and Six). Generally, Hera is mythologized, even deified, but Ellen's physicality prevents or at least limits this kind of representation – her all-too-human physical appetites and her bond with Saul Tigh are often presented as weaknesses. Her role as progenitor of the Cylons is emphasized at times, as when she talks of the baseship as 'a whole ship full of my children', but she too functions as software, and Cavil threatens to 'cut open [her] head' to find the secret of resurrection technology ('No Exit').

The other version of reproduction, by human–Cylon pairing, retains female difference in order to contain similar tensions and, as Gumpert notes (153), the sequence detailing the birth of Hera is edited into 'Downloaded', one of the first episodes to take viewers into Cylon society and to explore the downloading process as a version of re/birth. Discussing the birth of *Farscape*'s human protagonist John Crichton's son in relation to the birth of cyborg gunship Talyn, Battis argues that the former 'is an eminently natural reproduction meant to ameliorate (or erase) Talyn's more upsetting birth; but it is also a triumphant restaging of normalcy within the show, a mythical closure that reaffirms healthy, human reproduction, while trying to avoid the more threatening alien pregnancy that preceded it' (44). Though Hera's birth arguably functions as 'natural' in relation to the downloading of Six and Eight in this episode, her naturalness and normality are always in doubt – she is a Cylon-human hybrid. She is not generally seen as a person, a subject, tending to be mythologized as the saviour of both humanity and the Cylons. Caprica Six's insistence on her importance and the visions that Caprica Six, Athena and Roslin have of her in the Opera House culminate in her role as 'Mitochondrial Eve', when a flashforward demonstrates that she is the missing link that allows humans to evolve and Cylons to reproduce without resurrection technology ('Daybreak (Part Two)'). Unlike her mother's namesake, the goddess Athena who sprang fully formed from the brow of Zeus the father-god, Hera (named for the wife of Zeus) is the progenitor of a whole new species and does this, presumably, by physical reproduction, the labour (literally) of the female body.

The baseship Hybrid seen in Season Three is another development along the same lines. C. W. Marshall and Matthew Wheeland note that 'the pronoun "it" comes naturally' when discussing the Hybrid (103, note 4), yet gender is signalled here in several ways. The Hybrid, played by a female actor, apparently exists permanently in a modified resurrection tank. While other Cylons are born as fully grown adults, the Hybrid appears to be perpetually unborn, existing in a womb-like space, connected to the ship as a foetus is connected to the mother (almost every commentator calls the liquid in the tank 'amniotic', and Ellen uses the term 'amniotic fluid' in relation to resurrection in 'No Exit'). Hybrid speech seems to be nonsense, though Caprica Six tells Baltar that some Cylons believe it is religious revelation and at various points it functions this way to further the narrative. Her mode of speech and existence could be equated with Julia Kristeva's description of the semiotic, a pre-patriarchal, pre-symbolic mode that privileges the feminine and the chaotic. Marshall and Wheeland explain their choice of 'it' rather than 'she' to describe the baseship Hybrid because 'this stage of development does not seem human enough to be worthy of the courtesy of gender recognition that we extend our pets' (103, note 4). In science fiction, however, gender need not exist at all and their statement highlights how many humanoid Cylon models have strongly (or even over-) determined gender identities. The notion that the Hybrid is a primitive form of Cylon life, moreover, underlines her representation as a kind of Kristevan archaic mother (or a pre-Oedipal child, in contrast to Caeners' reading of the humanoid Cylons as Oedipally conflicted); her difference to the patriarchal, symbolic norm is writ large, in gendered terms.

Images of a wounded and comatose Anders effectively becoming a Cylon Hybrid in Season Four potentially offer a challenge to the feminized trend. Shot in the head during the mutiny aboard Galactica, Anders slips into a coma after brain surgery to remove the bullet. The other Cylons on Galactica suggest that plugging him in like a Hybrid might 'help him reset his neural net' ('Someone to Watch Over Me' 4.17). This leads him to function like a Hybrid for a while, but he does not regain his former self and eventually pilots the empty fleet ships to a fiery death in the sun ('Daybreak (Part Two)'). Part of the effect here is in the transformation of the active Anders into a neutered and blank conduit: one way to read this is that his hybridization feminizes him. He even has his brain drilled, the kind of invasive medical procedure previously associated with female characters. A similar dynamic is at work in the earlier 'Six of One' (4.02), which contains a montage of bloody surgery carried out on the Cylon Raiders under Cavil's orders to ensure they do not rebel. In other words, Cylon technology is feminized, even for male or ungendered Cylons.

Love, Romance, Family

Since reproduction in the show tends to be centred on the biological, it is 'naturally' aligned with the female. For Cylons, feminized reproduction is also associated with non-rational elements such as love and romance – elements that underpin patriarchal power and the traditional family in a heteronormative society. Religious belief demonstrates that Cylons are not simply rational technology and the implication that Cylon–human reproduction (followed as a religious commandment) requires love adds a further irrational dimension. As Helo explains, 'They have this theory: maybe the one thing they were missing was love. So Sharon and I . . . we were set up to—' ('The Farm'). Initially, love or lust is introduced as a tactic on the part of the Cylons, both for Helo and Athena, as a means to an end, and when Six seduces Baltar to gain the access codes needed for the attack on the Twelve Colonies. However, things do not go entirely to plan. As Lampkin observes, 'Love. Precocious evolutionary move, fashioning Cylons to be capable of experiencing it. I don't know if it was engineered as a tactical imperative, but . . . it's not for the faint-hearted, is it?' ('The Son Also Rises' 3.18). Being one half of a Cylon–human relationship makes for a unique experience, and writer Bradley Thompson observes that Caprica Six and Boomer 'probably messed up their chances for seamless reintegration into Cylon society' by falling in love with humans (in Bassom, *The Official Companion Season Two*, 93).

Cylons may feel both desire and love, yet both are focused primarily (though not exclusively) on female Cylons. This is not unusual in science fiction representation: compare the female replicants, especially Rachael, in *Blade Runner*, obvious antecedents for the Cylons. Battis observes that the 'female cyborg is often granted a liberatory and even recuperative sexuality within cyborg studies' (42), though this is not necessarily the case in science fiction, and indeed he argues that *Farscape* operates rather differently. In *Battlestar Galactica*, Six may appear to be an example of 'liberatory' sexuality, but a nuanced representation means that her (conventionally sexualized) visual representation could distract from other aspects, and most Sixes seem to be characterized by 'sensuality and physicality', even if these are portrayed in different ways, as actor Tricia Helfer explains (in Bassom, *The Official Companion Season Two*, 121). Thus Six can be both a femme fatale and an angel, as well as points between, encompassing a range of female roles, conventional and otherwise. Male Cylons are less obviously sexualized, perhaps a play on the typical science fiction split between male rationality and female (sexualized) physicality. Leoben's relationship with Kara, for instance, is characterized by hostility and violence in an exaggerated version of the eroticized antagonism that underlies other liaisons. In only a handful of scenes do we see a (known) male Cylon engaging in sexual activity. Before she is revealed as a Cylon, Ellen exchanges sexual favours for the release of Tigh on occupied New Caprica ('Occupation' 3.01). This explicit scene with Cavil clearly demonstrates a gendered power dynamic: Ellen 'uses the only skills she has, her feminine wiles', to help her husband, observes actor Kate Vernon (in Bassom, *The Official Companion Season Three*, 41). This is not straightforward sex, 'It's more violent. Ellen wants to kill this man', says Vernon (34). The meaning of this scene is revisited in Season Four when we realize that Ellen is/was a Cylon and it becomes part of an ongoing hostility between the two ('No Exit'); she even mentions 'the swirl' from 'Occupation' to Boomer, Cavil's new sexual partner. Another scene, showing Cavil with Boomer, is still, apparently, about power, since he introduces her to D'Anna as his 'pet Eight' ('The Hub' 4.09). Cavil's enmity with first Six and then Ellen is partly driven by the familiar opposition between the machine perfection he seeks and the (abject) messy emotions and sexuality that Ellen valorizes, or Six's religious belief and sexualization.

A recent article describes Eight as the 'love model' of Cylon (Pegues), and it is certainly true that if Six and Ellen are (primarily) sexualized, Eights are objects of love in several relationships. Boomer's early liaison with Tyrol is represented as physical, but the aftermath implies that it was based on love. From the outset, Athena's relationship with Helo is presented as love and is situated within a context of traditional heteronormativity, down to their marriage (she takes his name and becomes Sharon Agathon; compare this with Cally, who becomes – at least in *The Official Companion* – Cally Henderson-Tyrol) and the birth of their daughter. The 'forbidden love' aspect reinforces this: Athena defects to the humans to be with Helo, while he endures distrust for being a 'toaster-lover'. Roslin assumes that it 'would be disastrous' in a strategic sense for Athena to raise Hera herself ('Downloaded') – another example of a science fiction pregnancy becoming a matter for public debate. Like Sarah Connor in the *Terminator* cycle, Athena is the mother of the future and her mothering is not simply a personal matter. Yet Athena (unlike the Sarah Connor of *Terminator 2*, 1991) is consistently presented as a good mother in the traditional, human sense. She sacrifices herself to reclaim Hera from the Cylons, persuading Helo to shoot her so she will be reborn on a resurrection ship and thus access the Cylon fleet ('Rapture' 3.12). Her (vision-induced) fears about Hera being abducted lead her to shoot the Cylon leader (a Six) when the truce is arranged in Season Four, an instance of her parental role overtaking her social duty ('Guess What's Coming to Dinner?' 4.07). A lingering transition between scenes in 'Sometimes a Great Notion' (4.11) shows Athena, Helo and Hera playing aeroplane in their quarters, presenting them as a genuinely happy family – soon to be shattered by the abduction of Hera.

Athena's character is set in direct contrast to Boomer, another Eight, whose sleeper-agent status left the lasting scars noted by Thompson. Boomer's conversion to Cavil's philosophy of Cylons as good machines is challenged when she meets former lover Tyrol again, and sees the shared projection of their possible future life. This image of domestic bliss might, for some, resonate with Leoben's disturbing 'playing house' with Kara during the occupation of New Caprica but it is presented initially as derived from love rather than controlling obsession. However, when Boomer gets Tyrol's help to escape from Galactica and a Cylon death sentence for treason and, unknown to him, abducts Hera, Roslin states that 'Sharon Valerii preys upon' feelings and emotions ('Someone to Watch Over Me'), a rather different reading of Eight. Even Cavil describes the Eights as 'self-destructive' and 'hyper-emotional' ('No Exit'). The comparison intensifies when Athena's self-sacrifice in trying to rescue her child is contrasted with Boomer's threat to kill Hera just to stop her crying, in 'a scene [from 'Rapture'] that proved highly controversial with the US Sci Fi Channel' (Bassom, *The Official Companion Season Three*, 73). The comparison is further developed during Boomer's escape when she passes herself off as Athena and has sex with Helo (who demonstrably cannot tell the difference) while the captive Athena watches, bound and gagged, from the closet. Boomer's kidnapping of Hera may present her as lacking maternal feeling, but they build an affinity and Boomer is the first to discover Hera can project like a Cylon ('Islanded in a Stream of Stars' 4.18). Boomer is partly redeemed when she rescues Hera from Simon's medical testing although Athena kills her anyway ('Daybreak (Part Two)'). Motherhood and loving relationships, then, are used as a means of distinction as well as connection between different Eights.

Caprica Six also puts herself in danger to save Athena and Hera (compare her debut in the miniseries as a baby-killer) by accompanying them to the human fleet, and D'Anna risks herself to take Hera and find 'true love' after the occupation dissolves ('Exodus (Part One)' 3.03). The very fact that Caprica and Tigh conceive a child suggests that they love each other, working on the model set up by Athena and Helo (though here both are Cylons). Certainly this is how Ellen reads the situation, and the tensions between her, Tigh and Caprica at least partly contribute to a miscarriage, leaving Hera again the only hope for the future of the Cylon race. All this suggests that the Cylons who become the most human are those who adopt recognizable gender and sex roles. Certainly, the notion of romantic togetherness (another fantasy of wholeness, to return to Gumpert's term) is used to reflect the union of Cylon and human, especially since two of three couples left at the end of the series are human and Cylon (Six and Baltar; Athena and Helo).

Hybridity, Wholeness

Hybridity is thus a key factor in this representation. The Cylons, as their name implies and the show insists throughout, are cyborgs. Cylon 'evolution' was achieved through hybridizing the human and the artificial ('Razor', 4.00), and the ultimate goal of Cylon reproduction appears to be Cylon-human hybrids such as Hera, seen by some as preferable to reliance on resurrection technology. Pregnancy itself can be seen as hybridity, a joining of selves, and intercorporeal exchanges 'blur the line between Cylon and human' (Catherine Waldby, in Leaver 140) further: Athena is given immunity to the virus affecting other Cylons in 'A Measure of Salvation' through her previous pregnancy. The hybridity of the cyborg (like human-alien reproduction) has often been taken as science fiction's way of addressing race and interracial rela-tionships (tackling miscegenation, for instance, or incorporating the trope of the 'tragic mulatto'), and Eight in particular could be read as a new version of this. Yet the Cylons are not concerned with purity of race, they are willing to continue their 'evolution' via hybrid reproduction; hybridity is, after all, their nature.

The human characters are most concerned with maintaining clear distinctions between human and Cylon and persistently refuse to see the Cylons as people. This is demonstrated in the genocide storyline of 'Torn' (3.06) and 'A Measure of Salvation', as well as in the arc concerning the threat that Hera might pose to human existence. In Season Four it is developed through tensions within the fleet following the truce with the Cylon rebels and acceptance of their help in maintaining the ageing Galactica. Baltar warns Admiral Adama against Galactica becoming a 'blended' ship because, in a neat image capturing the visceral side of Cylon technology, 'You are pouring Cylon blood into her veins', Both Adama and Roslin realize this blending has already happened when they see a Six posting a picture of a Cylon on the memorial wall where the ship's dead are remembered ('Deadlock' 4.16), but our sense of the ship as a hybrid construct also comes from the biomaterial used in repairs – the substance literally grows into the ship, making 'her' appear new or alien. Hera's hybridity is, as Christopher Deis notes, 'key to resolving the human and Cylon conflict' (164) and the eventual hybridity of the battleship Galactica mirrors the close relationship formed between Cylons and humans towards the end of the series, such that they become one species.

All this has happened before and all this will happen again, as the show continually reminds us, and Season Four reveals that the lost Thirteenth Tribe were Cylons, and then that hybrid Hera is 'Mitochondrial Eve' or the 'common ancestor' of all humans in the far future. Gallardo C. and Smith suggest that in the *Alien* films, 'patriarchy always desires what the woman has inside of her (her womb or her child) but never the woman herself' (153); here social constructions such as patriarchy and (to a lesser extent) gender are put into evolutionary perspective by a cyclical mythology. The emphasis on natural elements in the closing episode(s) on the fertile new Earth conflates the feminization of reproduction with Hera's role as 'Eve', rendering a vision of Mother Nature. Circularity brings together past and future and, although this conclusion is apparently all about reconciling oppositions, it insists on femininity as key to reproduction, evolution and survival of the species, maintaining binary constructions of sex and gender.

The feminization of soft technology in *Battlestar Galactica* subverts some stereotypes of gender, as the representation of birth as female simultaneously perpetuates others. It is notable, though, that the uncanny elements inherent in the humanoid Cylons are reduced by hybridity with humans and especially via conventions of love and family. The dynamic of realism (the show's aesthetic) and the fantastic (its genre) also creates tensions in representation: the science fictional space-travel setting defamiliarizes key areas of gender, sex and reproduction but naturalistic realism often denotes power as gendered. *Battlestar Galactica* is as much an origin myth as it is a representation of a futuristic society, and the description of Hera as 'Mitochondrial Eve' combines integral, and apparently contradictory, discourses of science and religious myth. The series cannot resolve the apparent paradox but it does show – extremely effectively – how traditionally patriarchal discourses, such as politics, science and religion, can be combined with science fictional imagery to render the complex ways in which gender is constructed.

Works Cited

Balsamo, Anne. 'Reading Cyborgs Writing Feminism.' *Cybersexualities: A Reader on Feminist Theory, Cyborgs and Cyberspace.* Ed. Jenny Wolmark. Edinburgh: Edinburgh University Press, 1999. 145–56.

Bassom, David. *Battlestar Galactica: The Official Companion.* London: Titan, 2005.

—— *Battlestar Galactica: The Official Companion Season Two.* London: Titan, 2006.

—— *Battlestar Galactica: The Official Companion Season Three.* London: Titan, 2007.

Battis, Jes. *Investigating Farscape: Uncharted Territories of Sex and Science Fiction.* London: I.B.Tauris, 2007.

Caeners, Torsten. 'Humanity's Scarred Children: The Cylon's Oedipal Dilemma in *Battlestar Galactica*.' *Extrapolation* 49.3 (2008): 368–84.

Deis, Christopher. 'Erasing Difference: The Cylons as Racial Other.' *Cylons in America: Critical Studies in* Battlestar Galactica. Ed. Tiffany Potter and C. W. Marshall. New York and London: Continuum, 2008. 156–68.

Doane, Mary Ann. 'Technophilia: Technology, Representation and the Feminine.' *Cybersexualities: A Reader on Feminist Theory, Cyborgs and Cyberspace.* Ed. Jenny Wolmark. Edinburgh: Edinburgh University Press, 1999. 20–33.

Gallardo C, Ximena and Jason Smith. *Alien Woman: The Making of Lt. Ellen Ripley.* New York: Continuum, 2004.

Gumpert, Matthew. 'Hybridity's End.' *Cylons in America: Critical Studies in* Battlestar Galactica. Ed. Tiffany Potter and C. W. Marshall. New York and London: Continuum, 2008. 143–55.

Kristeva, Julia. *Desire in Language.* Ed. Leon S. Roudiez. Trans. Thomas Gora, Alice Jardine and Leon S. Roudiez. Oxford: Blackwell, 1981.

Leaver, Tama. '"Humanity's Children": Constructing and Confronting the Cylons.' *Cylons in America: Critical Studies in* Battlestar Galactica. Ed. Tiffany Potter and C. W. Marshall. New York and London: Continuum, 2008. 131–42.

Marshall, C. W. and Matthew Wheeland. 'The Cylons, the Singularity, and God.' *Cylons in America: Critical Studies in* Battlestar Galactica. Ed. Tiffany Potter and C. W. Marshall. New York and London: Continuum, 2008. 91–104.

Moore, Robert W. '"To Be a Person": Sharon Agathon and the Social Expression of Individuality.' *Cylons in America: Critical Studies in* Battlestar Galactica. Ed. Tiffany Potter and C. W. Marshall. New York and London: Continuum, 2008. 105–17.

Newton, Judith. 'Feminism and Anxiety in *Alien.*' *Alien Zone: Cultural Theory and Contemporary Science Fiction.* Ed. Annette Kuhn. London: Verso, 1990. 82–7.

Nixon, Nicola. 'Cyberpunk: Preparing the Ground for Revolution or Keeping the Boys Satisfied.' *Cybersexualities: A Reader on Feminist Theory, Cyborgs and Cyberspace.* Ed. Jenny Wolmark. Edinburgh: Edinburgh University Press, 1999. 191–207.

Parks, Lisa. 'Special Agent or Monstrosity?: Finding the Feminine in *The X-Files.*' *'Deny All Knowledge': Reading The X-Files.* Ed. David Lavery, Angela Hague and Marla Cartwright. Syracuse, NY: Syracuse University Press, 1996. 121–34.

Pegues, Juliana Hu. 'Miss Cylon: Empire and Adoption in *Battlestar Galactica.' MELUS* 33.4 (2008): 189–209

Peirse, Alison. 'Uncanny Cylons: Resurrection and Bodies of Horror.' *Cylons in America: Critical Studies in* Battlestar Galactica. Ed. Tiffany Potter and C. W. Marshall. New York and London: Continuum, 2008. 118–30.

Sofia, Zoe. 'Virtual Corporeality: A Feminist View.' *Cybersexualities: A Reader on Feminist Theory, Cyborgs and Cyberspace.* Ed. Jenny Wolmark. Edinburgh: Edinburgh University Press, 1999. 55–68.

Stone, Allecquere Rosanne. 'Will the Real Body Please Stand Up? Boundary Stories About Virtual Cultures.' *Cybersexualities: A Reader on Feminist Theory, Cyborgs and Cyberspace.* Ed. Jenny Wolmark. Edinburgh: Edinburgh University Press, 1999. 69–98.

Wolmark, Jenny, ed. *Cybersexualities: A Reader on Feminist Theory, Cyborgs and Cyberspace.* Edinburgh: Edinburgh University Press, 1999.

Woodward, Kathleen. 'From Virtual Cyborgs to Biological Time Bombs: Technocriticism and the Material Body.' *Cybersexualities: A Reader on Feminist Theory, Cyborgs and Cyberspace.* Ed. Jenny Wolmark. Edinburgh: Edinburgh University Press, 1999. 280–94.

Disco Galactica
Futures Past and Present

BENJAMIN HALLIGAN

Lost in Reimagination

A liberal's case against monopoly-minded multinational media conglomerates, when it comes to decrying the paucity of quality in today's broadcast programming, often rests on the multiplicity of sequels, prequels, remakes, cycles, specials, tie-ins, one-offs and spin-offs. This characteristic is explained as a result of the acquisition of copyrights that comes with buy-outs or take-overs of other broadcast media companies – and their archives – as monopoly status is further consolidated. Yet if this industrial house style of television programming can be identified as typifying the Rupert Murdoch era, then the case for a 'national' television drama culture, one that attained a universality with (rather than despite of) an 'individual voice' – a case once made by Murdoch's implacable enemy, television dramatist Dennis Potter (22) – should be, by rights, long forgotten. And yet Potter's argument now seems, with the return of *Battlestar Galactica* and series such as *Curb Your Enthusiasm*, *The Office*, *Deadwood*, *The West Wing*, *24* and *The Wire*, impressively far-sighted. For Potter, real life was infinitely mine-able for the television dramatist, demanding a richness and complexity in its representation that both challenged and informed, and yet was accepted by the television viewer. Clearly something of this dynamic has survived, even with the contemporary propensity for the dilution of just such original programming, which structures an anaemic postmodern culture (and nowhere more so than in the besieged culture of popular television), in which nothing is understood to be new, or can usefully aspire to break new ground. Producing quality television, therefore, necessitates a tricky negotiation: to be both new, and yet to cast that problematic newness as accommodating the old – that is, new but often within the multiplicity of sequels, prequels, remakes, cycles, specials, tie-ins, one-offs and spin-offs. In this context, at first glance, the 2000s series of *Battlestar Galactica* represents an arresting achievement of just such a negotiation.

The vaunted 'reimagination' with which *Battlestar Galactica* was introduced, or reintroduced, suggests a dialectical relationship between the original, 1978–9 *Battlestar Galactica* series (hereafter abbreviated to *BSG1*, excluding the *Battlestar Galactica 1980* series of 1980) and the contemporary series of *Battlestar Galactica* (*BSG*, 2004–9). The latter is not entirely a remake of the former, and not entirely a sequel to it, yet it is also not entirely a self-contained text, as separate from it. *BSG* flags up thematic continuums and the very imagination of its reworkings of the motifs, characters and enemies, concerns and even vocabulary of *BSG1* as all still present – a continuity long after computer-generated imagery (CGI) has supplanted matt and model work. *BSG* is old and new; familiar and alien; of then but from now. The former haunts the latter, particularly in the all-important opening episodes, in which both series need to establish their narratives, introduce their characters, dazzle with their science fiction visions, and establish the grounds for a deepening and furthering of all these facets. The demands of television sci-fi necessitate a front-loading of wares – an immediate 'experience' – for the speed seduction of the virginal audiences. And in these opening salvos, large slices of *BSG1* are – and perhaps this is the most prosaic, and so most welcome description of the idea of a reimagination – simply rewritten for *BSG*. Once again, mankind's guard is unwisely down, enabling the Cylons to mount an attack of such ferocity and completeness that *once again* (to the extent that considering *BSG* as picking up the story where *BSG1* left off renders this moment in *BSG* comically implausible and dramatically ridiculous) the human race itself becomes an endangered species. And once again the Battlestar Galactica spaceship and its Colonial Viper space fighters are fired up to repel, or at least mitigate, this sudden attack.

To consider the dialectical relationship between *BSG1* and *BSG* in intertextual terms – an invitation extended by the continuums present in *BSG* – suggests an insight into the television series per se at the dawn of the twenty-first century: multi-platform grand narratives, created through and disseminated across a variety of media (DVDs and their extras, internet/ mobile phone downloads, exclusives for fan groupings, console or interactive gaming, and even the weekly television broadcasts of old). This replaces Potter's dream of television as the great, singular populist art form (the one vision, often shown just the once, for all) with a hydra-headed form of endless possible entry points into any number of variants of the narrative. But such intertextuality bolsters an enticing myth of reimagination: that the old series, shortcomings and all, is *reimaginable* – that the old series now speaks to us, via the new; the *BSG1* vision of a beleaguered humanity now never more relevant, so that the seeds of a visionary quality to be found in *BSG1* can only now be cultivated. After all, what is old, forgotten science fiction other than 'visionary' once it re-emerges in such critically praised contexts?[1] The suggestion of an intertextual reading of *BSG1*, in *BSG*, is selective: there is plenty in *BSG1* that does not receive the reimagination treatment. And those elements left behind point to the limitations of the surface political liberalism of *BSG*, and the way in which the process of reimagining reveals an ideological shift between the times that *BSG1* and *BSG* were created. It is from this perspective that this chapter will conclude by questioning the ideology of *BSG* in respect to *its* times.

Ditching retrospective intertextual readings returns a consideration of *BSG1* to its historical time and place: late 1970s West

Coast North America. That is, *BSG1* speaks of a popular television culture at the end of the celebrated phase of New Hollywood, with producers and television companies still unsure just what the kids want to see, but happy to follow discernible emergent market trends. *BSG1* follows the leads of *Close Encounters of the Third Kind* (1977) and *Star Wars* (1977) – in respect of the then newfound popularity of sci-fi – and, as with *Happy Days* (1974–84), subscribes to a reinvigorated, 1950s-era mythology for its young adult cast (preferable to the anti-establishment 1960s and the moral uncertainties of Nixon's 1970s). And yet, hedging their bets, and perhaps even taking guidance from market research, the producers were clearly reluctant to leave the militarism of *BSG1* unqualified by a mildly anti-establishment, slightly revolution-minded, consciousness. (The unapologetic militarism of the *Rambo* films (1982, 1985, 1988, 2008) and their like, which abandoned any such liberal kowtowing, were only a few years away – but after the dawn of Reaganism). Typically, the vehicle for just such a modish consciousness is the vicissitudes of fashion, and so *BSG1* seems to have imbibed, and regurgitated, elements from another part of the popular cultural scene of its target audience: disco. In this respect, with disco culture imported to provide a contemporary ambience, an ambience that works to temper the militarism, it becomes understandable why at least the *politics* of disco culture were not reimaginable. In fact, for *BSG*'s own contemporariness, in a series that goes to such lengths to suggest itself as a mirror to the post-9/11 West, and that was critically received as such (Tranter 49), the equivalent of a *Battlestar Galactica* disco culture is redundant. The regurgitated disco culture, as a means of access to and reverberation of a certain ontology of feeling flowing from a particular ideological reading of the world, has been excised from the micropolitics of *BSG*, banished in favour of the new seriousness with which the post-9/11 West is to be explored. A battle-hardened space warrior is required for *BSG*: a post-*Rambo*-ization of the libertarian-hedonist cosmic explorer of yesteryear – someone with no time for trivial recreations.

So what is abandoned? What did disco culture represent at the close of the 1970s that is unwelcome in a contemporary *Battlestar Galactica* – essentially unremakeable, and so seemingly lost in reimagination, as it were? At this juncture, such a trade-off seems to suggest an honest replacement of *BSG1* libertarianism with *BSG*'s tarnished liberalism, as befits popular drama, post-9/11. But, as Alex Cox observed in 'Blockbuster Barbarism', the tide of popular American fare seems to be actively dragging such tarnished liberalism away from its one-time Hollywood home, making way for once-unimaginable discussions on the legitimacy of torture. And such a shift has occurred through a greater creative collaboration between Hollywood 'movers' and the burgeoning industries and institutions of 'homeland security', post-9/11, as is now well documented. Is this shift to the right not the context for a consideration of *BSG*? After all, from this vantage point, such a shift could be understood as the price for the surprising renaissance in quality television drama. In this respect, the process of reimagination presents *Battlestar Galactica* as a useful example of this shift, from disco sci-fi to neoliberal sci-fi.

Disco Sci-Fi

The trappings of a late 1970s disco culture, with disco as signifying the look and feel of the new, can be readily discerned in *BSG1*. But the wider disco culture that *BSG1* drew upon was, for most commentators, the wrong one. It drew upon disco once it had sold out, once it occupied the top forty music charts rather than presenting an alternative to them; it was disco culture once it had become fully integrated into the discourses of corporate entertainment (of music, fashion, interior design and so on), the disco of the discotheques newly installed in franchised chain hotels, disco as 'Disneyland with tits', as it is described in the heavily sanitized disco movie *Thank God It's Friday* (1978). The ironic mode of *That '70s Show* (1998–2006) is a paean to this kind of disco. The 'right' (as in the culturally authentic) disco culture, as the soundtrack to, or even the enabler of, a carefree (pre-AIDs, pre-crack cocaine, pre-Reagan) idyll of sexual hedonism, resonates more in *Boogie Nights* (1997). In this latter respect, in disco culture comes a late flowering of the Summer of Love – a radical liberation to a state of depoliticized and freed desire – to be followed by the struggle for the reintegration of this dangerous turn into bourgeois mores. The dilution and selling of disco culture (that is, the triumphant emergence of the 'wrong' disco culture) represents a reshaping of disco culture in order to mitigate or neutralize the radical potential of the liberations of the body. These liberations from previous codes of 'straight' behaviour (particularly in relation to sexuality/morality) were founded on the liberation from the dictates of biological necessity: in the Western society of abundance, a generation after wartime austerity, the need for biological survival is overtaken by the drives of desire, with those drives now routed through the pleasure-oriented technologies where flows of intensities of feeling finally recalibrate the functioning of the body. In this, the agency of organs comes to be understood to be replaced by (or surrendered to) technology, creating new intensities of pleasure between the two (body and technology), so that Shapiro, in his history of disco, can claim 'disco is the ultimate cyborg music, the ultimate coupling of orgasm and machine' (103). Thus a new and ambiguous liberation comes from the very heart of the machine, springing from the allotted pleasure-times in advanced Western techno-capitalist societies.

Shapiro here journalistically invokes the notion of the 'body without organs', as outlined by Gilles Deleuze and Félix Guattari (165–84)[2] – something not unusual for critical considerations of the seemingly apolitical freeing of desires in the zone of mental and physical liberation of the disco floor. The invocation arguably holds good for a consideration of disco-induced bliss as 'plugging into desire, of effectively taking charge of desires' (Deleuze and Guattari 184), but it is questionable whether disco does not, in fact, induce one of the false doubles of the 'body without organs': those 'empty vitreous bodies, cancerous bodies, totalitarian and fascist' (183). Indeed, the concern of this chapter is exactly false doubling; the sold-out disco, the shammed emancipation that blocks the revolutionary potential of bodily liberation that an optimistic Marcuse had identified, as discussed below.

The radical potential was evident in the fledgling new life-styles and patterns of communalism that first emerged within, or even as, disco culture. Thus the 'right' disco culture – that of a hedonistic, post-moral, underground flowering of sexually 'problematic' lifestyle choices to the cold and machine-generated beats of (often European) twelve-inch mixes – was vanquished with the market's reimagination of its essence as sexual freedom per se; sexuality as the structure itself, and not the structuring agent. Hence the slightly prurient sexual scenarios of a post-moral world shown in many science fictions, such as *Logan's Run* (1976) – which mostly consists of an ease of moving between partners. But there is a sci-fi prehistory of the coupling of man and machine, desire and technology – after all, which other genre is best suited to explore such future scenarios? – that flourished between 1968 and the emergence of disco, and so complicates the relationship between inauthentic disco culture and science fiction. Such a vision of a dehumanized near-future is apparent in *THX 1138* (1971), *Dark Star* (1974) and, most notably, in *2001: A Space Odyssey* (1968). Miller traces the influence of *2001* across the 1970s, albeit with the lonely vision of the future man isolated in his computer-regulated environs reworked as an appealingly futuristic prospect in advertisements, and through architectural design (24–5). Thus the killer computer does not preclude human advancement or even regeneration – in fact, this contradiction is the very story of the domestic and erotic 'remake' of *2001*: Donald Cammell's *Demon Seed* (1977). The paradox is present in *Silent Running* (1972) too, which pits ecological and technologi-cal futures against each other, with its hippie protagonist going so far as to assassinate colleagues who opt for the latter, and then attempt to humanize his worker drones while maintaining his spaceship-greenhouse for the revegetation of a post-nuclear war Earth. In the world of *Logan's Run* the technological future gives on the one hand (a society entirely for the pleasure of its beautiful occupants) but takes on the other (since breeding has become a function of the HAL-run city-state, and to avoid the coming, disastrous overcrowding – one of the racist myths of the 1970s – no one may enter their thirties). Whereas science fiction once offered warnings (the dire shape of things to come, with the fight for humanity against the machine, or alien invasion, as the standard line of battle) – a warning that returns with BSG – this post-1968, pre-disco sci-fi sensibility expresses a cautious, anticipatory welcome: man can yet evolve for better or worse, rather than face extinction. The untameable spirit of man persists in this future – in the shambolic hippy 'crash pad' spaceships of Dark Star and The Hitchhiker's Guide to the Galaxy (the BBC television series, 1981), in Dr Hans Zarkov's defiance of brainwashing (clinging onto his indelible memories of the Beatles and sexual experiences) in Flash Gordon (1980), and later in Officer Murphy's usurping of his cyber-genetic programming in RoboCop (1987), and in the psycho-sexual sci-fi explorations of space, the 'sexual odyssey' of Starcrash (1979), Sleeper (1973), Sexmission (Seksmisja, 1984), On the Silver Globe (Na srebrnym globie, 1978-1988) and even Solaris (Solyaris, 1972). Here the cosmos is feminized, this final frontier as a sexual frontier: a vaginal darkness to be, like its siren female denizens, conquered by the bold males venturing ever forth, for whom both females and space represent the waiting, expectant 'other'.

However, the acceptance or even celebration of the radical potential of disco and the body without organs is rare, and certainly does not colour many Boogie Nights-style retrospective readings of the historical period.[3] Corporate disco culture required the reassurance of conservative revisions of disco culture: disco as a feel-good communalism, clean and depoliticized (unlike the murky and protest-minded psychedelic music that preceded it), and with sexual desire (via John Travolta's working-class hero in Saturday Night Fever (1977)) as a hetero- rather than homo- or pansexual concern. This phase of revisionism came between the 'death' of disco and the anti-disco backlash; between the high tide of disco fever following *Saturday Night Fever* and the beginning of the end of disco's stranglehold on the charts. Shapiro sees this process as culminating in 1979 (194, 226), which coincides exactly with ABC's original broadcast of *BSG1*, from September 1978 to April 1979.

Indeed, although *BSG1* – as a high-budget, primetime television series – effectively *is* one such revision, traces of the utopian dreams and aspirations of disco remain. Such traces are to be found, therefore, in the undercurrent of aesthetics, ambience, performance and space, and in the 'filler' in-between moments of narrative importance. Elsewhere *BSG1* simply recycles many of the familiar paranoias of Cold War science fiction, and in this sense is very un-disco. Indeed, it is at the very moment of intergalactic communalism – a detente coming together for the common good of all (the peace initiative with which the series, and European film version of *BSG1* start) – that a Cold War *realpolitik* emerges in this sci-fi context. The peace initiative is nothing more than a Cylon ruse to raze humanity once and for all. Repeatedly, thereafter, the human 'Hawks' have realism on their sides while the pacifists are dupes and patsies. The Hawks are thus emboldened to take executive decisions since the pacifists, with their democratic niceties, are recklessly gambling with humanity, have a track record of being dangerously naive, or are simply infiltrated by the enemy. This last belief was held by some on the right in relation to anti-nuclear activists and peace groupings and their infiltration by Soviet agents and far left groups throughout the 1970s and 1980s. *BSG1* accommodates and advances just such a reading; thus Tranter finds in *BSG1*'s Viper pilots an '. . . attitude straight from the pages of Robert M. Heinlein' (47). The bumbling civilian Council of Twelve repeatedly block military initiatives (resulting in the rapid formation of a political-military cabal of Adama, Apollo and Starbuck), with disastrous results. A rightist reading of the US defeat by the North Vietnamese resonates in this dynamic: the soldiers and generals undone at the hands of a meddling civilian leadership, and battlefield valour wasted and nullified by political appeasements. But such 'adjustments' to democratic norms by the cabal are not seen to undermine the democratic structure seriously – after all, the enemy is entirely totalitarian: the Cylon leader is a sole, enthroned figure. In these ways the subtexts and ideological positions of the dramatic narrative of *BSG1* are as reactionary as one could expect.

It is beneath this narrative, however, that an ideological position quite contrary to the aggressive military ethos can be discerned: in the frisson of vintage disco libertarianism. Even within the 'straitened' confines of a heterosexualized disco culture, the current of sexuality is *BSG1*'s very teleology (or its 'force' equivalent). (Homosexuality, rendered as camp behaviour and intonation, is left to asexual robots – also taking the *Star Wars* and, arguably, *2001* leads or, more problematically, marginalizing the gay origins of disco culture by now ascribing homosexuality to those not-quite-human figures still walking among us). This frisson is difficult to avoid, especially with the hindsight of some three decades, which invariably pushes the datedness of the set and costumes designs to the fore. There is a predominance of disco lighting; sensual reds and purples flood the sets. At other times, fairly empty sound stages are lent space and depth, and an aspirant science fiction artificiality, via the strategic placing of visible spotlights in the background, with their cross-flares arcing across the camera lens – an aesthetic device typical of disco (cameras often track or pan into flaring spotlights in disco-era promo videos, sometimes in anticipation of a lap dissolve or fade). Under or against or even lit by such a sensual colour scheme, Apollo and Starbuck have the look of Studio 54 busboys. Even when unlit and in action, their heterosexual posturing in their Vipers is undercut by cutaway shots to their manicured nails on the spaceship's fire and boost buttons. And this sexual identity extends beyond make-up and sexualized uniforms (with the belts worn at angles); Starbuck's tangled love life is a major theme in *BSG1* – even structuring whole episodes. Indeed, in a way unthinkable in *BSG*, substantial subplots in *BSG1* concern, or are given over to, the pursuit of pleasure. This is particularly so in the visit to the alien disco in 'Saga of a Star World' (*BSG1*

1.01–03), during which Starbuck considers managing the resident disco singers on 'the star circuit', and another character is accused of 'smoking plant vapour'. It is no exaggeration to say that, in the context of the plot, these party-going exploits endanger the existence of humanity. And the theme persists elsewhere, in terms of the overriding pursuit of pleasure: the (romantically) disruptive reappearance of Aurora, Starbuck's old flame, now a Baader-Meinhof-style revolutionary moll, in 'Take the Celestra' (*BSG1* 1.23); Starbuck's gambling and his flirting with his (female-voiced) Viper onboard computer, even when in peril (and 'she' reciprocates; 'anything you say, honey'); his willingness to put the mission on a backburner in favour of a cache of bootleg vintage liquor in 'The Long Patrol' (*BSG1* 1.07); his use of a Viper as a place of lovemaking; and the way in which Apollo's soldierly concern for Serina's wellbeing soon merges with a seduction of her. Even in the early, desperate hours, the checking of human survivors turns into a cruising-like social activity – indeed, a party is discovered to be in full swing.

The pursuit of pleasure coincides with the pursuit of women in *BSG1*; the series was remarkably free of exclusively male patterns of behaviour: the kind of male bonding and whooping it up that could be expected in the wake of repelling enemy attacks. And so the disco aesthetic is strongly present in the desired female, conveying their presence and availability in terms of the sexual pleasure of, or as, the future female. And the futureness of these females indicates the kind of shopping mall-coloured vision of things to come also specific to the West Coast in the late 1970s. The blueprint for such females is based on the figure, hair and skin pallor of the actress-model Farrah Fawcett-Majors, particularly in *Charlie's Angels* (1976–80). Here the female is decorated and clothed so as to be animated or ventilated by a Big Sur breeze – through the off-the-shoulder gown, through the fluffed hair, blowing stray strands from the face to reveal clear WASP eyes, set against the reds and purples of a summer sunset. This is the quintessential *Playboy* woman of the 1970s: the PA on nightclub hours, the beach tan and halter dresses, shimmeringly orgasmic yet entirely domesticated – that is, born into that first post-war generation of the newly classless, upwardly mobile, leisure time-rich society, able to move from the beach to the office and back again.

The ambiguous position of this female in the context of the end of Second Wave feminism, at the end of the 1970s, is apparent in Fawcett-Majors' own mysterious role in another disco science fiction touchstone: *Logan's Run* (in fact, it was the role that propelled her on into *Charlie's Angels* – chronologically, then, a contemporary reframing of the future woman). Her *Logan's Run* role essentially serves no purpose; in terms of the dramatic narrative, she is redundant. But on the level of a future vision of frictionless free love, her role is pivotal: the future (female) form of pleasure, presiding over a painless plastic surgery clinic able to alter appearances entirely (that is, manipulate the body independent of its organs), for reasons of pleasure (or, for fleeing Logan, disguise).[4] As with *The Graduate* (1967), *Logan's Run* offers an LA-based, LA-styled vision of the near-future (the film was even partly shot in a shopping mall), so that the post 1968 'LA woman', in Fawcett-Majors, becomes the access point to this future – as found in both (in the words of the *Logan's Run*'s introduction) the coming '. . . ecologically balanced world [in which] mankind lives only for pleasure, freed by the servo-mechanisms which provide everything', and on and in the contemporary fashions of the disco floor. This LA woman does not break with the evolution of the female form of pleasure (something attempted by *Star Trek: The Motion Picture* (1979), with its bald female, or a number of female and female–alien hybrid characters in *Space 1999* (1975)), but remains true to its texture – the Aryan, outdoors-healthy, full-lipped and toothsome blondes of, say, Pirelli's 1969 calendar portfolio.[5] As a kind of 'end of history' aesthetic, the LA woman extends from that first post-war generation (with its aesthetic institutionalization of the sexualized, domestic blondes of the pin-ups taken by US servicemen abroad to Europe, where women typically did not match this model), and on into the future. Indeed, *BSG1* opts for the big-haired receptionist/PA type rather than her counterpart, Jessica (Jenny Agutter) of the *Logan's Run* film, whose sexual liberation is tempered by a sense that there must be more to life – a dangerously subversive notion that eventually propels her out of the pleasure-domed future Garden of Eden. The first *Logan's Run* television series (1977–8) also eradicates such a counterpart; Heather Menzies' Jessica melds Fawcett-Majors' appearance with Agutter's role as Logan's love interest and sidekick.

Here, the LA woman represents the horizon of the libertarian imagining of a technological, pleasure-bound, post-feminist, post-late capitalist society. Cassiopeia (Laurette Spang) in *BSG1* fulfils and extends such a role; her 'liberated' sexual status, emphasized with her disco-red dress, is also institutionalized in the world of the series. She is seemingly a reformed legal prostitute (precision is hidden beneath the coyness of the sci-fi terminology employed) so that, once on missions towards the end of the first series, it is her interpersonal (rather than laser gun-wielding) skills that matter to the males. Femininity serves pleasure first and militarism as an afterthought. Much the same could be said for Colonel Wilma Deering (Erin Gray), Commander of the Earth's Defences – the combat Earth Mother in silver jumpsuit and lip gloss – of *Buck Rogers in the Twenty-Fifth Century* (1979–81).

Spaces Exploration

Starbuck, despite Cassiopeia's wishes, inevitably womanizes. The size of the interiors of Galactica, and of the other spaceships in the fleet, and the remoteness of the planets encountered and visited, with their scattered human or alien populations, creates and allows for such an opportunity. Neither disco culture nor this sense and use of sizeable physical spaces make it into *BSG*; indeed the two – disco culture and space – are interconnected. The physical space to roam across the dancefloor, making eye or body contact with those seen and encountered, asserts itself in the sets of *BSG1*. This space odyssey is one in which endless possibilities present themselves – possibilities that necessitate substantial physical spaces for their staging, a space that restores agency to the characters, and gives freedoms to their free wills. It is in the sizeable physical space that the body is free to explore, and free to gravitate towards the loci of desire: the sexually available other bodies. For late 1970s science fiction, this was no radical or particularly new departure; Captain Kirk's love odyssey in the original 1966–9 *Star Trek* series (the clichéd subplot involving a girl on every planet) tempered the stiff, scientific exploration (forever logged and star-dated) of the encountered galaxies with a more physical and communal interaction with beings on/of other worlds. With the dawn of disco, only a few years later, this sensual type of galactic exploration becomes a chief mode for the exploration of other galaxies and interactions with their inhabitants. And such wide-ranging explorations, across such spaces, presuppose a general enlarging of scale: bigger spaceships, bigger spacescapes, bigger space 'action'.

Such bulk and size, in the late 1970s, was closely allied with the fantasy 'wow' factor of sci-fi: the enormity of the UFO at the climax of *Close Encounters of the Third Kind*, for example,[6] or the Gothicism of the cathedral-sized interiors of *The Black Hole* (1979), or James Bond in the shuttle launching bay, and orbiting spaceship, of *Moonraker* (1979). Biskind goes so far as to locate the beginnings of Reagan-era cinema (bombastic, escapist and fantastical) in the opening scene of *Star Wars* – the giant space freighter that rumbles over the heads of the cinema audience (experiencing this rumble via the newly fitted and prerequisite stereo sound system), and onwards to the galaxy vanishing point (337). It is as if enormity had taken the place once occupied by straight special effects and miniatures against matts – the special effects of earlier eras of fantasy.

This 'wow' factor for the late 1970s is predicated on the integration of a dramatic use of size and space into the sci-fi narrative itself. The maze of Galactica's interior or the ruins and architecture of societies and civilizations found on other planets offer space for an infinity of narrative possibilities and surprises:

the geographical scope for unending sagas. The same is often true of *Dr Who* from this time; in 'The Pyramids of Mars' (1975, 13.08–12), for example, the action jarringly shifts from Tardis space travel to an English country house in 1911, to Martian interiors and to a meta-space outside time occupied by Dr Who's nemesis. The enormous spaces of *The Black Hole* encompass previous generations of space explorers, both living (Maximilian Schell's Kurtz-like Dr Hans Reinhardt) and dead (the zombie robot workers), and previous generations of technology (earlier models of robot). To traverse this space, or simply to exist in this space, is the condition of the picaresque adventure. Edmund White described the 1980 New York underground gay disco clubs The Mine Shaft and The Anvil in just such terms (269–85): cruising ever onwards into darkened corners, basements or back rooms, encountering the (newly discovered and entirely available) others. In the resultant collective happening, individualism melts away into events that occur with the synchronization of movements across groups of people, across ethnic categories and even across different classes. Space and exploration are united in this new communal eroticism, with disco culture as (in its earlier manifestation) progressive unifier so that, for White:

> . . . it was more than just the sexual body that disco was concerned with. The dance floor is nothing if not communal, and this group body was a polymorphous, polyracial, polysexual mass affirming its bonds in a space that was out of reach of the tentacles of the church, state or family. At the discotheque, the rigid boundaries imposed by such institutions were thrown out with the careless disregard of someone discarding a spent popper bottle... in the discotheque the seventies practiced what the sixties preached: the communion offered by the dance floor was the embodiment of the vision of peace that the sixties yearned for.   (White 185)

This 'what the sixties preached', as utopian wishful thinking at least, was the point at which, for Marcuse in *An Essay on Liberation* (originally published in 1969), the:

... new sensibility has become ... *praxis*: it emerges in the struggle against violence and exploitation where this struggle is waged for essentially new ways and forms of life: negation of the entire Establishment, its morality, culture; affirmation of the right to build a society in which the abolition of poverty and toil terminates in a universe where the sensuous, the playful, the calm, and the beautiful become forms of existence and thereby the [sic] *Form* of the society itself ... [and at this point] the hatred of the young bursts into laughter and song, mixing the barricade and the dance floor, love play and heroism.   (Marcuse 33)

The spirit of this future form, in the sense of its animating force or its *praxis*, was to be the nascent disco culture: a 'oneness' that arises with and from shared rhythm or feeling – something that, like the 'force', transcends normative modes of communication, becoming a cosmic bonding agent, an 'interplanetarianism' (as an intergalactic variant of cosmopolitianism), free (in the sense of depoliticized, non-partisan) love, an organless harmony between man and machine – the latter as an emancipatory instrument for the former. The 'force', of *Star Wars* vernacular, is an appropriate description of Marcuse's *praxis*: a new metaphysical motor for a secular age, promising fulfilment for those who surrender to it – which is also to surrender to their own desires, since this force permeates and guides the 'good' half of the galaxy. And where else could this permeation be at its purest other than on the dancefloor? Thus the force is relayed from *Star Wars* into The Real Thing's 1979 disco hit, 'Can You Feel the Force' ('People who make war are making love instead / This could be the dawning of another time'), and informs Starbuck's own libertarian-hedonist philosophy: '[We] may as well live for today – we might not have many left' (*BSG1*, 'War of the Gods (Part One)', 1.13).

While *BSG1*'s formal metaphysics are somewhat more prescriptive, so that Ford can readily map them onto Mormon theology,[7] the world of *BSG1* is clearly in the *umma*, as it were, of the force. In this crucial respect (and in respect of a post-structuralist reading), the Hawkish militarism of *BSG1* is immediately diminished. Its nominally foundational position in the text is almost always soon forgotten once the new mission begins, with disco values now recontextualizing militarism as a rearguard action – vanquishing the threatening, amassed enemies in order that the dancing can go on, so to speak. Such a recontextualization of the vehicles of war occurred with The Village People too, dancing on an active warship for the video for 'In the Navy' – a highpoint in the queering of military aesthetics. This overall balance of values is articulated in the introduction to each BSG1 episode: in Patrick McNee's patrician storyteller tones, the idea of a creed ('There are those who believe . . .') and communion ('brothers of men') of humanity is understood as the guiding intelligence of the mission; the fight is for the good 'dawning', to borrow The Real Thing's term. In this respect the fight ultimately subordinates military action to the ideological and metaphysical coordinates of a galactic mission of love – BSG1 as a sci-fi variant of The Love Boat. Thus material comfort remains an integral part of this world; BSG1 opens with a meal for the Quorum, complete with waiters, flowers on the table and velvet curtains.

Two decades later, BSG will open with military hardware-style computer data flashed across the screen, over images of spaceships (rather than BSG1's psychedelic galaxies and abstractions of cosmic gases and clouds) – that is, the point of view is shifted from that of McNee's benevolent observer/chronicler to that of Viper pilot, mid-dogfight.

POV-CGI

How best to describe the profound difference that marks, from this opening moment onwards, the reimagined Battlestar Galactica? It is not so much a matter of the quality of the new aesthetic, nor the careful strategies (possibly even reckless, in relation to the timidity typical of US network television channels) of parleying the particulars of contemporary conflicts into the storyline – most notably with the colonized planet of New

Caprica, post-Cylon attack, as occupied Baghdad (complete with night-vision footage of house raids), and the Cylons themselves as technological blowback. Indeed, the eye-catching nature of these achievements, in themselves, seem to obscure the more fundamental shift between BSG1 and BSG.

The beginnings of an answer to the question comes in the collision of two strategies that are in constant operation in BSG: CGI and point of view (POV). That is, the moment of action, of attack, of catastrophic destruction, of incoming ordnance, of movement in space, of encounters with the Cylons – those moments of 'high-octane' drama, the very 'money shots' of science fiction – often arise from computer-generated imagery seen from the point of view of a protagonist. It is often in this way that the danger of the world of BSG is communicated, and the viewer involuntarily measures his or her own dexterity in relation to it: the POV shot positions us in front of the goaded Cylon, places us in the cockpit of the Viper as debris and missiles hurtle past – a gaming rather than framing aesthetic tendency. This POV-CGI aesthetic is quite different to the use of CGI in Hollywood blockbusters, especially those that illustrate the influence of the Spielberg and Lucas recalibration of experiential cinema at the end of the New Hollywood phase. In this later strain, CGI use is given over to the visualization of the spectacular: the view beheld, and the exactitude of this fantastical sight, as primarily realized on the screen via (*pace* Orson Welles' *mise en scène*) deep focus and depth-of-field shots. It is often used for sequence shots, or elevated establishing shots, with figures or clusters of civilization lost or dwarfed in the enormity of the landscapes. In this is an echo of the aesthetic tradition of German Romanticism: the framing of the world, as encountered, often by a new set of eyes (those of the explorer, or the discoverer of ancient ruins) – the world is found and presented, therefore, essentially objectively, and distanced, and to be surveyed. Thus Spielberg and Lucas remade their lost worlds, or attempted to realize new ones fully.

When this kind of framing occurs in BSG (which, after all, 'classically' concerns a civilization, en masse and in transit), typically with the parade of spaceships à la *2001*, the camera revolts. It suddenly and artlessly lurches into the image, a CCTV-like speed zoom, breaking the vista and restoring an urgency to, and introducing movement within, the image. The imagery of *BSG* is not to be surveyed but to be rapidly scanned – the establishing shot now as a field of data concerning battle – to inform the need for an instantaneous repositioning of the subject (the subject whose POV is used for such shots) so as to outmanoeuvre imminent danger.

When this kind of framing occurs for establishing shots on New Caprica, the onlookers rapidly retreat – into prison-camp tents and huddles of insurgents. The field of battle is no longer the geographical space beheld by the onlooker, necessitating a military leader's reading of that space (natural defences and blind spots in the landscape, possible supply routes and so on). Rather, the field of battle now exists on the level of human interaction. So the spaces for movement – which in *BSG1* allowed for communalism and exploration, and can be equated to Marcuse's 'Form' – are squeezed, and the characters locked down; an individualism of a paranoid kind returns, in the final analysis, with Cylons now disguised as humans, each character can only vouch for themselves.[8] And back inside the mothership, in the mole tunnel corridors of Galactica itself, space is closed in, ditch-like, like the space afforded by the trenches of the First World War. The resultant bunker aesthetic enforces intimacy of an imprisoned rather than erotic kind. And, as with the intimacy of the chamber drama (Ibsen's or Noël Coward's living rooms, or in Sartre's *Huis Clos*), human qualities come to the fore. Ironically, for a series that transcends the typical future war sci-fi scenario of human flesh vs. alien hardware by positing an immortal artificial intelligence that lives on when the hardware it inhabits is destroyed, the old-fashioned quality of the human being becomes all-important.

So the structuring of the aesthetic of *BSG*, via POV CGI, is misleading in terms of theorizing this vision of the future. In short, it is not what is seen, but who sees it. And the seer is locked down, closed in, guarding the premium position of his or her flesh and blood in this world of constantly de- and re-territorializing cyberspace technology. So the fundamental shift between *BSG1* and *BSG*, conceptually and in terms of the concerns of the episodes themselves, is the difference between the human bodies in each series, original and reimagined. The 'message of love' of *BSG1* occurs as, despite the near-complete annihilation of the human race, the bodies of the survivors remain impulse driven, self-possessed (in the usual sense, but also literally) and recreationally (in both senses) minded. Thus the bodies of *BSG1* were at ease in their surroundings, something also lost in reimagination.

The Micropolitics of Apocalyticism

One searches in vain for bodies at ease in *BSG*: not making love (although the love rivalries usual in television series are present and correct, in spite of the Cylon sex dolls thrown into the mix), not in the spaceship's bar (under the wing of a Viper, with most revellers ever-ready in their combat uniforms), not in contemplation (the 'chapel' which, with its innumerable photos of the dead, seems like a variation of Orwell's *Nineteen Eighty-Four* 'hate hour', or a sci-fi holocaust museum) and not sleeping (more than a plague of fantasies come to the fore; the infiltration of the human mind by Cylon psy-ops). Rather, the bodies of *BSG* are taut, limber and anticipating action. Clothing, therefore, is utilitarian: combat uniforms over a variant of gym clothing; the work-out outfit beneath, and for, combat preparedness. Hair is practical; long gone is the big hair, now replaced by manageable crops, or hair tied back into a ponytail. The quality of the skin is rougher too; stubble, blemishes, lines and dark under the eyes rather than the moisturized evenly tanned skin, glossed lips and the general male grooming of *BSG1*. The teeth, however, are impervious to any new, scuzzy digital realism; there is clearly still one frontier sci-fi is reluctant to cross. Much the same set of differences apply to the Cylon robots, old and new – rust has now overrun the shine in these Gothic (rather than pop, and specifically disco, with their vocodered voices) creations, and their weapons.

Thus the reimagined state of war, or more precisely this new future era of war, a total war, a war seemingly without end, in which the battleground is the organic and the physiological – the very existence of the human body in itself – impacts at all moments, on all bodies. The human body is the last line of defence and the zone of resistance: the body attacks and is attacked, it is appropriated (by the Cylons who remain undetected as mock humans) and in adversity regained. The very tactile humanness of the human body – even in sickness and tiredness – is all we have left; it is seen in the blood of bloodied Commander Adama after his surprise bout in the boxing ring, blood that confirms the necessity of his example of self-criticism in keeping the collective guard up.

In the final analysis, the measure of the gravity of the threat to humanity is evident in the way in which there is no longer any territory to defend. War is literally deterritorialized and the only remaining uncrossed frontier or outpost is that of flesh and blood, and its continued existence in the light of the possibility of elimination altogether. The human body that survives under these circumstances is one that invites a consideration of it as, micropolitically, fascist: the message of war, having usurped the message of love, is the very operator, as it were, of the body. That is, the elements of a rightist sensibility of *BSG1* have come to determine the behaviour, use, understanding and ethics of the body rather than prompt the formation of bureaucratic organs of totalitarian fascism of yore (in the cabal formed to overturn the Council of Twelve). The future shock in *BSG* occurs inside the spacesuit, not outside it: the body, in extremis, contorted in its technological shell, as it fights for the survival of the fittest in the cosmic arena. This is crystallized in the abovementioned boxing match: violence as generative, recreational, the moment in which 'the moral' is delivered; violence as the moral and existential index of humankind. Verhoeven's *Starship Troopers* (1997), which also diagnoses a militarized future of intergalactic fascist imperialism for humans and contains an array of suitably repulsive space foot-soldiers, baulks at this final frontier. For Verhoeven, what little optimism there is can be eked out from the wavering of the human proletariat – their humanity just about intact, despite the bombardment of scare-mongering infotainment (a virtual 'false consciousness') and the fascist historical revisionism alive and well at their military academy. However, Verhoeven also factors in massive military incompetence as beginning to engender dissent within the ranks; *BSG* collapses the distinction between the military and the non-military, substantially curtailing such a possibility.

In order to secure the imperilled flesh and blood, the human body itself is caged in; the small spaces in which the human form now fits dominate *BSG*. There are dormitory bunks (rather than the carpets, armchairs and cushions in the living quarters of *BSG1*), cockpits, the mock living rooms of the Cylon prison-flats, tunnels and tents, with the body continually jostled or strapped in or strapped down. All spaces close in. The captain's deck resembles a dingy submarine interior rather than the expansive Cape Canaveral-style control room of the *Star Trek* Enterprise bridge, the settlements of occupied New Caprica resemble a cheek-by-jowl squatters' camp, the winding corridors are now bottlenecked, and even the battlestar's landing bay seems diminished in size – its psychedelic landing lightshow replaced by a modest area for vertical ascents and descents. This pervasive claustrophobia erodes the space for physical action and movement, for expansiveness and dancing, pacing and yelling to colleagues; it blocks off big gestures and the bolting and rolling across the flight deck as it rocks from the impact of Cylon missiles. In short, the diminished space of these sets further clamps down on the body, squeezing the leg-room needed for knee-jerk, instinctive survival-oriented actions: the dodging and diving manoeuvres that, surely, represent one front of spontaneous, tissue intelligence – the human edge on the artificial intelligence of the automatons.

As spaces shrink, the spectrum of possible actions tightens: the humans rely almost completely on the virtual imaging capacities of their armour hardware and computer weapons systems. They only furtively glance out of the cockpit when necessary, and then from under the brims of bulky helmets, to clock the whereabouts of fellow pilots. As space is compacted, the space for secrets goes too. Hiding places disappear and, in the microscope *mise en scène* that emerges, all is seen: the recurring image of the human alone, flooded with white interrogation light (often from above and often blindingly) that returns the imagery of the film to the very texture of the skin – a closeness from which refractions of light across irises are visible. These scrutinized humans, like those of H. G. Wells' novel *The War of the Worlds*, feel observed and experimented upon, their body resistance faltering and failing, fearing that they are merely colonies of bacteria serving a momentary purpose for a ruthless higher intelligence.

This is the magnitude of the future catastrophe that elicits such a response in the future bodies that fight it. For this collective mindset, micropolitical fascism thrives on intertwined complexes that, considered without their science fiction trappings, are far from futuristic: communal persecution and victimhood, survivalist-tinged foreign policies and the invisible enemy as having infiltrated into everyday life.

Mirror to Mirage

It is from this vantage point that a series of more satisfactory connections can be seen to the 'war on terror' than those suggested by the narrative of *BSG*; connections that are not thematic, but textual. The militarized future of *BSG* is presented as an unfortunate necessity – the result of a paradigm shift in warfare so extreme as to prompt, in one much-discussed episode, the suicide bombing of occupying forces. *BSG*'s recontextualization of such future military action therefore presents it as an exception, even to the point of such an aberration as 'our side' engaging in suicide bombing; an exception, but one born of unfortunate necessity. In this, *BSG* effectively dramatizes and fleshes out the grand narrative political myth that critical theorists of globalization understand and have recognized to be in operation. The total war of *BSG* is one in which war is no longer the continuation of politics by other means (to quote Clausewitz) but simply *is* the means of politics so that, today, '. . . war has passed from the final element of the sequences of power – lethal force as a last resort – to the first and primary element, the foundation of politics itself' (Hardt and Negri, *Multitude*, 21).

This new foundation necessitates the indefinite suspension of formal norms in the name of such an 'omni-crisis' (Hardt and Negri, *Empire*, 189), creating a 'state of permanent exception' (17) from the particulars of peacetime rule, which impinges on human rights, judicial norms and so forth. The new norm is now an endless and constant, unlimited war, attaining the level of a '. . . global state of war' (Hardt and Negri, *Multitude*, xi):

> . . . a perpetual and indeterminate state of war . . . with no clear distinction between the maintenance of peace and acts of war. Because the isolated space and time of war in the limited conflict between sovereign states has declined, war seems to have seeped back and flooded the entire social field. *The state of exception has become permanent and general*; the exception has become the rule, pervading both foreign relations and the homeland.
> (Hardt and Negri, *Multitude*, 7; italics in original).

Hardt and Negri share this reading with Baudrillard, where Baudrillard characterized the contemporary era as that of the Fourth World War (Hardt and Negri, *Multitude*, 37).[9]

The bodies of *BSG* are bodies capable of operating in and for the state of permanent exception and are bodies modelled after it, since this is the world in which the state of permanent exception comes to be the actually existing (rather than, as read by anti-war activists, effectively) norm. The achievement of *BSG* is one in which a future speaks of such abstractions, making them concrete in its ontology, even experienceable. And, in this materialization, the diversionary nature of *BSG*'s surface liberalism is revealed: the progressive political mode of *BSG* when compared to *BSG1* – from '. . . a militant theocracy . . .' to 'the human civilisation of the "Twelve Colonies" [which] appears pluralistic, secular, and remarkably similar to contemporary society . . .' (Tranter 49) – is effectively incidental.

Such approaches to *BSG* hold to the classic analytical model for theorizing science fictions, where the envisaged future is no more than a mirror to our present (a model I have adhered to throughout this chapter), or the present as once envisaged in our past (with that 'old' sci-fi now offering, to paraphrase Jameson, 'archaeologies of the future'). For *BSG* as Bush-era popular entertainment, the symmetries are apparent: neoliberal sci-fi that dreams of the good battle, and heroism in the face of the attacks on civilization; the discourse of apocalyticism with 'freedom' over 'human rights', moralism as ideology. In respect of the fictional realization of the state of permanent exception, *BSG* seem to accept the parameters of the debate of the 'war on terror', despite the gestures towards dissent identified above. These occur in local instances of implied or implicit criticism (such as the brutal nature of occupation and subjection) – criticism that, in the best liberal tradition, seeks to present both sides of the argument, or, rather, simply withholds comment. Therefore *BSG* in its micropolitical fascism first normalizes the exception *before* – and irrelevantly therefore – offering limited measures of criticism against it.

One area for further consideration is raised when we revisit the classic analytical model for theorizing science fictions with an appropriately postmodern sensibility – which is apt when confronted with *BSG* and its deterritorialized warfare and loss of cognitive certainties across a cosmos-wide cyberspace, a contemporary science fiction trope identified as a 'radical capitalist . . . gnostic-digital dream' by Žižek (5). What, exactly, is mirrored? The classic moral structuring of sci-fi (usually a warning about the atomic age – as in *Them!* (1954), for example) does not seem to be in operation. And, in the context of *BSG*, any such moral or warning would be pre-empted by the prior acceptance of the new parameters of the permanent state of exception. Rather, the relationship between the fantasy and the actual it mirrors has changed: the mirroring is of the fantasmatic ideological underpinnings of that society, presenting the mirage of society (as Situationists would have it) as it now presents itself to its disoriented inhabitants.[10] In this respect, *BSG* seems more akin to the propaganda model of red scare films of the 1950s, but with the menace now firmly ensconced within Western society, and on the verge of victory. And the mirage itself – the fully militarized, self-defending fortress commune of civilization in the wastes of the hostile desert, its survivors a dwindling cohort that it is possible to number (at the outset of most episodes, in the 'survivor count') – how is this to be understood in the context of popular television drama? The Retort collective, discussing the nature of the 'US–Israel bond' finds the Bush-era neoconservative White House bedazzled by an 'exemplar of a society in which total militarization and spectacular modernity were fully compatible [to the extent that] Israel has mirrored and mesmerized the American state for nearly four decades' (Retort 110) In this light, and the light of the nature of its break from *BSG1*, *BSG* seems not so much mesmeric, but an exercise in mesmerism. But this is an exercise that – usefully – reveals the contours of the fevered imaginings of a future life in the permanent state of exception.

Notes

1 In other, marginal viewer contexts – nostalgic, amateur sociological and cult; *Mystery Science Theater 3000*, the Something Weird DVD company, etc – the answer can be 'camp', of course.

2 Shapiro seems not to be the only figure who draws on these figures in passing; is *BSG*'s own Felix Gaeta a reference to Félix Guattari?

3 Two examples do come to mind: Verhoeven's fascinatingly subversive *Showgirls* (1995), and French pop group Daft Punk's

concept Manga film, *Interstella 5555: the 5tory of the 5ecret 5tar 5ystem* (2003). (Indeed, one of the Daft Punk duo seems to model his appearance on a *BSG1* Cylon). Here, Manga comes to function as a doubly alienating aesthetic: the 'otherness' of its 'Orientalism' (from the Western perspective unused to Manga), and the otherness of its retrospective aesthetic (highly anachronistic late 1970s-styled cartoons illustrating Daft Punk's late 1970s-styled Eurodisco).

4   From this perspective, the prescience of *A Clockwork Orange* (1971) becomes particularly notable; Allen Jones' sculptures – women in submissive positions, used as tables or drink dispensers in the milk bar sequences – ironically recast and deaden the notion of beauty in this literally domesticated future female form.

5   Shot by Harri Peccinotti for Pirelli on, appropriately enough, Big Sur (see Larkin).

6   Trumball, who provided the *Close Encounters* special effects, would go on to design the space ship, integrated into the lightshow, of the Times Square disco Xenon in summer 1978. The space ship was intended to descend from the ceiling and hover above the dancers.

7   Indeed, it is the religious pretensions of *BSG1* that first attracted critical attention, with James E. Ford's reading of this world 'somewhere beyond the heavens' as creatively indebted to Mormon theology. Deleted scenes from *BSG1* (archived on the DVD release) reveal that more overtly religious (and homoerotic) material was removed.

8   In a telling intertextual joke, therefore, it is the paranoiac Dwight of the US version of *The Office* (who winds up appointing himself as his own assistant on the grounds that he cannot trust anyone else) who expresses how much he is 'into' *BSG* on more than one occasion.

9   This is summarized in Baudrillard's *The Spirit of Terrorism*: 'The first two world wars corresponded to the classical image of war. The first ended the supremacy of Europe and the colonial era. The second put an end of Nazism. The third, which has indeed taken place, in the form of cold war and deterrence, put an end to Communism' (11–12). The third, note Hardt and Negri, was relatively quiet: 'it seems to many today that the global order of our recent past, the cold war, was paradoxically the last moment

of relatively peaceful global cohabitation . . .' (*Multitude*, 352). The fourth occurs in relation to antagonisms within the drive to globalization, a '. . . *triumphant globalization battling against itself*. In this sense, we can indeed speak of a world war – not the Third World War, but the Fourth and the only really global one, since what is at stake is globalization itself' (Baudrillard 11, original emphasis) For the genesis of the notion of permanent exception cf. Passavant and Dean (166–7).

10   Or, with the final plot twist of *BSG* (which shares with the 'rebooted' *Star Trek* of 2009 a return to the origins before the originals), then in purely thematic terms the mirroring is of the historical-mythical-metaphysical underpinnings of what *had* seemed to be the coming society of the distant future. And this society, at the close of the series, is suddenly revealed to predate our backwards present, rendering these underpinnings as a newly revealed mythology (a device akin to the suggested Egyptian origins of the space colony of *BSG1*). In the context of this critique, could it not be said that – with the spliced biological/robotic origins of man – what appears to have been just micropolitically fascist is unmasked as DNA-encoded or molecular fascism? At any rate, this belated arrival in the early twenty-first century also confirms the eradication of the actual prehistory of *BSG*, as argued here; the pedant could note that this visit to actual planet Earth had or has already occurred, in *Battlestar Galactica 1980*.

Works Cited

Biskind, Peter. *Easy Riders, Raging Bulls*. London: Bloomsbury, 1998.

Baudrillard, Jean. *The Spirit of Terrorism*. London: Verso, 2002.

Cox, Alex. 'Blockbuster Barbarism,' *Guardian*, 6 Aug 2004 <http://arts.guardian.co.uk/fridayreview/story/0,,1276537,00.html>.

Deleuze, Gilles and Félix Guattari. *A Thousand Plateaus: Capitalism and Schizophrenia*. London: Continuum, 2007.

Ford, James E. '*Battlestar Gallactica* [sic] and Mormon Theology,' *Journal of Popular Culture* (Fall 1983): 83–7.

Hardt, Michael and Antonio Negri. *Empire*. London: Harvard University Press, 2001.

—— *Multitude*. London: Hamish Hamilton, 2005.

Jameson, Fredric. *Archaeologies of the Future: The Desire Called Utopia and Other Science Fictions*. London: Verso, 2007.

Larkin, David (designer). *The Complete Pirelli Calendar Book*. London: Pan Books, London 1975.

Marcuse, Herbert. *An Essay on Liberation*, Middlesex: Penguin Press, 1973.

Miller, Mark Crispin. '2001: A Cold Descent,' *Sight and Sound* 4, 1 (Jan 1994): 18–25.

Passavant, Paul A. and Jodi Dean (eds). *Empire's New Clothes: Reading Hardt and Negri*. London: Routledge, 2004.

Potter, Dennis. *Waiting for the Boat: On Television*. London: Faber and Faber, 1990.

Retort [Iain Boal, T. J. Clark, Joseph Matthews and Michael Watts]. *Afflicted Powers: Capital and Spectacle in a New Age of War*. London: Verso, 2005.

Shapiro, Peter. *Turn the Beat Around: The Secret History of Disco*. London: Faber and Faber, 2005.

Tranter, Kieran. '"Frakking Toasters" and Jurisprudences of Technology: The Exception, the Subject and *Techné* in *Battlestar Galactica*,' *Law & Literature* 19, 1 (2007): 45–75.

White, Edmund. *States of Desire: Travels in Gay America*. London: Picador, 1986.

Žižek, Slavoj. *In Defence of Lost Causes*. London: Verso, 2008.

The Military Organism

Rank, Family and Obedience in *Battlestar Galactica*

ROZ KAVENEY

Science fiction has one of its roots in the utopian tradition
– the exploration of how things might be different and better
if the polity were only more rationally constructed. One of the
reasons why that tradition also includes so many nightmares is
that we learned long ago that rationally constructed societies
are often rules of the saints, in which not only the poets ejected
by Plato from his Republic, but ordinary fallible people, have no
place. Given that one of the prevailing modes of science fiction,
particularly the Anglo-American tradition of sci-fi, what I have
elsewhere called 'dialectical metonymy', is the echoing of an
earlier text in order to confute it, one of the things that science
fiction regularly does is critique utopian fictions and demonstrate
that the difference between utopia and dystopia is often merely a
matter of perspective.

The reason why the bloodless heavens offered by such fictions
retain an appeal is that utopias offer a way out of certain
intolerable aspects of consensually accepted reality, and one of
those realities is war. Rejecting that appeal – and those grounds
for that appeal – has always been one of the more difficult tasks
set by its anti-utopian bloodymindedness for the populist strain
in science fiction. It is a hard saying, and probably not true,
that to exclude the possibility of armed conflict is to abandon

a part of what makes us human. It is a claim that much science fiction has tried to reject or soften by claiming, for example, that armed conflict will only be necessary when human beings find themselves in a war for survival against aliens – and often aliens whose appearance or ancestry renders them repulsive, such as H. G. Wells' large-brained octopoid Martians in *War of the Worlds* (1898), or R. A. Heinlein's insectoid Bugs in *Starship Troopers* (1959) – or genocidally parricidal robots, like those in all versions of *Battlestar Galactica*.

In a post-9/11 era, the inhuman and repulsive enemy can look just like us, whether it is a terrorist in *24* or a 'skin job' Cylon in *Battlestar Galactica*; the show explores a vein of paranoia that science fiction has exploited since the McCarthyite 1950s, a key text here being Heinlein's *The Puppet Masters* (1951), in which humans are controlled by alien slugs that ride them like beasts of burden. And in Heinlein, and the strain of sci-fi that derives from him, the answer to such an insidious threat is total war without ifs or buts or conditional surrender – 'The free men are coming to kill you'. The constant references to the Cylons as 'toasters' or 'skin jobs' and the paradoxical use of torture and rape by the crews of Galactica and Pegasus while maintaining that the Cylons they torture and rape are mere machines are good examples both of the licence given to people in general, and to the military specifically, by paranoia, and of its implicit bad faith.

If war is a matter of survival and the enemy is not human, ethics, it is often argued, can be cast aside and war can be entirely virtuous – and of course it has always been possible to argue that, in some sense, enemies are not human, or not truly human, which has led to many of the worst atrocities of actual war. Often the same texts will both register that truth and ignore it, in the way that Ron Moore's version of *Battlestar Galactica* opposes rape and torture of particular Cylons in whom we happen to be emotionally invested while having virtuous characters such as Adama and Roslin cheerfully contemplate the genocide of the entire Cylon species through biological warfare in 'A Measure of Salvation' (3.07) only seriously, though effectively, opposed by

Helo. Adama, it is true, regards it as an issue on which civilian authorities will have to sign off. The fact that the Cylons also commit acts of torture and rape is, of course, further evidence that – however much ideology on both sides claims that they are machines – they are human, all too human.

Some military science fiction – notably Joe Haldeman's *The Forever War* (1974) – expresses scepticism about the worth of war as a means of resolving conflict even with the utterly alien: the war ends when the human race has become something else. Most military sci-fi, especially since Heinlein's *Starship Troopers*, celebrates military virtue as a school for other civic virtue; in Heinlein's novel, only veterans have full civil rights. One of the subtexts of military science fiction is almost always this kind of militarism: by learning to be a good soldier, the protagonist learns to be a better man or woman. One of the assumptions of the reimagined *BSG* is that this is true – Lee Adama becomes the leader of humanity with the authority to argue for the abandonment of technological civilization because of his long service as a loyal officer as much as his comparatively brief foray into civilian politics, and Gaius Baltar is finally redeemed when he stops talking and picks up a gun.

More generally, the strain of military science fiction, a subgenre that in large measure Heinlein started, are stories about the young hero or heroine coming to maturity in a military structure, and learning to be extraordinary – Gordon R. Dickson's *Dorsai* and David Weber's 'Honor Harrington' novels for example. This is an important strain in Heinlein's novel, but his hero Johnny Rico is unlike most of his literary descendants in not being a military genius and only rising to be a officer in command, albeit of a unit in which his chief NCO is his own father – and therefore, we are assured only metaphorically, something like his wife (Kaveney ch.8). Bill Adama's relationship with Saul Tigh is the subject of major jealousy on the part of both men's female partners, for example Ellen Tigh in 'Deadlock' (4.16).

As we will see, Ron Moore's reimagined *BSG* is both influenced by, and subversive of, this strain of published science fiction.

Adama is a not a military genius, and strategic brilliance is shown as essentially a sign of imbalance: Starbuck's capacity for bright ideas is contaminated by her drunken slovenliness and occasional hallucinations, and Admiral Cain is arguably objectively insane, and certainly someone in whom military brilliance has become decoupled from any kind of moral compass. The show is innately distrustful of anyone in whom professionalism is at the expense of a rounded personality. The obvious example of this is Baltar, but the same is true of Romo Lampkin, who is shown as seriously delusional in 'Sine Qua Non' (4.08); Bill Adama is someone that a populist distrustful of 'fancy people' can trust as a military commander.

Part of this populism is a surprising level of tolerance for disrespectful behaviour among his subordinates; it is as if he has chosen to balance its consequences against the overall good presented by his easy-going manner. His tolerance creates real problems: Simon Bradshaw has suggested that one of Starbuck's greatest flaws as an officer is her selective, and conditional, respect for other officers, particularly Tigh – whom she despises for flaws such as drunken ill-temper that she possesses herself; she is blind for a while to Cain's major faults because Cain is like a version of herself without the vices.

There is thus a pronounced double edge to Adama's decision to hand to his son Lee the law books of his own father Joe; one of the reasons – as far as we can tell, and the prequel show *Caprica* may make this more complex – why Adama opted for a military career was the extent to which his father's career as a lawyer had involved him in endless compromises with the criminals he defended. Lee's regard for constitutional proprieties, whether in freeing Laura Roslin after his father has had her arrested, or insisting on Baltar's right to a proper defence, is something Adama often finds himself instinctively reacting against, even though Lee usually manages to persuade him in the long term.

In his personal life, of course, Adama is drawn into a sexual relationship with the woman he had earlier had arrested, a relationship that for a while is put into abeyance precisely because of their feeling that their responsibilities are made too complex by it; it only becomes openly sexual at points where Roslin is out of power or when she is too ill to perform her presidential duties. Caught up as he is in political complexities in which being 'a simple soldier' is potentially as much a piece of game-playing as Zarek's pose as a freedom fighter or Baltar's as a man of the people, we never doubt – because we have seen him in private moments with Lee and with Roslin – that Adama's preference for soldiering over the shifts and complexities of civilian life is entirely genuine. In this, he is entirely in the tradition of Heinlein's soldiers; elsewhere in Heinlein, of course, in *Double Star* (1956) or *The Moon is a Harsh Mistress* (1966) a rather different view of the political realm is taken, one far more favourable to the career of politics. In one flashback in 'Daybreak (Part One)' (4.19), Adama rejects a potentially lucrative civilian job simply because it involves having his integrity assessed, and therefore questioned.

Logically, the show ought to be, far more than it is, about the personal evolution of Lee Adama to a point where he sees what needs to be done and persuades the rest of humanity of his correctness; this would be far more in keeping with the traditions of military science fiction than the show ends up being. Part of the reason for this is that Jamie Bamber's portrayal of Lee, while more than adequate, is lacking in charisma and that the show spends so much time on his messy and destructive relationships with his wife Dee and with Starbuck; the standard fan reaction to the Lee/Dee/Starbuck/Sam relationship in Season Three was to refer to it as the Quadrangle of Doom[1] and regard it as a waste of space and time. The weakness of all of this made the show's most effective love interests the perverse relationship between Baltar and Caprica Six and the middle-aged partnership of Laura Roslin and Bill Adama.

Another strain of science fiction is what John Clute calls the Edisonade, specifically the tale of the boy inventor and his marvellous machine, but often, by extension, the whole body of sci-fi that celebrates vast machines and their romance. There has been a clear link between this and the military strain ever since Garrett P. Serviss' *Edison's Conquest of Mars* (1898), whose eponymous hero – the real Edison endorsed this potrayal of him – mounts a punitive expedition in the aftermath of the invasion portrayed in Wells' *War of the Worlds* (1898); another Wells story, 'The Land Ironclads' (1903) described tanks over a decade before they were introduced to warfare. Great vessels such as the battlestars and basestars and resurrection hubs of *Battlestar Galactica* are not just there as the weapons with which space war is fought – they have a romance all of their own. It is worth remarking here that one of the things that made the reimagined series possible was the advanced computer graphics technology of the decade in which it was conceived.

Some years ago, in a survey of 1970s science fiction for the magazine *Foundation*, I devised the term 'Big Dumb Object' to describe a particular common trope of written science fiction; it is a useful description of large artefacts that serve, often simultaneously, as the location of a science fiction plot, as that plot's McGuffin or driver and as one of its controlling metaphors. One of the major *BSG* websites takes its name from my coinage – perceptively because the battlestar itself fills all the conditions of my description. The battlestar, and the other battlestar, Pegasus, are not only hunks of metal; they are also, metonymically, symbols of their crews, and of the complex of relationships that make up both chains of military command and more general human interactions.

At a crucial point in 'Blood on the Scales' (4.14), Galen Tyrol shuts down the battlestar's faster-than-light drive to prevent the mutineers who have temporarily mounted a political and military coup against its commander and his partner, humanity's president. As he does so, he notices that the structure of the ship has become hopelessly cracked and compromised. The divisions within the community of surviving humanity are paralleled and manifested as damage to the ship that is its protector.[2] Ruskin mocked as the pathetic fallacy the use of landscape as correlative for human emotion and states of mind; when the landscape is entirely artefactual, it is legitimate to reinstate such correlation.

Galactica is presented to us throughout the four seasons of the show as a refuge for and protector of the hopeless, a damaged correlative to the shattered remnants that are all that is left of humanity after the Cylon's largely successful nuclear genocide. At the same time, it is a home and a ship of war, just as Commander (later Admiral) Bill Adama commands what is at the same time a military organization and, in some senses that transcend but include the literal, a family – a family that has the right patriarch in control. Similarly, in the political realm, the show largely endorses Laura Roslin as the righteous leader who will bring humanity to a safe haven in spite of the fact that she will presumably die before they reach the Promised Land.[3]

If we doubt Adama's fitness to command humanity's last hope – and the show gives us every reason to at many points – we have only to look at the various other commanders that the show presents us with. We have Admiral Helena Cain of Pegasus, Gaeta and Zarek who lead the attempted mutiny/coup, and John Cavil, the model who is the closest thing that the Cylons have to a leader and proves latterly to have manipulated vast areas of the show's plot simply by knowing what no one else does and for entirely personal agendas. All of these – with Gaeta only a partial exception – regard command as an opportunity to indulge their ego, where for Adama it is a matter of self-discipline and obligation. All commanders send the men and women who serve under them to their deaths, what Churchill called 'paying the butcher's bill', and Adama is no exception, but for him it is always a serious matter to do so, rather than something he takes thoughtlessly for granted, or positively welcomes.

His preparedness to do this balances out that tendency to nepotism that can be seen as his major weakness as a commander: he appoints his surviving son Lee as CAG, in charge of Galactica's pilots, and later on as commander of Pegasus, but it is self-evident that Lee is a highly competent officer who happens to be Adama's son. Adama has protected the career of Kara Thrace from her endless self-destructive escapades, not only because she was at one point his potential daughter-in-law, but also because she is an extraordinarily gifted pilot and warrior; her crucial role in defeating Gaeta's mutiny is only one proof of this.[4] He also takes people under his wing as if they were family where there is no such link. Saul Tigh, his executive officer, is the man he has chosen as brother-in-arms whom he protects and continues to honour in spite of Tigh's alcoholism and occasional drunken rages. Sharon 'Boomer' Valerii is as much his adoptive daughter as Starbuck, however much of a traitor to him she eventually proves – in 'Daybreak (Part Two)' (4.20) we see the original incident in which he made her his dependant by forgiving her a military error. His replacement of her with another Eight in the shape of Athena is not even slightly a mistake.

Adama promotes people who are highly competent, and regards them as having a duty of loyalty to him. Sometimes these people gradually become assimilated to his extended family; for example, Dee marries Lee and does her best to make that marriage work, even when it becomes clear that his real interest is in Starbuck. Though there are times when the audience questions his non-negotiable loyalty to Tigh, though that loyalty is regularly endorsed in the last analysis, the point is regularly and convincingly made that a desire for Adama's approval is one of the things that makes Tigh pull himself together. The great exception to this is perhaps the most competent of all Adama's officers, Gaeta, who saves the ship and the fleet time and time again, but ends up ordering Adama's death and being executed for treason. It is hard to say why Adama never warms to his incredibly competent technical officer unless it is simply his competence, something of which television science fiction is often suspicious.

Simon Bradshaw, a former serving engineering officer in the RAF to whom I am much indebted to for insights about military culture as applied to this chapter suggests that:

Gaeta comes across as the sort of officer that more traditional military types tend to see as technician first and officer second.

Adama respects Gaeta, but fundamentally he views him as someone who will solve problems by intelligent application of specialist knowledge rather than by leadership or strategic insight; this puts Gaeta outside Adama's circle of officers whom he sees as true military leaders. In this context, it's worth noticing how fast Kat comes from nowhere to a senior position; despite her flaws, it seems clear that Adama regarded her as a true combat leader. This also explains a lot about Adama's sheer outrage not only at the coup but that Gaeta, of all people, is leading it. Adama is not only furious that one of his officers is betraying him, but clearly is shocked and almost offended that it is someone he does not rate highly as a leader or commander.   (Bradshaw interview)

It is significant that Boomer is so much a part of this sense of family that people trust her when it is foolish to do so, when she has betrayed humanity to the Cylons, and then betrayed not only the peace party that she helped create among the Cylons but also her entire line of Number Eights; it is, in the end, another Eight, Athena, who decides that enough treachery is enough, and executes her when she changes sides yet again by bringing back the child Hera that she had stolen during an earlier feigned repentance. It has to be her other self who kills her finally – an earlier murder of her by Cally in 'Resistance' (2.04) was a piece of domestic violence that did not take.

If at times Adama is overly prepared to forgive Lee and Kara gross insubordination, it is in part because on the principal occasions when they disobey him, they turn out to be right and he turns out to be wrong, and in part because they choose to obey other imperatives, such as respect for the civilian authorities. When Lee quarrels with him to a point where Adama questions Lee's fundamental integrity as an officer (in 'Crossroads (Part One)' 3.19), it is Adama who finds himself obliged to back down when he responds to Lee's speech at Baltar's trial by voting for Baltar's acquittal. Adama is not the sort of commander who persists in error for the sake of unquestionable authority. The only person he does not, in the end, forgive is Felix Gaeta, who did not merely question, but actually overthrew his authority and ordered his execution.

He will forgive even active disobedience if it produces genuine success. Kara chooses to obey Roslin rather than Adama in 'Kobol's Last Gleaming (Part One)' (1.12) and returns with the Arrow of Apollo and news of human survivors on Caprica in 'Home (Part One)' (2.06); Adama does not quarrel with this success, even when it is rooted in disobedience. Even though her return from the dead is highly suspicious, and her sanity open to question, Adama allows Kara (in 'Six of One' 4.02) a garbage scow to pursue her search for an alternative route to Earth. Adama's loyalty to those he chooses as family is unconditional and his forgiveness of them limitless; the show regularly endorses his choices as correct, even when they are apparently entirely irrational.

Further, his preparedness to forgive extends productively to the genocidal enemies of humanity; he is in no position to forgive Boomer for attempting his assassination as he is still in a coma when she is shot by Cally, but he reserves judgement when another Cylon of the same model turns up on Galactica as a dissident and as partner to Helo. In due course, Adama even commissions her as an officer; significantly, when accepted by the other pilots, this Cylon, presumably as monotheist as her coevals, takes the name of a goddess worshipped by humans, Athena. When Starbuck brings the crippled basestar to the fleet, Adama accepts that there should at least be a conversation; if part of leadership is a capacity to think outside the box, he has that ability to a remarkable extent.

Adama throws a major fit of rage and sorrow when it is revealed that Saul Tigh is one of the Final Five, but he gets over it as soon as he realizes that Saul is the same man he always was, and that his loyalty is one of the unchanging things in their world, whatever Saul's nature. Similarly, in 'No Exit' (4.15) he asks Tyrol to return to duty as Galactica's chief, in spite of the fact that Tyrol is another of the Five, and Adama accepts, however reluctantly, that the only possible way to heal the broken Galactica is with a semi-organic Cylon resin. He accepts, in other words, that the only way forward is hybridity; in a later episode 'Deadlock' we see that Cylon pilots fighting for the alliance have established their own memorial wall where they post photographs of their dead, next to the wall where human pilots have always been memorialized – and more importantly, that the human pilots have accepted this from their former enemies.

With all his undoubted flaws, and in spite of his many mistakes, Adama has over four seasons lived up to the trust placed in him; Napoleon asked about officers whom he was considering for promotion to marshals of France 'is he lucky?' but Adama's luck is perhaps at times excessive. He has transcended the mediocre military record that led to his being beached for a while at the end of the Cylon War[5] and left him at the end of his career a mere commander in charge of a battlestar about to be mothballed as a museum. Even that position is to some unspecified degree his reward for the morally ambiguous actions he performed for his superiors in the episode 'Hero' (3.08), in which he was instructed to take actions that were a technical breach of the armistice with the Cylons and in doing so sacrificed one of his pilots and friends to the greater good. It is perhaps because of the element of disappointment and disillusion in his career that he is flexible rather than rigid; for all his disapproval of his lawyer father's involvement as a defence lawyer for criminals, Adama – who is prepared to lie to the entire fleet about the existence of Earth at the very start of their quest – has himself a complex relationship with truth.

Adama has proved adaptable to changes in circumstances and prepared to back down gracefully and without looking weak from positions he would earlier have considered non-negotiable. Examples of this are numerous enough that a list of them would be a significant summary of large parts of the series' plot – he backs down from the military take-over with which he responded to the president's giving officers under his command instructions behind his back, for example, and he comes to an accomodation with Chief Tyrol's strikers after threatening to shoot those of them who are serving crew on Galactica. This flexibility prepares us for his decision to accept a truce and then an alliance with the rebel faction among the Cylons, an imaginative act that is clearly necessary but which is part of what drives a significant part of his crew to open mutiny.

He is a military commander in a way few other starship commanders in television science fiction are,[6] but he deals with a considerably larger military unit. Most of the shows in the *Star Trek* franchise are sceptical of military hierarchy – Kirk is often insubordinate to his superiors and leads his crews by example and moral fibre rather than by hierarchical right.[7] Sisko in *Deep Space Nine* and Sinclair and Sheridan in *Babylon 5* are both Chosen Ones, messiahs as well as commanders, in a way that Adama never becomes; the Chosen Ones of *Battlestar Galactica* are Roslin and Starbuck, and arguably Baltar and Hera, but never stolid old Bill Adama. Of the *Star Trek* commanders, only Picard comes close to being in the military mainstream – and in him it is an effect maintained by some deliberately Royal Navy-esque affectations such as his tea-drinking and his perpetual 'Make it so'.

Blake and Crichton are outlaw civilians who lead by virtue – *Farscape* is a show in which all military hierarchy is seen as destructive and dysfunctional and Crais is not the only 'insane military commander' in it. Though Mal Reynolds and Zoe served together in their war, *Firefly* is another show about outlaws – 'to live outside the law / You must be honest' – and part of the drama of the show derives from the fact that many of Serenity's crew have individual secrets that threaten the welfare of the crew as a whole. However much he sometimes indulges particular men and women under his command, Adama is always someone whose role is primarily that of a man at the head of a structure; he possesses moral virtue but it is not through it that he has a right to rule.

At the same time, he is the only commander to whom a sense of his command as family is quite this important, perhaps, paradoxically, because of the military structure in which Adama is embedded. Outlaw crews are familial in the sense of being a band of brothers (and sisters) but not in terms of having a stern father in control. This is partly a matter of Adama's having 'the Nelson touch' often ascribed to the best commanders – a capacity to make each member of his crew feel respected as a part of the whole and as having a personal relationship with the admiral – and partly a matter of the inherent protocols of a television show: Adama needs to be this particular sort of commander to be acceptable to the audience. For a civilian audience, and the sci-fi audience tends to be at the more liberal end of politics, to find the line of command acceptable as a given in a show, it has to be combined with this sort of emotional authority.

The show makes effective use, at some key moments, of the problems inherent in this acceptance of military hierarchy. Bill Adama is the only military commander in television science fiction whom one can imagine accepting as he does without question being superseded by a military superior when Galactica and the civilian fleet it shepherds meets up with Pegasus under the command of Admiral Cain.[8] Moreover, Adama continues to accept Cain's right to command once it is clear that she only grudgingly and conditionally accepts the claim of Laura Roslin to the presidency, or of civilian authority in any form.[9]

Further, it becomes clear to him that Cain has a sense of her military mission that is wholly and solely about revenge on the Cylons and not even slightly about the preservation of the human race; she has, indeed, forcibly conscripted civilian specialists, set civilian passengers adrift without resources after stripping their ships for parts and ordered the shooting of those who dissent or resist. Under the plea of military necessity, she has become not only a war criminal, but effectively someone who by killing humans has become complicit in the Cylon genocide. It is nonetheless with the most profound reluctance that in 'Resurrection Ship (Part One)' (2.11) Adama accepts Roslin's view that Cain has to be assassinated; Cain, meanwhile, determines on Roslin and Adama's deaths with incredible ease, even if she later withdraws her orders in the aftermath of the destruction of the Cylons' resurrection ship.

Once she is dead – murdered by her Cylon former lover whom

she had had repeatedly raped and tortured as much out of pique as for any military purpose – Adama takes no reprisals against those of her crew who, like Kendra ('Razor' 4.00), had committed clearly illegal atrocities against civilians, and indeed integrates the crews of Pegasus and Galactica. This is a decision he makes partly on pragmatic grounds – he has, after all, to crew his ships – and partly through a belief that they were obeying orders from a legitimate source of authority; no Nuremberg nonsense on Galactica, clearly. This is not necessarily his wisest decision: the former crew of Pegasus remain a problematic element, from the involvement of Cain's former executive officer, Fiske – briefly commander of Pegasus – in the black market ('Black Market' 2.14), right down to the mutiny in 'The Oath' (4.13), where Cain's rape squad joins the mutineers in order to pick up where they left off. Even after the mutiny and its bloodshed Adama restricts reprisals to the leadership, Gaeta and Zarek.

Adama regards the life and death authority of command as something to be used incredibly sparingly – his treatment of the strikers is relevant here, as is his endorsement of the amnesty in the aftermath of New Caprica. Cain, by contrast, shoots her original executive officer out of hand for disobeying a probably illegal order, and the Cylons have a habit of resolving disagreements in military matters with guns and nuclear weapons. Zarek uses murder – of the chief who has replaced Tyrol – as a way of blooding the mutiny and giving Gaeta no room to compromise or back down. Adama is arguably almost too merciful, but it is seen as a virtue by comparison with the behaviour of those rival commanders who are trigger-happy.

It is worth mentioning at this point the extent to which the reimagined *Battlestar Galactica* follows the tradition of most written sci-fi in regarding space war as either straightforwardly a sort of naval warfare or that particular kind of naval warfare that involves the extensive supplementary use of air power. There has always been a colossal debt owed on the part of science fiction to that genre of historical novel that deals with the naval warfare of the Napoleonic era – E. E. Smith's 'Lensman' novels of the

1940s acknowledge that debt to the extent that his young officer Kinnison has a loyal sidekick called Buskirk in clear tribute to the 'Hornblower' novels of C. S. Forester, produced in the same period, where Hornblower has a lieutenant called Bush.

Both the battlestars and the Cylon basestars are essentially a combination of battleships, in possession of massive batteries of medium-range artillery, and aircraft carriers, with a complement of fighters and heavier craft – the human versions of these are Vipers and Raptors. The battlestars have a complement of marines; Galactica's complement was almost minimal and ceremonial at the start of the show, which is perhaps why they are so rarely mentioned and serve principally as guards in the brig. Landing groups seem only occasionally to include a marine contingent – the tribunal set up in 'Litmus' (1.06) is headed by Sergeant Hadian. When Pegasus is destroyed, Galactica acquires its far larger complement of marines: one of these, Erin Matthias, recurs in a number of episodes before being killed during Starbuck's expedition in search of Earth.

A battlestar is commanded by its commander, with the help of an executive officer, who is a colonel, and the crew of the combat information centre (CIC), which also acts as the equivalent of a bridge. The pilots of the Vipers and Raptors are under the command of the commander, air group (CAG), who answers to the battlestar commander, as does the chief, an NCO, of the 'knuckledraggers', the ground crew who service the Vipers and Raptors. These structures are largely copied from the US Navy, without any particular attention to logical nomenclature, with the exception of the NCO status of the chief. This is something that Ron Moore copied from *Deep Space Nine*, where Chief Operations Officer Miles O'Brien is an NCO. In this he failed to think through that *Deep Space Nine* has a minimal crew and that, with a structure as large as Galactica or Pegasus, a more appropriate structure would be that of the Starship Enterprise, where the head of engineering is a commissioned post; much drama derives from the lower status of the engineering crews, but at the expense of logic.

Both Lee Adama and Starbuck serve as CAG at different points and both are shown as highly competent in tactical planning and, generally speaking, in the provision of training and the maintenance of group morale. One of the strong points of the show is that such matters get proper consideration, and that their command styles are shown to be as essentially different as their piloting habits. Lee is generally cautious and sensible, whereas Starbuck is dashing and charismatic; his besetting weakness is caution and hers is recklessness. In general the show is more indulgent of him than of her. Lee is good at managing his crews, Starbuck rather less so, partly because she would always rather be the hotshot pilot than the thoughtful commander. She can be a competent CAG but often falls short – she is a brilliant planner of missions – such as the attack on the resurrection ship in 'Resurrection Ship (Part One)' – and excellent in emergencies like the mutiny, but has a short attention span for some of her other duties.

It is significant that she is the Galactica crewmember that Admiral Cain most obviously takes to – there may, of course, be an element of sexual attraction here on Cain's part – and the worrying aspect of this is that both regard command as in some degree an oppurtunity to indulge their egos in general and their death wishes in particular. Starbuck is riddled with guilt about her neglect of her highly abusive mother and her treatment of Zack Adama, and on several occasions her guilt is directly linked to suicidally reckless behaviour, as in 'Maelstrom' (3.17). This also contaminates her judgement: she effectively suggests atonement through suicide to Kat, an almost equally reckless pilot who can be seen as her shadow and who has a past as a drug dealer, in 'The Passage' (3.10). Starbuck's arrogant treatment of her crew on the garbage scow, and her obsession with painting star patterns at the expense of explaining herself, leads to a mutiny ('Faith' 4.06) (and yet Starbuck, who has, after her repeated rapes, more reason to hate the Cylons than most, shows real insight into the overall strategic situation when she agrees to a truce with the Cylon rebels). One of the reasons why the eventual revelation that, since her death in 'Maelstrom', Starbuck has been an angel is ludicrous, is that her behaviour shows no sign of this whatever. Certainly it has not made her a better commander than she was before.

To summarize, then, the reimagined *Battlestar Galactica* is a show to which portrayal of military/naval organizations, their personnel and their structures is far more central than is the case with other television science fiction shows portraying starship crews. At the same time, it tries to make this more palatable to a civilian audience by showing the battlestar as an organic community, a family with the right members in command; in this it draws on the tradition of written sci-fi, but takes things rather further in this direction than is generally the case. One of the show's central figures – arguably its protagonist – is Bill Adama, who is shown as extraordinary in his moral uprightness, but not exceptional in his talent for command; his portrayal by Edward James Olmos has a craggy gravity that derives, in part, from our sense that he is a man who begins the show at the end of his career, a career in which he is forced by circumstances to continue well past retirement, a retirement from which he is dragged a second time by the arrival of the Cylons on New Caprica.

For all that will be said in my chapter later in this volume about the faults and follies of the show's last phase, one of the strengths of its final episode 'Daybreak (Part One/Two)' (4.19/20) is the sight of Adama summoning his followers to one last mission, the raid on the Cylon base to rescue Hera, and the sight of him calm and resigned at Laura Roslin's grave, his command at an end and Galactica sent into the sun. If the ending is generally a ludicrous mistake, it is a mistake to which the sense of Adama's authority as portrayed by Olmos is by no means a contribution; he is, as always, unfailingly excellent.

Notes

1 See, for example <http://mutantreviewers.com/blog1/battlestar
   -galactica-al-and-lissas-ten-moments-worth-talking-about-and-
   five-where-you-can-save-your-breath/>.

2 Similarly, the divisions among the Cylons are paralleled by physical
   damage to the basestar home of those rebel Cylons who form an
   alliance with humanity.

3 The original show was explicitly caught up with Judaeo-Christian
   and Mormon mythology; the reimagining continues this tendency
   to at least the extent that we are allowed to see Roslin as a prophet
   endorsed by God as well as a politician who has jumped from
   deputy secretary of education to president purely because of the
   vagaries of who happens to survive a nuclear war. If at times there
   are complexities to our reaction to this, they come in part from
   the way that some American Christians were stating, during the
   years that the show was broadcast, that the contentious elections
   which brought G. W. Bush to the White House and kept him there
   were the hand of God working in US history. Adama's position
   as commander of Galactica is at least positioned in a rationally
   accountable process of promotion: he is one of science fiction's
   most convincing portrayals of a Necessary Man.

4 Others include her return from shipwreck inside a butchered
   Cylon Raider, her retrieval of the sacred arrow from Caprica
   and her ultimately successful attempt to find Earth, however
   disappointing that proves.

5 This is made more clear in deleted scenes on the DVDs than in
   broadcast canon.

6 Not surprisingly, given that only the short-lived series *Space:
   Above and Beyond* (1995–6) celebrates military values in quite the
   same way as *BSG* in contemporary sci-fi television.

7 It does not feel out of keeping with the television show's canon
   when, in the 2009 *Star Trek* film, Kirk takes the captain's chair
   of Enterprise for the first time as a personal act, though one
   endorsed by consensus.

8 Sheridan in *Babylon 5* secedes from Earth the moment he dislikes
   the elected government.

9 Adama has no great regard for constitutional forms himself – but
   his short-lived seizure of power at the end of Season One was

at least genuinely provoked by Roslin's meddling with military matters.

Works Cited

Kaveney, Roz. *From Alien to Matrix*. London: I.B.Tauris, 2005.

Real-imagining Terror in *Battlestar Galactica*

Negotiating Real and Fantasy in *Battlestar Galactica*'s Political Metaphor

STEVEN RAWLE

Call it 'Naturalistic Science Fiction.'
    This idea, the presentation of a fantastical situation in naturalistic terms, will permeate every aspect of our series.
        (Moore, '*Battlestar Galactica*: Naturalistic Science Fiction')

In a posting on his blog in March 2006, Ronald D. Moore outlined the vision for the reinvented *Battlestar Galactica* (*BSG*), detailing the aggressive retooling of not only the show itself, but the very core of the science fiction genre. He explained that:

> Our goal is nothing less than the reinvention of the science fiction television series. We take as a given the idea that the traditional space opera, with its stock characters, techno-double-talk, bumpy-headed aliens, thespian histrionics, and empty heroics has run its course and a new approach is required. That approach is to introduce realism into what has heretofore been an aggressively unrealistic genre.
>   (Moore, '*Battlestar Galactica*: Naturalistic Science Fiction')

It was intended that the reimagined show would avoid the conventional clichés of formulaic genre television; part of this was undoubtedly an attempt to distance *BSG* not only from classic examples of television science fiction such as the various incarnations of *Star Trek* (which Moore had worked on for several years), but also from the previous incarnation of the *Battlestar Galactica* format. If one were looking to characterize the earlier series, 'stock characters, techno-double-talk, bumpy-headed aliens, thespian histrionics, and empty heroics' might go some way to describe the series, which quickly left the Cylons behind to visit a series of friendly and not-so-friendly planets where Apollo and Starbuck would invariably help the local inhabitants overcome crises. With the new *BSG*, the universe is a cold and empty place, with no inhabited planets, just the relentless Cylon pursuit. It was even rumoured that, should a 'three-eyed alien' ever have walked through the doors of the combat information centre (CIC), Edward James Olmos would have immediately quit the show (Bassom, *The Official Companion*, 101).

However, despite Moore's defiant stance on the naturalism of the new *BSG*, cracks do appear in the realist picture created by the rationale for the series' stylization, although there is clear metaphorical and political motivation for these deviations from the overriding stylistic tenets of Moore's manifesto. Towards the end of 'Scar' (2.15), we begin to hear the low-key sounds of John Williams' score from *The Deer Hunter* (1978). In the pilots' lounge after finally dispatching the raider Scar, Kat is celebrating the kill and her new standing as Galactica's top gun. Starbuck pours the first drink and leads a toast to the fallen pilots whose names she had claimed not to remember earlier in the episode: 'to BB, Jo-Jo, Reilly, Beano, Dipper, Flattop, Chuckles, Jolly, Crashdown, Sheppard, Dash, Flyboy, Stepchild, Puppet, Fireball'. Apollo, who also couldn't remember their names, stands to second the toast 'to all of them'. After a shared 'so say we all', the music from *The Deer Hunter* begins to play quietly in the background through the following scene between Helo and Starbuck until the end of the episode. In a show general devoid of overt references to contemporary Earth culture ('All Along the Watchtower' aside), this intertextual reference to classic film seems a little out of place. This is, however, until we consider the political implications of a reference to a classic Vietnam War film. The thematic links between a remembrance for fallen comrades and the damaging mental consequences of war on America in the 1970s hardly need restating, although the sequence does restate *BSG*'s continued commitment to explore contemporary and historical consequences of conflict on a jaded and damaged populace, reminding the viewer explicitly of the pre- and post-9/11 environments on which the series comments.

The unusual inclusion of an intertextual reference in 'Scar' is juxtaposed with a strong example of the show's commitment to naturalism. Whereas references to other cultural texts tend to make films and TV shows less realistic, and therefore remind us we're watching a constructed text, the overt documentary realism of a show such as *BSG* produces a significant 'reality effect' that stresses the 'reality' of the events being depicted. We see both effects in the closing scenes of 'Scar'. Just after Starbuck has made her toast to old friends, Apollo stands and takes a step closer to the camera. When he does so, the shot very briefly goes out of focus, before pulling focus on Apollo. This stresses the 'accidental' nature of the shot – the implied message is that this isn't rehearsed, not constructed, but is a 'real' moment. This is a strong example of Moore's commitment to realism that he outlines in his manifesto for the overall visual aesthetic. Nevertheless, we're still all aware that this is a science fiction television show, rather than a documentary about space pilots: as Moore himself notes, 'a casual viewer should for a moment feel like he or she has accidentally surfed onto a "60 Minutes" documentary piece about life aboard an aircraft carrier until someone starts talking about Cylons and battlestars' (Moore, '*Battlestar Galactica*: Naturalistic Science Fiction') Here we experience the conflict between the traditional fantasy elements of the science fiction genre and the realism of style and narration that attempt to suppress the fantasy elements in order to engage better with the show's ongoing commentary about our own world, where fantasy is non-existent in a conventional science fiction sense.

This chapter will examine the implied confrontation of real and fantasy in *BSG*'s generic allegorization of contemporary political and ideological conflict. Playing close attention to the aesthetic stylization of the series and narrative arcs such as Season Three's Cylon occupation of New Caprica, in which the dynamic of earlier seasons is reversed, the article will argue that the political and religious allegories of *BSG* function in a constant negotiation between the generic fantasy elements and realist sensibilities of the show, as in this momentary clash of realism and non-realism in 'Scar'. The science fiction 'fantasmatic backgrounds' of *BSG* form a backdrop to the 'reality' of the series' exploration of contemporary subjects. Therefore, the chapter will situate *BSG* as a significant example of sci-fi television, while also locating the show within a broader cultural thread of media texts that has responded to changes in the recent political climate in both form and content.

'Machines Shouldn't Feel Pain. Shouldn't Bleed, Shouldn't Sweat'

Battlestar Galactica is a significant addition to the canon of science fiction television. Science fiction is a genre that traditionally deals in fantasy subjects, speculative science, utopian and dystopian societies, alien 'others', and contemporary social and political allegory. *BSG* tends to deal with a heavy cross-section of the conventions of the genre: spaceships, technology, 'alien' enemies and a dose of both utopian and dystopic fantasy (the images of Caprica throughout the series generally constitute an image of a progressive utopia, although whether this is meant to symbolize a pre-9/11 America is unclear). Thus, *BSG* is thoroughly grounded in fantasy, as much so as the original vision of the series. Much of Moore's vision for the show revolves around the removal of fantasy elements to emphasize the realism of the series in spite of the fantasy background that the show is built around. One of the key, if seemingly minor, changes to the format of the show was to assign real names to the characters. In the original show, characters were know simply by their allegorical names – Apollo (referred to more than once as the son of Zeus; something Tom Zarek does in 'Bastille Day' 1.03), Starbuck, Athena, Cain, Baltar – with little or no reference to first names or family names. While this reinforced the fantasy and quasi-religious allegory behind the series, there was little attempt to ground the characters in a contemporary Earth-style reality (until the failure of the short-lived *Galactica 1980*). The new *BSG* has significantly diminished this overt allegorization of its main characters, giving its characters 'real' names – Lee 'Apollo' Adama, Sharon 'Athena' Agathon, Gaius Baltar. What were previously discrete names become family names, or simply call signs, calling to mind conceptions of the Colonial Fleet as a reflection of the US Navy, or at least the one familiar to viewers from *Top Gun* (1986). While these points may seem minor additions to the format of the show, they represent a significant part of the series' attempt to diminish its obvious basis in fantasy in order to emphasize the 'real' aspects of the concept that relate to the deep vein of political and religious allegory that runs throughout the series; much of this political motivation can be seen in its standing as a key example of post-9/11 visual culture.

The relationship between fantasy and notions of what constitute the 'real' have altered since the epoch-changing events of 9/11. In his collection of essays, *Welcome to the Desert of the Real: Five Essays on September 11 and Related Dates*, the Slovene philosopher Slavoj Žižek talks about Hollywood's reaction to the destruction of the World Trade Center (WTC) towers by Al-Qaeda terrorists. Žižek draws on the commonly made links between Hollywood disaster movies 'from *Escape from New York* to *Independence Day*' that he contends make up Hollywood's 'ideological fantasizing' about the very events that became 'the unimaginable Impossible' on that day in 2001 (15). The most common reaction to the tragedy was that it was 'like a movie', an intrusion of fantasy, culled from Hollywood's unconscious imagination. Žižek argues that the attacks actually worked in the

opposite direction, a consequence of most Western inhabitants'
life in 'the desert of the real', as though trapped in the 'Matrix'.
Žižek contends:

> We should . . . invert the standard reading according to which the
> WTC explosions were the intrusion of the Real which shattered
> our illusory Sphere: quite the reverse – it was before the WTC
> collapse that we lived in our reality, perceiving Third World horrors
> as something which was not actually part of our social reality, as
> something which existed (for us) as a spectral analysis on the
> (TV) screen – and what happened on September 11 was that
> this fantasmatic screen apparition entered our reality. It is not
> that reality entered our image: the image entered and shattered
> our reality (i.e. the symbolic coordinates which determine what
> we experience as reality). The fact that, after September 11, the
> openings of many 'blockbuster' movies with scenes which bear a
> resemblance to the WTC collapse (tall buildings on fire or under
> attack, terrorist acts . . .) were postponed (or the films were even
> shelved) should thus be read as the 'repression' of the fantasmatic
> background responsible for the impact of the WTC collapse.
> (Žižek 16–17)

Jean Baudrillard, the postmodern theorist, echoes Žižek's
argument in *The Spirit of Terrorism*, of a reality 'everywhere
infiltrated by images, virtuality and fiction' (Baudrillard 28).
Similarly to Žižek, he refers to 9/11, as a 'Manhattan disaster
movie', (29) again evoking an image of fantasy subverting
what we once thought a stable reality. Žižek's contention that
the disruption of Hollywood release slates was an ideological
response to the events of 9/11 is particularly significant when we
consider the depiction of science fiction in *BSG*, something very
consciously conceived by Moore and David Eick. The style and
content of *BSG* function very much to repress the 'fantasmatic
background' of the show. As previously mentioned, the use
of real-sounding names for its characters ensures a greater
grounding for the series in a reality that is not so unlike our own
(Lou Anders (87–8) makes a similar point about fashion in the

series). The comments of Michael Rymer, producer, director of the miniseries and principal director of much of the series (twenty-three episodes), imply that the production of the miniseries was aimed towards creating a visual aesthetic that fitted with the meshing of fantasy and realist styles: '[Moore] and David [Eick] were both very clear that they wanted a more naturalistic approach than other sci-fi shows. Our main references were *Black Hawk Down, Band of Brothers, 2001* and *Alien*' (in Bassom, *The Official Companion*, 28) On one hand, Rymer's comments suggest a continued commitment to canonical examples of the science fiction genre in *2001: A Space Odyssey* (1968) and *Alien* (1979), both of which engage, although very differently, with classical sci-fi themes of the relationship between humanity and technology and other species/intelligences outside our common experience. *Black Hawk Down* (2001) and the television miniseries *Band of Brothers* (2001) both appeared around the time of 9/11 (*Band of Brothers*' first episode was broadcast two days before the attack) and depicted war zones in an immediate, handheld documentary style, often using desaturated images and an overall verisimilitude reminiscent of *Saving Private Ryan*'s (1998) Omaha Beach D-Day sequence. *BSG*'s overall aesthetic represents a blending of these two styles, the 'fantasmatic background' of the science fiction genre, and the gritty verisimilitude of these recent war dramas.

The constant negotiation between these two elements begins right at the opening of the miniseries (M.01). The first shot introduces us to a familiar-looking spaceship, the first of the miniseries' many nods to the original *BSG*. In keeping with Moore's conceptualization of the look of the show, the shot appears to be taken from a camera mounted on the side of the ship as we watch the ship dock with the armistice space station. As the captions provide key narrative exposition on the background of the human–Cylon conflict, we see the interior of the space station, as the Colonial envoy waits futilely for the Cylon representative, reviewing documents and looking at photos of his family. The shots are a combination of styles: still, slow-zooming long shots of the space station interior combined with nervy, handheld close-ups of the envoy, his photographs and the papers on his desk. Eventually he hears a sound – the Cylons have arrived. The sequence with Six and the Centurions continues this stylistic tone, combining conventional longer shots from low angles to suggest the menace of the Centurions, with motionless close ups of Six as she asks the envoy if he is 'alive' before kissing him, and the wobbly close ups of the envoy. The Cylons here seem to take the burden of the fantasy elements of this opening scene, shot in a menacing, but conventionally dramatic style, while the human representative is shot throughout with an anxious, jagged handheld vérité style. The attack on the station by the baseship is similarly handled in a conventional space effects shot. The scene cuts outside the space station, to a low-angle shot as the Cylon baseship manoeuvres above the station. The shot begins to zoom out as a missile arcs around the station, destroying it. In keeping with Moore's ideas for the shooting of space scenes, though, these exterior shots are mostly silent. This quick shift from the possible spaceship shot that opened the scene, to the 'impossible' special effects spectacle of the station's destruction demonstrates the fluid style of *BSG*'s negotiation of fantasy elements, here closely aligned with the Cylons, the show's ultimate 'other', and the 'real' elements, aligned with our human protagonists. It is these real elements that will continue to hold sway throughout the political allegories that run throughout the series.

However, the opening of the miniseries is marked by a bravura display of realism when we are first introduced to the interior of Galactica. Following the title caption, we zoom from an extreme long shot all the way around a meteor into the battlestar (another 'impossible' special effects shot), before cutting to Starbuck jogging through the busy corridors of the ship. What follows is an impressive long take, lasting over three minutes, which carries most of the burden of introducing our main characters (including the controversially female Starbuck) and the technological make-up of the ship and its role in history. The shot begins by tracking back with Starbuck as she jogs past the camera, encountering a PR executive with a group of journalists. We track with Doral (later

Cylon model Five) for a while as he provides key exposition for the audience by explaining Galactica's historical background. As Landing Signal Officer Aaron Kelly passes the camera, it begins to track with him, before quickly encountering Commander Adama coming through a door, rehearsing his decommissioning speech, which he will continue to do throughout the shot with interruptions to talk to Kelly and Starbuck. The camera follows Adama as he chats first with Kelly, then with Starbuck, before following her until she passes three of the deck hands (Cally, Socinus and Prosna), who we follow for a while, before picking up our interest in Adama again. The camera follows him into CIC, where he discusses communications details with Lieutenant Gaeta, whom we now follow out into the corridor. Here, we are introduced to Colonel Tigh, drunk and supporting himself against the wall. The camera tracks with Tigh for a while, until we re-encounter Doral, still with the journalists. He gives us some key technological exposition regarding the lack of modern technology on Galactica, a hangover from the previous war with the Cylons: 'a reminder of a time when we were so frightened by the capabilities of our enemies that we literally looked backward for protection'. This tour de force shot significantly introduces the key realist aesthetic of the show, the deep commitment to 'the use of extending takes and long masters which pull the audience into the reality of the action rather than . . . distract[ing] through the use of ostentatious cutting patterns' (Moore, 'Battlestar Galactica: Naturalistic Science Fiction').

Writing in the 1950s, the French critic André Bazin praised filmmakers who shot in depth, using long takes, producing whole scenes like this one from the miniseries, shot in one take. Bazin claimed that the one-take sequence shot 'brings the spectator into a relation with the image closer to that which he enjoys with reality. Therefore it is correct to say that, independently of the contents of the image, its structure is more realistic'. (Bazin 35) Bazin's contentions about the long take still hold sway today, as shots like this undoubtedly bring the viewer into a closer relationship with the image similar to that which he or she would share with the world around them. Although heavily directed by the passage of the camera from one character's business to another, the viewer can still revel in the atmosphere of the battlestar, the bustling environment, the military operations in CIC, the preparations for the decommissioning, the sheer spectacle of the structure of the ship. The master, close-up, close-up, two-shot, master pattern that Moore saw as 'ponderous' in the *Star Trek* universe ('*Battlestar Galactica*: Naturalistic Science Fiction') is washed away in the introduction to Galactica in the mini-series, producing a very different reality effect – even very different to that of the opening scene of the miniseries.

Where this combination of fantasy genre elements and realist aesthetic is most pronounced in *BSG* is during the episodes that engage most with the contemporary allegory that underpins the whole series. The producers of *Battlestar Galactica* are not alone in this instance, however. Many other contemporary texts have used a particular style of vérité documentary technique or realist narrative structures to engage with the contemporary zeitgeist. Popular television shows such as *24* (2001–) and films such as Paul Greengrass' *The Bourne Supremacy* (2004), *The Bourne Ultimatum* (2007) and *United 93* (2006) have utilized realist styles and narrative structures while exploring or reflecting contemporary political tensions. *24* especially, although its appearance just predates the events of 9/11, turns a gimmick of 'real time' episodes – avoiding overt manipulations of time through slow motion – into a 'limited, containable, and survivable crisis' (Herbert 87). The discourse of post-9/11 America is turned into a microcosm of the ongoing political ambiguity and instability initiated in September 2001 and extended by the ongoing wars in Afghanistan and Iraq. Unlike the political and moral uncertainty of *BSG*, *24* tends towards the heroic, suggesting a world in which abuse of enemy combatants is justified.

Whereas non-network shows such as *BSG*, *The Sopranos* (1999–2007) and *The Wire* (2002–8) have been exploring the moral uncertainty of our times, *24* collapses the moral ambiguity and ambivalence. Therefore, when Starbuck's torture of Leoben in 'Flesh and Bone' (1.08) leads to empathy between torturer and victim, resulting in uncertainty for the perpetrator of violence, she even prays for his soul: 'Lords of Kobol, hear my prayer. I don't know if he had a soul or not but, if he did, take care of it'. Likewise, Tigh's torture of Tyrol in 'Resistance' (2.04) is without results (although Tyrol does doubt his humanity), despite the irony that we eventually discover both to be Cylons. The torture in 'Resistance' is not only morally ambiguous, but these are actions by our supposed 'heroes', and they are pointless, as Tyrol's humanity is never really called into question, although it does reveal Tigh's growing paranoia and lack of control in command of the fleet. Torture in 24 always brings positive results, something that Jon Wiener in The Nation refers to as 'a fantasy of total knowledge and power'. In this sense, 24 becomes a better argument for torture than America's leader could ever make. The realism of the narrative structure then helps to reinforce this message. BSG portrays torture as counterproductive, full of wasted energy, stimulating doubt, fear and displacing fantasies of 'total knowledge and power'. Its own realism builds on this absence of power (on both human and Cylon sides, as in Tigh's interrogation in 'Occupation' 3.01), demonstrating a lack of polish, stable camera angles and definitive narrative progression – we often learn more about characters than we do about tactical and strategic information in BSG's torture scenes.

While a television show such as 24 offers a fantasy of control and governmental effectivity, BSG offers just the opposite: a narrative in which governmental authority is repeatedly questioned while fantasies of control and power are undermined or problematized. Even the Cylon occupations of the Colonies and New Caprica are exposed as unattainable political and military goals. In 'Occupation', Six explains on Colonial One that the holocaust has been an error, a fatal miscalculation. 'We're here because a majority of the Cylon felt that the slaughter of mankind had been a mistake', she explains. Cavil tells her that she and Boomer are 'all living in a fantasy world'. 'Delusional machines', he exclaims. 'What's the universe gonna come up with next?' This contradicts the Ones' declaration in that 'it's been decided that the occupation of the colonies was an error'. He later explains:

Cavil (1):   Our pursuit of this fleet of yours was another error. That's two for anyone who's keeping score. Both errors led to the same result. We became what we beheld. We became you.

Cavil (2):   Amen. People should be true to who and what they are. We're machines. We should be true to that. Be the best machines the universe has ever seen. But we got it into our heads that we were the children of humanity. So instead of pursuing our own destiny of trying to find our own path to enlightenment, we hijacked yours.
             ('Lay Down Your Burdens (Part Two)' 2.20)

This fundamental lack of coherent decision making, countering the logic of the 'empty heroics' of conventional narratives (the 'good' characters make 'good' decisions, 'bad' characters can only make 'bad' decisions) avoids the traditional Manichaean dynamic of most television drama, especially sci-fi such as the original *Battlestar Galactica*, where the decision making of either good or bad characters is never called into question explicitly – characters would simply fulfil their designated narrative role. Of course, 'Lay Down Your Burdens (Part Two)' ends with the occupation of New Caprica, while the subsequent narrative strand involving the Cylons has them descending into chaos, as the fourth season opens with the Cylons' growing self-doubt (or self-realization) and civil war becomes an inevitable outcome of the machines' growing individuality. The decision by the Six known as Natalie to remove the 'telencephalic inhibitor that restricts higher functions in the Centurions' (a contravention of Moore's decision to avoid technobabble) on the baseship during the dispute over consciousness of the Raiders becomes a shocking act of rebellion that comes at a point where the lines between good and bad in *BSG* have been totally eradicated ('Six of One' 4.02). The 'fantasy of total knowledge and power' could not be further away at this point, as the Colonials are split by Starbuck's return and Baltar's growing status as a messianic figure. Internal conflict becomes the key dramatic theme in Season Four, as the previous distinction between self and other is blown away altogether. The binary of self and 'other' is central to motifs of torture, where the victim is othered in order to dehumanize them. That othering has always been problematized in *BSG*, from Boomer's initial struggle with her growing awareness of her otherness (partially echoed by her ethnic background, in both diegetic and pro-filmic senses), to the sudden realization of otherness in Tigh, Anders, Tyrol and Tory, who, more than anyone else, seems to revel in her new found role of villain, murdering Cally ('Escape Velocity' 4.04) and siding with Baltar ('The Road Less Traveled' 4.05). However, while some humans are becoming more 'other', some Cylons are becoming less so, proposing a truce with the humans and a new, shared road to Earth.

What we glimpse with the collapse of self and 'other' – the 'big other' in this case, the enemy itself (Dunn 131) – is the undermining of the stability of identity, something echoed in the style of the show, which tends to undermine the audience's recognition of identifiable markers of the science fiction genre. Just as Rymer pointed to the show's 'main references' as cited above, the intrusion of fantasy into realism, or realism into fantasy in this case, is mirrored in both the characters – who find their 'realities' disturbed by growing realizations of otherness – and the style of the show, which partially suppresses its own basis as a fantasy show dealing with killer cyborgs, intergalactic space travel and scientific speculation. These two positions – one for the subjects within the text, another for the viewers – echo both sides of Žižek's argument. One sees, as many suggested in the aftermath of 9/11, the intrusion of reality into the fantasy realm – the destruction of the fantasmatic arena that many felt constituted the closed West – and the other the suppression of reality by the fantasy, the images from television screens and movies entering the environment we saw as a real space. In many ways, both sides are the same, as Žižek implies: 'the symbolic coordinates which determine what we experience as reality'. (16) are in some way fictional anyway, contingent upon the maintenance of very specific ideological frames of reference that combine to make up what is seen as the capitalist Western world, itself a space of illusions and political masquerades.

So, as many of our 'heroes' in *BSG* find their existences undermined by the realization of their own 'fantasmatic backgrounds', their Cylon identities, their own 'symbolic coordinates', are shattered. Their reality is fundamentally altered, as the fantasy comes rushing into the reality they previously viewed as stable, self-evident and unchanging, despite the destruction of the Colonies. Their 'reality' was built on a belief in a reality that is shaken, but not broken, by the events in the miniseries. That is, until Boomer's initial recognition of her possible unconscious sabotage aboard Galactica ('Water' 1.02). Even when Boomer downloads and return to Caprica in 'Downloaded' (2.18), she refuses to give up on the coordinates that previously defined her particular universe. She 'returns' (although technically she had never been there before) to the apartment where Boomer had once lived in Caprica City. She continues to treasure the artefacts of her previous life, such as the hand-carved elephants given to her by her mother the day she left for the Fleet Academy. But, as she observes, it's all 'fabricated', a 'lie' to help her succeed in her mission as a sleeper agent. Nevertheless, she continues to hold onto the reality that she now understands was a fantasy of a perfect life in order to help her achieve her Cylon goal. This confusion is signified in the following speech, which suddenly moves from present tense to past tense, as she recogizes the new reality to which the realisation of her otherness has lead her:

> This is love. *[looking at a picture of the Galactica crew]* These people love me. I love them. I didn't pretend to feel something so I could screw people over. I loved them. And then I betrayed them. I shot a man I loved. Frakked over another man, ruined his life. And why? Because I'm a lying machine. I'm a frakking Cylon!
>
> ('Downloaded' 2.18)

'Boomer' wasn't a simple performance by a Cylon agent; Boomer was 'real' person, a subject forged by her experiences, rather than a program carrying out its preset objectives. When the program finally emerged, it became an unconscious performance at odds with the personality – a 'fabrication' that shattered Boomer's 'symbolic coordinates', undermining the stability of her identity.

'And When That Life Turned Against Us, We Comforted Ourselves in the Knowledge That it Wasn't Really Our Fault, Not Really'

Many of the issues surrounding identity and otherness map onto *BSG*'s discourse surrounding the 'war on terror'. George W. Bush himself set the tone for the war, and the separation of self and other that runs throughout *BSG*, although in a much less stable state than Bush himself would have intended. In Bush's 20 September 2001 'Address to a Joint Session of Congress and the American People', he warned the world: 'Every nation, in every region, now has a decision to make. Either you are with us, or you are with the terrorists.' This war, in which enemy combatants are defined intellectually by their politics rather than visibly by the uniform they wear, is clearly reflected in *BSG*'s political and religious allegory. There is repeated imagery of terrorist tactics such as suicide bombings on both sides (Doral in 'Litmus' 1.06; Duck in 'Occupation'), while atrocities, such as the torture and murder of dehumanized and disenfranchised 'others' are carried out by those we expect to see as heroes (heavily associated with events on Pegasus, such as the brutal abuse of Gina ('Pegasus' 2.10), and the murder of civilian resisters ('Razor' 4.00). The complex religious conflict between the polytheists and monotheists also fits with popular conceptions of the central religio-political grounds covered by the 'war on terror'. While it seems obvious to link the events of *BSG*, especially the narrative arc of late Season

Two and early Season Three, via 'The Resistance' webisodes, as a metaphorical reflection of contemporary situations in the 'war on terror' and Iraq, Moore has resisted attempts to label the show in these narrow terms, emphasizing the broader metaphorical concerns of the show:

> A lot of people have asked me if the Cylon occupation was our way of addressing the situation in Iraq, but it really wasn't . . . There are obvious parallels, but the truth is when we talked about the episodes in the writers' room, we talked more about Vichy France, Vietnam, the West Bank and various other occupations; we even talked about what happened when the Romans were occupying Gaul.   (in Bassom, *The Official Companion Season Three*, 31)

The ending of 'Lay Down Your Burdens (Part Two)' was also intended to reflect this broader metaphorical scope, as the invading Cylons were intended to echo the 'Nazis marching into Paris in 1940' (Bassom, *The Offical Companion Season Two*, 103). Nevertheless, the parallels between the Coalition invasion and occupation of Iraq and the Cylon invasion and occupation of New Caprica are plain to see: surges in terrorist activities, local security forces targeted as collaborators, suicide bombings, rises in prison populations, abducted civilians, diminished quality of life, multiple deaths of occupying forces and a deeply unpopular president.[1] The Cylon occupation also proves to be unpopular with many of the occupying Cylons, as noted above, who see the occupation as 'an error'. However, it is the insurgency that wins, with help from Galactica and Pegasus ('Exodus (Part Two)' 3.04). Although this has to reflect the morality of the overall narrative of the series, the tactics employed by the insurgency on New Caprica, especially the suicide bombing of the security force graduation and Tigh's murder of his wife for collaboration ('Exodus (Part Two)'), reflect the complex morality of the narrative arc that spans Seasons Two and Three, reflecting the problematic morality of the Iraq war and the tactics employed by both sides in that real-life situation. In his reading of the insurgency, via

Frantz Fanon's radical anti-colonial theory, Dan Dinello has argued that the more general view of historical occupation is a reflection of 'the brutal, racist nature of occupation, its inevitable provocation of an indigenous revolt and the ensuing spiral of violence that devours combatants and civilians alike' (Dinello 188). *BSG* projects this matrix onto its own generic situation, using contemporary and historical allegory to marry the real with the fantasy, a typical strategy of the sci-fi genre, which tends to reflect contemporary concerns metaphorically in generic situations and characters. So, while Moore has tried hard to distance his new show from those on which he has worked in the past, as well as the formulaic Manichaean dimensions of the television sci-fi genre, this feature of the reimagined *BSG* locates the show as a classic example of science fiction television, a fact reflected in its Peabody Award win in 2005.

The collapse of the Manichaean dynamic of traditional dramatic television can be seen in the three-episode arc of the second half of Season Four, 'A Disquiet Follows My Soul' (4.12), 'The Oath' (4.13) and 'Blood on the Scales'. The events of the mutiny led by Felix Gaeta and Tom Zarek offer both a summary and a resolution to the political narrative of the series, before metaphysical and eschatological concerns become its primary focus. Mirroring the Cylon civil war of the first half of Season Four, the mutiny underlines the collapsing boundaries between humanity and the Cylons, especially as the loss of resurrection technology has effectively erased species difference between the two. When Zarek orders two marines to murder the Quorum after their refusal to sanction his power ('Blood on the Scales'), we're afforded an effective repeat of the rebel Cylons' use of the Centurions to gun down the Ones, Fours and Fives. In addition, Gaeta's role in the mutiny echoes his own role in his earlier participation in the New Caprica occupation and his decision to perjure himself in the trial of Baltar. The conversation between Baltar and Gaeta towards the end of 'The Oath' refers specifically to their 'little secret', one signed with a 'special pen'. Other moments in the episode refer back to this narrative arc at the end of Season Three. The return of Romo Lampkin to try Adama reflects the role he played in Baltar's trial, while Adama's threat that there would be 'no forgiveness, no amnesty' for the actions of the mutineers reflects Lee's speech in 'Crossroads (Part Two)' (3.20):

> So did he appear to cooperate with the Cylons? Sure. So did hundreds of others. What's the difference between him and them? The President issued a blanket pardon. They were all forgiven. No questions asked. Colonel Tigh. Colonel Tigh used suicide bombers, killed dozens of people. Forgiven. Lieutenant Agathon and Chief Tyrol. They murdered an officer on the *Pegasus*. Forgiven. The Admiral? The Admiral instituted a military *coup d'état* against the President. Forgiven. And me? Well, where do I begin? I shot down a civilian passenger ship, the *Olympic Carrier*. Over a thousand people on board. Forgiven. I raised my weapon to a superior officer, committed an act of mutiny. Forgiven. And then on the very day when Baltar surrendered to those Cylons, I, as Commander of *Pegasus*, jumped away. I left everybody on that planet alone, undefended, for months! I even tried to persuade the Admiral never to return. To abandon you all there for good. If I'd had my way, nobody would've made it off that planet. I'm the coward. I'm the traitor. I'm forgiven. I'd say we're very forgiving of mistakes.

The Gaeta/Zarek mutiny seems to be the final statement on this morality and in particular the relationship between government and the military. The earlier *coup d'état*, from Tigh's instigation of martial law ('Fragged' 2.03), split the fleet, while the mutiny (variously referred to as a 'reckoning', a 'revolution', as well as a 'coup') finally collapses the difference between human and Cylon. Tyrol's trip into the bowels of Galactica's engines also brings the plot arc that will eventually signal the demise of the ship, but only after it too is repaired with Cylon technology, another erasure of difference in the series. Other events are resurrected during the mutiny: tensions between Galactica and Pegasus crews; the abuse of Cylon prisoners, specifically the horrific sexual abuse of Gina;

labour disputes on the tylium refinery ('Dirty Hands' 3.16), when the ship jumps away after refusing the Cylon upgrade; and the use of the launch tube for executions ('Collaborators' 3.05). *BSG* has repeatedly debated issues of power and control, by military and the government, and has often returned to its neoliberal humanist agenda – nowhere more so than in the conclusion. The Gaeta/Zarek mutiny plot draws a line under the political debate in the show, its exploration of the relationship between military and state and the unilateral actions of both. The executions of Gaeta and Zarek at the end of 'Blood on the Scales' signify an erasure of difference, and the uncanny sense that all of this *has* happened before, and presumably will happen again. Gaeta's final exorcism of the pain of his amputation – close-ups of him scratching at the socket of his prosthetic leg are a visual motif of all three episodes – is the exorcism of difference and signifies the ending of the political disputation of the entire series. By resurrecting the key narrative points from earlier in the series, 'The Oath' and 'Blood on the Scales' particularly emphasize the similarities between this rebellion and the Cylon civil war and debate the issues of authority, militarism and civil liberties that have existed since the very beginning of the series. The final act of military justice signals an end of militarism, looking forward to the utopian ending of the show, which focuses entirely on the mythic-religious dimensions. The difference and otherness that have been constantly shifting concerns throughout all four seasons come to an end, with one final warning, appropriately on the streets of New York ('Daybreak (Part Two)' 4.20), as a reminder of the 9/11 subtext of the show. Indeed, Magali Rennes may see this as the series coming full circle, as she argues that 'categories of difference start[ed] to crumble' with the kiss that opened the miniseries (64).

The episodes depicting the Gaeta/Zarek mutiny are some of the most frantic and realistic of the series, down to the use of documentary-style captioning of the time throughout the episodes. The mutiny is fairly short-lived, from 0620 hours in 'The Oath' to 1532 hours in 'Blood on the Scales'. While this is a typical use of realism in the show, it also provides an impetus to the narrative that underlines its pace and action. *BSG* has continually used its style to reflect post-9/11 concerns, perhaps even more than in its metaphorical narrative content. Much of this is directly concerned with the relationship between the real and fantasy aspects of the show. A philosopher such as Žižek sees the relationship as one which is concerned with an image of reality that is constructed, purely symbolic in an ideological sense, while the images of realism, a key carrier of ideology, in *BSG* are also constructed, but in a way in which the camera becomes an overt presence. At times, the imitation of documentary and news reportage, particularly in scenes of space battles and action sequences, reflects the show's main allegorical content onto the style as well as the content. In many respects the double-episode Season Three opener, 'Occupation/Precipice' (3.01/02) is a key example of this use of realist, documentary style to emphasize the real within the sci-fi scenario. By focusing predominantly on the planet-side action, and minimizing events on the two battlestars, the show is able to focus very much on developing a documentary aesthetic, which also draws on the news reporting that viewers have come to associate with coverage of both of the Gulf war conflicts.

At the beginning of 'Precipice', following the suicide bombing of the security force graduation, the Cylons clamp down on the inhabitants with a series of nighttime raids on key human personnel. The sequence in which Cally and other figures are abducted by the security forces is shot predominantly using a green night-filter. In his podcast commentary on the episode, Moore is again quick to distance this stylistic choice from the immediate political context of Iraq. He maintains that the choice to shoot in the limited green-and-black palette of 'night scrubs' was a choice of the director, Sergio Mimica-Gezzan, but was not 'a deliberate attempt to evoke Iraq'. The use of night-vision photography, Moore contends, is simply the way that the audience is 'used to looking at' night scenes, from shows such as *Cops*, from footage from Iraq, and scenes from around the world with troops battering down doors and abducting people. Again, while Moore aims to distance his show from the immediate political context, he confirms the referent, although he is deliberate in his attempts not to make Iraq the *only* political referent. He also draws an analogy between the show's space sequences, with its losses of focus, rough framing and handheld look; the style 'intuitively tells you that it's a real object, this is really happening'. Thus, the stylistic choices are intended to bring 'a sense of verisimilitude, of truth': they are not motivated politically, but by what is most effective dramatically (Moore, '*Battlestar Galactica* Episodes 3.01–3.02 Commentary'). Nevertheless, the sequence is not necessarily motivated by the realism of the text. Prior to the use of the night-vision shooting, we see the New Caprica Police (NCP) preparing, Jammer speaks with Cavil about the need to 'break the cycle of violence' (reiterating a comment from one of the NCP soldiers), and we see the NCP put on their night-vision goggles for the raid. Here, Mimica-Gezzan switches to the green filter reminiscent of news footage of bombings in Baghdad, firefights between American soldiers and insurgents, and assaults on insurgent targets, easily accessible from nightly news or twenty-four-hour news channels or, with the increase in internet video sharing, freely available on sites such as YouTube. The dramatic choice seems motivated more by the need to draw a parallel with this real-life footage as an intertextual reference than a need for verisimilitude. While the audience sees through the filter of the night-vision goggles, we do so without being offered a point-of-view shot from any of the NCP. The camera takes a detached perspective, as it had done in the previous sequence with Jammer and Cavil. Therefore, the switch to night vision doesn't offer the audience an identification with any of the NCP (which was one of Moore's goals in 'Precipice', a dramatic counterpoint to the insurgency perspective in 'Occupation'), but suggests the continued presence of an observational documentary camera crew, documenting the raids rather than participating in them. Thus, the switch to night vision, despite seeing the NCP put on their goggles, is an arbitrary device to suggest an analogy with news footage, rather than simply motivated by what we see in the events of the narrative. Nevertheless, like the space footage, this brief sequence offers the viewer an image of what is perceived as a reality – our reality, rather than the reality of *BSG* – again avoiding the fantasy basis of the show.

Geoff King has shown how visions of the events of 9/11 have been shaped by broadcasters to demonstrate 'a 'cinematic' construction of spectacular impact.' These, he contends, are mixed 'with many traces of the authentically real. These include unsteady camerawork and awkward zooms and slightly different visual quality of the images, taken from different cameras' (King 53). Like Žižek and Baudrillard, King sees the events of 9/11 as a blending of the real and the fantasy, although for King this is largely the effect of broadcaster manipulation, which reconstructed the events from multiple media and user-generated sources to fit pre-existing cinematic rules of continuity and spectacle, but with unavoidable markers of the real, quoted above. *BSG* fits very much with the model King outlines, with a mix of effectively cinematic qualities, spectacular imagery and realist techniques, such as handheld camera, the illusion of 'accidental' framing and focus, long takes, night vision, over-exposed lighting, and disjunctive cutting. In so doing, the makers of *BSG* have created a show that very much fits with the zeitgeist of post-9/11 culture, as well as with other products of that culture.

'All of This Has Happened Before, and All of it Will Happen Again'

Throughout the majority of its run, *Battlestar Galactica* carefully negotiated its basis in fantasy television with the realist techniques it utilized to comment on our reality, as well as to critique the stability of that reality for many of the characters who inhabit that world. Issues of identity and gender are key ideological messages that were explored throughout the show, so, while the final episodes of the series shifted focus from the overt political metaphors of earlier episodes in Season Four, this should not be seen as a displacement of politics or an invalidation of the themes debated throughout the show. The liberal agenda of difference and disenfranchisement was always at the heart of the show, so while these two threads may have become separate – even losing dramatic impetus – the resolution of *BSG* brought a conclusion to the negotiation of real and fantasy as well as between mythic and political. So, while the explicit political metaphors may have ended with the Gaeta/Zarek mutiny, the ideological utopianism of the ending offered a fantasy of liberation from difference, oppression, fear and technology. Nevertheless, this is offered in close proximity to a warning, embedded in the 'real', of contemporary experimentation with robotics meant to foreshadow the development of Cylon slavery. So, while a 'fantasmatic background' is offered over political metaphor, the ending cannot avoid an explicit ideological statement that is a reflection of contemporary concerns.

Note

1   Detailed statistics on military, economic, quality of life and security data can be found, compiled month by month at <http://www.brookings.edu/saban/iraq-index.aspx>, up to 20 August 2009.

Works Cited

Anders, Lou. 'The Natural and the Unnatural: Verisimilitude in *Battlestar Galactica*,' *So Say We All: An Unauthorized Collection of Thoughts and Opinions on* Battlestar Galactica. Ed. Richard Hatch, Tee Morris and Glenn Yeffeth. Dallas: Benbella, 2006. 83–94.

Bassom, David. *Battlestar Galactica: The Official Companion*. London: Titan, 2005.

—— *Battlestar Galactica: The Official Companion Season Two*. London: Titan, 2006.

—— *Battlestar Galactica: The Official Companion Season Three*. London: Titan, 2007.

Baudrillard, Jean. *The Spirit of Terrorism*. London: Verso, 2003.

Bazin, André (1967). *What is Cinema?*. Ed. and trans. Hugh Gray. Berkeley: University of California Press.

Bush, George W. 'Address to a Joint Session of Congress and the American People.' 20 Sept 2001 <http://www.whitehouse.gov/news/releases/2001/09/20010920-8.html>.

Dinello, Dan. 'The Wretched of New Caprica.' Battlestar Galactica *and Philosophy: Mission Accomplished or Mission Frakked Up?* Eds Josef Steiff and Tristan D. Tamplin. Chicago and La Salle: Open Court, 2008. 185–200.

Dunn, George A. 'Being Boomer: Identity, Alienation, and Evil.' Battlestar Galactica *and Philosophy: Knowledge Here Begins Out There*. Ed. Jason Eberl. Oxford: Blackwell, 2008. 127–40.

Eberl, Jason T. (ed.). Battlestar Galactica *and Philosophy: Knowledge Here Begins Out There*. Oxford: Blackwell, 2008.

Hatch, Richard, Tee Morris and Glenn Yeffeth (eds). *So Say We All: An Unauthorized Collection of Thoughts and Opinions on* Battlestar Galactica. Dallas: Benbella, 2006.

Herbert, Daniel. 'Days and Hours of the Apocalypse: *24* and the Nuclear Narrative.' *Reading* 24: *TV Against the Clock*. Ed. Steven Peacock. London and New York: I.B.Tauris, 2007. 85–95.

King, Geoff. 'Just Like a Movie?': 9/11 and Hollywood Spectacle.' *The Spectacle of the Real: From Hollywood to Reality TV and Beyond*. Ed. Geoff King. Bristol: Intellect Press, 2005. 47–57.

Moore, Ronald D. '*Battlestar Galactica* Episode 3.01–3.02 Commentary (Enhanced) Podcast'. 2006. <http://galacticasitrep.blogspot.com/2006_03_01_archive.html>.

—— '*Battlestar Galactica*: Naturalistic Science Fiction or Taking the Opera out of Space Opera.' 2006. <http://galacticasitrep.blogspot.com/2006_03_01_archive.html>.

Potter, Tiffany and C. W. Marshall (eds). *Cyclons in America: Critical Studies in* Battlestar Galactica. New York: Continuum, 2008.

Rennes, Magali. 'Kiss Me, Now Die!' Battlestar Galactica *and Philosophy: Mission Accomplished or Mission Frakked Up?* Eds Josef Steiff and Tristan D. Tamplin. Chicago and La Salle: Open Court, 2008. 63–76.

Storm, Jo. *Frak You! The Ultimate Unauthorized Guide to* Battlestar Galactica. Toronto: ECW, 2007.

Wiener, Jon. 'Fox Show '24': Torture on TV.' 2007 <http://www.alternet. org/story/46757/>.

Žižek, Slavoj. *Welcome to the Desert of the Real: Five Essays on September 11 and Related Dates*. London: Verso, 2002.

Butch Girls, Brittle Boys and Sexy, Sexless Cylons

Some Gender Problems in *Battlestar Galactica*

MATTHEW JONES

Battlestar Galactica and Me

I don't belong on *Battlestar Galactica*. Somewhere between the present day and the future that the programme presents, the likes of me (a short, chubby, bespectacled young thing) were seemingly wiped out, eradicated from human diversity in favour of the perfectly square jaw lines and the bulging, muscled torsos that constitute the men of the ship. Where the less than perfect specimens are permitted to exist in the future they are the wallpaper, the background of the shot, forced to live somewhere off camera, only glimpsed in passing on some nameless civilian ship. Only rarely does someone I can identify with, someone who isn't sculpted to perfection, affect, let alone carry, the narrative. I like *Battlestar Galactica* but, much to my chagrin, it does not seem to like me.

Finding my particular, albeit unconventional, breed of masculinity pushed out of the plot and onto a civilian ship somewhere on the sidelines, I started to wonder what exactly it is about certain types of people that prevented them from becoming the action heroes of this saga, charging the frontlines shoulder to shoulder with the beautiful people. What is it about their constitutions, about how they define and present themselves, that means they are not welcome onboard this last ark of humanity? There is, it seems, a problem with the representation of non-normative gender lurking at the heart of Galactica. Somewhere at its core, beneath all the military manoeuvres and the political wrangling, something is rotten. As an inquisitive audience, as active participants in the consumption of the programme, we ought to be taking a good, hard look at these men and women, at who belongs in this future, who does not, and why.

The Bad Doctor

Gaius Baltar clearly does not belong. It was Baltar, after all, who facilitated the annihilation of human civilization as we know it. It was, of course, the Cylons who actually launched the attack on the human colonies at the start of the series, while Caprica Six utilized her penchant for espionage to speed things on their way, but it was Baltar who engaged in the rather questionable practice of trading sensitive defence information for sex, thereby making the massacre possible. Two seasons later, in 'Lay Down Your Burdens (Part Two)' (2.20), it is Baltar again who endangers all of mankind, leading the last human survivors to colonize an only marginally habitable planet where, after a period of hardship and lack, the Cylons find and conquer them. Wherever Baltar is allowed to play a significant role in the narrative, it seems, misfortune and privation are not far behind.[1]

In truth, the series does its best to keep steeping as much responsibility as it can for the troubles of mankind at Dr Baltar's door. Not content with implicating him in the destruction of the Twelve Colonies, the programme goes on to show that, among various other more or less questionable activities, Baltar attempts to negotiate for the enemy in 'The Eye of Jupiter' (3.11), engages in sexual activities with the adoring members of his own

personal cult in 'He That Believeth in Me' (4.01) and regularly
seeks the advice of a potentially hallucinatory, possibly invisible
and ultimately angelic seductress who appears to him in the
body of a Cylon. Fear not the Cylon clones living within the fleet;
we have a human traitor in our midst far wilier (weaker? more
human?) than those pesky machines could ever be. The truth of
the matter is that, however brave the square-jawed heroes of the
military are, they can only do so much to protect humanity while
Baltar is sleeping with the enemy within. Indeed, in a series that
concludes by eschewing technology as the root of all humanity's
troubles and sending the icons of that technology – the ships of
the fleet – into the sun to burn ('Daybreak (Part Two)' 4.20), it
is no accident that Baltar, the man who takes such an unequal
portion of the blame for these troubles, is a scientist by trade. He
was, it seems, doomed to be a weak and treacherous man from
the very start.

So, then, what exactly is it about Baltar that makes him eligible
for this kind of bedevilment? If we are to understand what it is
that renders some people unworthy of residence aboard Galactica,
then finding out what makes Baltar the target of such sustained
criticism must be our first step.

Baltar's troubles stem from an incident in the first episode of
the miniseries that began the reimagined programme, wherein
he succumbs to his own sexuality and the advances of a beautiful
Cylon woman. Though Baltar could not have known that Caprica
Six was the enemy, disguised as she was by her human form,
paying for this sexual encounter with state secrets was still a
clearly dangerous, demonstrably immoral and probably criminal
activity. It is important to recognize, however, that, in connecting
Baltar's sexual and military misdemeanours, the series ties
together notions of sex and guilt. Through sleeping with Caprica
Six, Gaius not only trades in the security of the colonies but
he also displays weakness in the face of his biological drives.
Since military and sexual transgressions are here indivisible,
the condemnation we steep upon him is never solely aimed at
his culpability for the attack on humankind, but is also aimed

at his inability to resist engaging in the sexual act. While Baltar is certainly not an innocent man, sex plays a significant role in eliciting our criticism of him.

For anyone else onboard Galactica, sexual contact is a blameless act, the natural urge of a normal human being. The morally irreproachable Lee Adama visits a prostitute in 'Black Market' (2.14), an act for which he receives no condemnation. Even the heads of the military and the civilian government, William Adama and Laura Roslin, are allowed to enjoy sex without condemnation in 'A Disquiet Follows My Soul' (4.12). For Gaius, however, sex is never allowed to come free from consequence. His ill-conceived sexual encounter with Caprica Six at the opening of the series marks the beginning not only of his own mental decline but also of his culpability for the grim fate of mankind.[2]

If sex in the fleet at large is blameless, then perhaps it is the type of sex that Baltar engages in that renders him a threat. His crime, it seems, is not only the handing over of secret military information but also the sexual submission that accompanies it. Baltar makes his mistakes not because he wishes malice on mankind but because he allows a woman to hold power over him, using his desires to puppet him like a marionette.[3] The reason that Baltar's transgression with Caprica Six has such a uniquely negative impact seems to be that, in opposition to her strong, sexually aggressive femininity, his identity as a man is consequently entangled with notions of sexual influence and availability in such a way as to render him the subject of this influence rather than the bearer of it.

Worse still, however, are the implications of this act of submission. Not only does Baltar allow a woman to hold power over him, but in so doing he also inverts the male seduction fantasy. No longer is the woman weak and available at the hands of the powerful, dominating male, but the male's sexual desires place him at the mercy of the domineering female seductress. Gaius is, in effect, the receptive partner, allowing Caprica Six to have her way with him in both a sexual and intellectual sense. What Baltar does is – in the ideology of masculinity the series presents – far worse than simply selling the military down the river; he transgresses societal customs and boundaries, successfully overturning traditional gender roles.[4] Six is not merely a powerful and manipulative woman, she is the contents of a Pandora's Box that Gaius opens by allowing a female to usurp the male sphere, to attain dominance of the sexes.

Indeed, it takes Gaius the entire series to rectify this mistake. If Baltar's crime was allowing a woman dominance over him, and as such allowing masculinity to be rendered weak at the hands of femininity, then the path to redemption can only be found in reasserting the dominance of traditional masculinity and forcing the woman who did this to him to submit. In 'Daybreak (Part One)' (4.19) this is exactly what Baltar achieves. Giving up his promiscuous cult and his former cowardice, Baltar refuses the chance to flee from the final battle with the Cylons and remains on Galactica to fight. Gun in hand, Baltar cuts a very different silhouette to the cowering, treacherous scientist of the early seasons. In the eyes of the series, this is Gaius Baltar finally making amends for his crimes against masculinity and returning to the normative male ideals that he has so long avoided. Furthermore, Baltar gives up his questionable twin pursuits of science and sex to perform manual labour on his own farm with Caprica Six by his side ('Daybreak (Part Two)'). Having operated successfully in both military and manual spheres, two areas claimed by traditional masculinity as its own, Baltar's decision to settle with Caprica Six, and, importantly, only with Caprica Six, makes this relationship as close an approximation of the traditional family unit as Baltar could perhaps have hoped for. In this construction, Caprica Six fills the role of his dutiful wife, tamed at last by Baltar's adoption of a normative male identity. Only by adopting this new identity can Gaius rebalance the series' approach to gender, restoring the prescriptive patriarchal model that the programme had so long criticized him for avoiding. Only by returning to the fold, by giving up his sexually promiscuous and submissive ways, can Baltar once again be accepted by the world of the series.

If, prior to his redemption, the programme viewed Gaius as a failure, it is not simply because he failed to protect mankind from the Cylon bombardment, but is also because he failed to protect patriarchy and, therefore, failed as a man. It is little wonder that a series that places such store by traditional masculinity should seek to blame Gaius for the fate of humankind.

Brittle Boys

It is no surprise, then, to find that Gaius becomes a feminized object within the visual logic of the series. Longhaired, bumbling and with an English accent, Baltar appears to be at complete odds to the idealized image of manhood onboard the fleet.[5] The perfectly toned military men, such as Apollo and Helo, spend their days practising their martial and mechanical skills, increasing their might in their suitably masculine pursuits. If we were to read the series in Freudian terms it is not hard to see what could be made of Apollo, a pilot, penetrating the void of space in his sleek, pointed vessel. The symbolism here speaks for itself. Even his job connotes the type of sexual virility and testosterone-fuelled masculinity that he embodies. As Apollo rises through the ranks of the military, ultimately becoming commander of Pegasus in 'The Captain's Hand' (2.17), it becomes evident that, in order for a man to succeed in the fleet, this particular variety of traditional, normative masculinity is essential. Baltar, by way of contrast, passes the early seasons in laboratories making his name via the pursuit of knowledge, a cerebral rather than manual activity. He spends his days cooped up inside with his equipment (another Freudian metaphor, perhaps?). In the later series he becomes a quasi-religious figurehead for a cult of adoring (and often nubile) young women, a role that is treated not as the fulfilment of his male virility but as a cowardly retreat from all that is important to the survival of the fleet. Neither of these roles, nor his doomed political career in Seasons Two and Three, in which he is reduced to a powerless pawn of the Cylon occupation forces, allow him to exercise his body or his masculinity in the way that is afforded to his counterparts in the military. As such his physique is much less muscular, and therefore much less powerful, than his military equivalents. He is, in short, a very different kind of man to those of which the series seemingly approves. The programme's condemnation of Baltar can thus be read as a rejection of the particular variety of masculinity that he embodies in favour of more traditional gender identities, such as those projected by Apollo and Helo.

If Gaius becomes some form of un-man, a compromised aberration against so-called real masculinity, then Apollo and Helo come to stand for what the series believes these real men should be. When Helo protects his pregnant lover from Starbuck's gun, despite the fact that she is a Cylon ('Kobol's Last Gleaming (Part Two)' 1.13), he effectively becomes an image of moral faultlessness. Similarly, when Apollo plots to smuggle the wrongly imprisoned President Roslin off Galactica against direct orders ('Resistance' 2.04), the audience is asked to recognize him as decisive, rational and unfalteringly honourable. These incidents are not isolated but are mere examples of the myriad ways these characters place themselves above moral reproach throughout the series. Slowly but surely an image of what a man should be develops.

It is no coincidence that these men are both perfect physical specimens; onboard Galactica, physicality is a guide to the mental world of a subject.[6] From this standpoint, the reason why it is necessary for the sculpted physiques of these military men to stand in such sharp opposition to the long, gangly body of Gaius becomes clear; in every sense he is their opposite, but far from their equal. While these men are strong in both body and mind, Gaius is feminized (read weak), not only in his appearance, but also in his compromised position as a traitor. His taking up of both the gun and the plough at the end of the series ('Daybreak (Part Two)') comes with the promise not only of his moral restoration, but also of his physical development, too. It is not merely coincidental that both bodily and ethical revolutions occur simultaneously; in the world of *BSG* they are the same thing.

The Consequences of Hybridity

This system is disrupted by the transformation of Samuel T. Anders into a Hybrid, the techno-biological creatures that are capable of interfacing with Cylon technology, effectively running their basestar spaceships, and who, surreally, spend their time prophesying the future. Prior to Anders' conversion, we have witnessed two different varieties of Hybrid. All the Hybrids that we see on the modern Cylon basestars are depicted as female. Long hair and female features and voices give these creatures the semblance of being women, though their actual gender, or even the presence of gender and biological sex in such creatures is never discussed or verified by the series. The potential complexity of these beings is discarded and instead we are presented with a collection of signs and signifiers that code these Hybrids as female.

In a series that has constructed masculinity as a combination of bold adventurism, implacable loyalty and ruthless militarism, these Hybrids, creatures that spend their days lying naked in baths of goo, talking in incomprehensible code about possible future events and unable to defend themselves physically, stand as a counterpoint to all that the men of the fleet should be. It should come as little surprise, then, to discover that all of the modern Hybrids are coded female.

When we do see a male Hybrid, however, he is also prevented from portraying the type of normative masculinity that the series upholds. The prototype Hybrid, produced during the first Cylon war and seen in 'Razor' (4.00), is presented as an elderly man. This functions as a cunning ploy to disregard the threat that casting a male as a Hybrid could pose to the series' conception of manliness. The fact that this Hybrid is both old and a prototype renders him outside the realm of traditional masculinity. His body, now past its prime, cannot compete with those that exemplify dominant masculinity, namely Helo and Apollo. His status as a prototype, as an isolated aberration that is born out of gruesome and violent experimentation on prisoners of war, casts him as an outsider to the moral righteousness of the ideal specimens of his sex. As far as the series sees gender identity, this Hybrid, though presented as male, is no man.

The Hybrids, then, are prevented from holding the masculine identity that has been championed by the series. They are predominantly coded as female, and where they are not they remain incompatible with prescriptive masculinity. The conversion of Anders, a muscled, dedicated and fearless soldier, into Galactica's own Hybrid, then, is problematic. A sports star before the assault on the Colonies, Anders quickly adapts to a life of armed combat, becoming the leader of a resistance group on occupied Caprica ('Resistance') and taking up this mantle again on New Caprica ('Occupation' 3.01). Anders' muscular physique and doggedly militaristic mindset allow him to merge with ease into the ranks of Galactica's military upon his arrival at the fleet. To find such a clear embodiment of the type of masculinity that the series suggests is both necessary and correct placed firmly within the female sphere through his transformation into a Hybrid does indeed pose problems for the representation of gendered ideals in *Battlestar Galactica*.

It is important to remember, however, that this transformation is not performed in isolation from other events. Indeed, by the time that Samuel Anders receives a gunshot wound to the head and begins his journey towards becoming a Hybrid ('Blood on the Scales' 4.14), a context for this change has already been created that allows it to make sense within the show's gender politics. Anders' masculinity has been covertly undermined by events that render his eventual fate less subversive and more in keeping with the ideology of the series.

The principal moment that precipitates Anders' feminization is the revelation in 'Crossroads (Part Two)' (3.20) that Anders is one of the five humanoid Cylons that have yet to be discovered. The subsequent events of Season Four, with the reconciliation between the rebel Cylons, the humans and the enigmatic Final Five, cast the exposure of Anders' Cylon nature in a more positive light than it might have come under otherwise. In this final season, with the series' moral compass swinging once more, the programme eventually allows the Cylons redemption and integration with the human survivors, thereby rendering Anders' true nature less problematic than it previously had been. Accepted though he may eventually be by the human race, his being a Cylon still distances Anders from the viewer, making him something unfamiliar, an unknown quantity that holds the key to many long-buried secrets about the very nature of the Cylons themselves. Once Anders receives his fateful wound he begins to remember details about the lives of the Final Five, information that had previously been wiped from their memories, indicating to the viewer that, as much as they may know about Anders, there is still much, much more that they are unaware of. Anders is placed in the uncomfortable position of being both familiar and unfamiliar at once. He is the man we have known since 'Resistance', but he is also something strange, uncanny and possibly threatening. To see such a character feminized by conversion into a Hybrid, and indeed further emasculated by the revelation that the surgery to remove the bullet from his head left him with almost no brain activity ('No Exit' 4.15), can be seen as an attempt by the series not merely to undermine his masculinity but to render safe his challenging difference. If a normatively masculine man were to embody such a tenuous position between the humans and the Cylons, between 'Us' and 'Them', then the series' construction of masculinity itself would be called into question.[7] As such, after Anders' revelation, the only option left for the series is to both emasculate and feminize him, erecting new boundaries to separate him from the traditional masculinity that he had previously been allowed to exhibit. His conversion into a Hybrid is merely the physical embodiment of this. Though some of the Cylons might have come around to the human way of thinking, it is too far a stretch for the series to allow them access to its privileged breed of masculinity.

The Problem with Tigh

There are, of course, other men within the fleet who, for various reasons, are not deemed to deserve the exalted masculinity that is so respected by the military. They may not all encounter such a dramatic fate as Samuel Anders or such utter debasement and astounding redemption as Gaius Baltar, but each of them is emasculated in their own particular way.

Saul Tigh, existing somewhere between a strong, masculine physique and the less flattering stages of the ageing process, occupies the middle ground in the masculinity divide between Apollo and Baltar, being at once decisive, powerful, flawed, drunk and a Cylon. In a simplistic reading of the character, Tigh is a combination of masculine and feminine ideas (militarily active but emotionally weak), and as such is sometimes glorified, sometimes castigated. However, Tigh's role in the particular negotiation of maleness that the series enacts runs far deeper than merely being a buffer zone between what is and is not to be considered a man. In truth, he demonstrates the consequences of breaking the codes of masculinity, of transgressing the boundaries the series enforces. While Gaius exists in a feminized space all of his own, never adopting even a semblance of the rigid masculine identity required by the fleet until the very end, Tigh reveals what happens if a man's man dares to weaken.

Unlike Baltar, Tigh never belongs to a purely feminine space, but still he manages to betray the fleet by drinking at its helm in 'Fragged' (2.03). As a strong male character his actions could be seen as contradictory in the context of the normative gender system I have identified. However, in a world where danger is ever present and the enemy can attack at a moment's notice, the primary human need, and consequently the primary requirement of masculinity, is the provision of protection. What are these muscled men that populate the military for if not to protect? Tigh's drinking, then, can be read as a dereliction of masculine duty, as a move from providing the fleet with protection to facilitating its endangerment. At the bottom of his bottle Tigh does not find absolution, he finds his feminine side. By rendering himself unable to protect he in turn becomes one who requires protection. He trades in the supposedly masculine traits of competency and responsibility for the feminine sphere of reliance on others.

Once the series ceases to signal his drinking as a problem, Tigh is further rendered problematic by the revelation that he, too, is a Cylon. Why, then, does Tigh not suffer a similar fate to Anders? If Anders' conversion into a feminized Hybrid was a way of shoring up traditional masculinity, of denying the Cylon Anders the same unregulated access to it that he had previously enjoyed, then Tigh does not require such a fate as he was never allowed this access to begin with. Whereas Anders needed to be removed from the masculine sphere, Tigh was never even permitted to occupy it.

Significantly, Tigh's wife Ellen plays a role in his emasculation both before and after it is revealed that they are both members of the Final Five. Early in the series, Tigh sees the return of his wife to the fleet in 'Tigh Me Up, Tigh Me Down' (1.09) and allows her to function as his unofficial adviser. Consequently Tigh's decisions are compromised within the logic of the series, not only by his drinking, but also by the influence of Ellen's femininity and supposed weakness. It isn't long before she has him at the bottle again, rendering the fleet at risk once more.

After they both come to understand that they have been Cylons all along, Tigh and Ellen reconstruct the same scenario that once led to the downfall of Gaius Baltar at the hands of Caprica Six. Some time after Ellen's resurrection after her death on New Caprica, she is taken back to the fleet, where she is reunited with Saul once more ('Deadlock' 4.16). Tigh, unable to resist his biological urges, makes love to Ellen despite the fact that Caprica Six is pregnant with his child. Just like Baltar, Tigh is incapable of denying his sex drive, no matter what the cost. Whereas Baltar paid with the lives of billions of humans on the Twelve Colonies, Tigh pays with only one life, that of his unborn child, the miracle baby conceived by two Cylon parents, a set of circumstances previously considered impossible. The series' mantra, 'all this has happened before; all this will happen again', has never been more true. Tigh repeats Baltar's mistakes, and so is condemned to the same punishment: emasculation. If the primary male duty in the fleet is to protect the innocent, then the fact that Tigh's inability to control his libido causes the death of an unborn child can only be read as the most severe dereliction of his duty as a man.

The message here seems clear: once traditional masculinity is compromised, be it by Tigh's drinking, by his being a Cylon or by his inability to resist his biological urges, the security of the fleet is compromised. For a man to occupy a supposedly feminine space in the world of *BSG*, no matter if it is through sexual passivity or undue female influence, is not only undesirable, it is downright dangerous.

An LGBTQ-less Future

It is worth noting that this system of binary opposition, where traditional masculinity stands as the reverse of femininity, is left unchallenged by homosexuality, bisexuality, transsexuality, transgenderism or queer characters of any sort. These things, which one might reasonably assume could destabilize the artificial division between the masculine and feminine in *BSG*, are supposedly non-existent in this particular future, wiped out as the archaic products of a bygone era.

In the solitary episode where such characters do appear, they are immediately and unceremoniously vilified or punished. 'Razor' takes the promising step of suggesting that lesbianism has not been completely eradicated in the *BSG* universe. Indeed, Admiral Helena Cain of Pegasus has a lesbian relationship of her own. She is, however, not a non-heteronormative role model.

We have met Cain before, though then we were unaware of her sexuality. In 'Pegasus' (2.10), Cain was introduced as the leader of another group of survivors aboard their own battlestar, mirroring the programme's heroic crew. Soon, however, things went awry. Before the episode is completed, Cain has proven herself to be a cold, callous individual by ordering the execution of both Tyrol and Helo before launching a full-scale assault on Galactica, the only other survivors of her own race.

As if this were not bad enough, Cain has an even darker secret locked up in the bowels of her ship. Gina Inviere, a Cylon model Six, languishes in the brig, frequently beaten, whipped and gang raped in an attempt to elicit information from her. As we discover when we are later told of Cain's history, Gina was her lover before her Cylon identity was unmasked. Cain then rapidly suppressed her feelings for Gina and ordered her torture at the hands of her crew.

To make matters worse, however, this is the only explicit representation of a non-heteronormative relationship that we get in the series, and not only does it end badly, it ends with the complete degradation and brutalization of one of the women involved. With no positive representations of alternative sexualities to counterbalance this, one is forced to conclude that this is simply the effect of lesbianism. Not only does it lead to Gina's torture, these episodes also imply that Cain's cold, hard nature is a product of her lesbian affair and the betrayal that concluded it. If lesbianism does not have serious physical consequences for Cain in the way it did for Gina, it certainly takes a serious psychological toll.

Indeed, the series goes to great lengths to indicate that it is not the fact that these two form a close friendship that causes these problems, but rather it is the fact that this friendship is then allowed to become sexual. This can be made clear through a comparison of the relationship between these two women and the friendship between Saul Tigh and William Adama. This is another close relationship, though this time purely asexual, between two people of one sex where one is human and the other is eventually revealed to be a Cylon. In this way, Tigh and Adama can be seen to mirror Gina and Cain, but with the key difference that these men never become sexually involved.

There are numerous moments within the series that are designed to display the closeness of this friendship, but, as the series reaches its conclusion, some characters begin to say some rather curious things about Tigh and Adama that highlight the intensity of their friendship. For instance, in 'The Oath' (4.13), Felix Gaeta tells Adama that he is 'a sad old man that has let his heart and his affection for a Cylon cloud his judgement'. The Cylon they are discussing is, of course, Tigh and the relationship that Gaeta is describing seems to be something much, much more intense than an ordinary friendship.

Later, Ellen says to Caprica Six, her husband's pregnant lover, 'do you see, little girl? There is something in the universe that he loves far more than you or me, and that's Bill Adama. It's Bill Adama and the ship and the uniform and everything else takes second place' ('Deadlock'). Though Tigh's fondness of Adama is here tied to his sense of duty, it is still clear that, if his wife and girlfriend both have to take second place to Bill Adama, then this friendship must be based, no matter how much they would undoubtedly protest it, on love.

The significance of this is that we are presented with two very close friendships between two sets of people of the same sex, both based on love. The reason that Gina is repeatedly raped and Cain is shot while Tigh and Adama make it to the finale's paradise planet, Earth, is that Tigh and Adama's love remains platonic while Gina and Cain allow theirs to become sexual. Within the gender politics of the series, same-sex friendships are allowed to become very close indeed, but the moment that sex is introduced, thereby raising the possibility of homosexuality, the relationship becomes unhealthy.

This contrast of the healthy relationship between Tigh and Adama and the unhealthy relationship between Gina and Cain casts lesbianism as a corruptive force that challenges the pro-gramme's gender model by negating the need for the masculine. In the world of *Battlestar Galactica*, where normative masculinity is the ultimate goal, lesbianism threatens to render men in gen-eral useless. Taking this argument to its natural conclusion, if the women of the fleet are content by themselves, why would they need the programme's prized maleness at all? Consequently, in order to once again secure masculinity, the series ensures that lesbianism operates as an evil in itself.

Though this explains, but does not excuse, the series' disturbing portrayal of lesbianism, it still does not explain the absence of overt male homosexuality, transexuality, transgenderism or queer characters of other identities aboard the fleet.

Failed Fantasies

The series uses other tools, too, to eradicate any challenges to the dominance of masculinity, and Baltar's corruption of the male seduction fantasy is not the only time that the series has done this by denying its characters and viewers their dreams and desires. Indeed, there have been a number of occasions where the series has had to respond, often violently, to fan interpretations of its characters and scenarios in order to exert the supremacy of its masculine ideal.

Admiral Cain, as we have seen, was first introduced in 'Pegasus', where her sexuality was not discussed, before returning two years later in 'Razor', where her sexuality had become a security concern. In the intervening years, during the period when Cain's sexual preference was not canon, a number of fans had started to suggest on online discussion boards that she might be a lesbian. Similarly, there was much fan debate of Lieutenant Felix Gaeta's sexuality before his death in 'Blood on the Scales'.[8] There have been occasional hints within the series that Gaeta's sexuality might not match up to the expectations of the fleet, but these have never been made in a manner that would allow a definitive conclusion to be reached, always contained in allusion and visual code. As such, fan speculation, perhaps invigorated by anger at the treatment of Cain, has filled in the blanks, drawing a conclusion where the series would not. Gaeta became gay to many of the programme's viewers, whether the writers liked it or not.

In this way, Gaeta's presiding over a violent and regressive revolution and his eventual execution can be read in much the same manner as Cain's demise, as the punishment doled out to those who dare to challenge the primacy of heterosexuality and, by extension, masculinity. Whether the production team had intended Gaeta to be gay is not the issue here; once the fans had interpreted the character in this way he posed the same threat as Cain, canon or not, and so the viewer's fantasies had to be shut down as soon as was possible. Gaeta's execution is the violent redemption of the masculine ideal from the claws of the fan community.

In much the same way, the characters themselves sometimes engage with fantasies in a way that can become threatening to the aims of the series and, as such, must be eradicated. The threesome that occurs between Caprica Six, D'Anna and Baltar in 'Hero' (3.08) could easily be read as Baltar living through one of the more commonly discussed male fantasies. Once again, however, Baltar finds himself in a more complex sexual fantasy than he had at first realized. There is an intricate power dynamic at work in this entanglement of bodies. Baltar has again fallen under the sexual allure of a dangerous woman who asserts dominance over him; only one episode earlier, in 'A Measure of Salvation' (3.07), D'Anna had been Baltar's torturer. D'Anna is here playing the same role as Caprica Six did in the first season, doling out both pleasure and pain.

This situation is further complicated when Baltar leaves Caprica Six, the woman he seems to care for most in the universe and who the viewer has started to suspect might actually care about him too, in order to follow D'Anna and her quest for forbidden knowledge of Cylon history. Whether it is the quest or the implicit promise of sexual experimentation that tempts Baltar, it is possible to see D'Anna's seduction of him as revenge against Caprica Six for killing her with a rock in 'Downloaded' (2.18). D'Anna uses her sexuality to manipulate Baltar, removing him from the male fantasy threesome and placing him instead in a complicated power game that renders him once again the passive partner to a dominant and domineering woman. To give Baltar the pleasure of fulfilling his sexual fantasies would be too much for a series that disapproves of his breed of masculinity, and so his dream is corrupted into a nightmare that once again denigrates him in the eyes of the show.

Leoben, a Cylon model who shows a particular interest in Starbuck, also signs away his masculine dominance in return for the fulfilment of a sexual fantasy. When Starbuck is kept prisoner on New Caprica at the start of the third season, she is held in an apartment and forced to live in a parody of domesticity with Leoben. They play the roles of husband and wife, sitting down to eat dinner together in the evenings, though during this charade she takes the opportunity to stab him with her knife and watch him die. Being a Cylon, however, Leoben is able to return the next night and the whole performance begins again, repeating itself as often as the viewer is willing to presume. There is something in this performance of physical dominance and fatal submission that suggests Leoben as a glutton for punishment, as a willing victim who returns time and again to receive whatever Starbuck deems to throw at him. His repeated visits to the apartment and her violence against him suggest a desire on his part to participate in this painful subjugation, hinting at a pleasure to be found in the pain. Not only does Leoben reverse the gender roles through his submission, but he actually enjoys doing it.

In this sense his situation is comparable to Baltar's. They are both allowed to live the fantasy, to participate in and even enjoy the act itself, but in hindsight the dream becomes a nightmare that subverts gender norms and consequently requires retribution. Whereas Gaius paid for his transgression by being ostracized from the rest of society, Leoben's punishment is built into the crime; he is violently murdered night after night. Once again, *Battlestar Galactica* reasserts the dominance of normative masculinity via the eradication or punishment of its detractors.

The Problem with Gaius

If any challenge to the masculine ideal has been erased, then this demonstrates more clearly the nature of Gaius' crime, my original point of investigation. He connotes the possibility of an unconventional brand of masculinity that involves the embracing of some feminine ideals. Though Tigh crosses this gender boundary from time to time, it is left to Gaius to live exclusively on the wrong side of the division. If he were allowed to exist as a viable entity then the entire system on which *BSG* builds its understanding of gender roles would be incapacitated. It is of no surprise, then, that we are asked to accept that the woes of the galaxy are, ultimately, his fault. Heavy-handed though it may be, the series has found a way to condemn the corruption of men by what it sees as the weakness of femininity. *BSG* not only promotes normative ideals of masculinity, it punishes those who don't (or can't) conform and creates its own monsters out of the margins of social uniformity.

Butch Girls

If masculinity in the series is brittle (push it too hard and it shatters into traitors and drunks) then femininity tells a very different story. It would seem reasonable to assume that if the series enforces a traditional brand of male identity then female identity might be fixed in a similar, conventional fashion. Indeed one look at Ellen Tigh at the bar in 'Colonial Day' (1.11) – all sparkling jewellery, perfect blonde curls and big, blue eyes – is enough to persuade us that in this dim and distant future our concept of femininity has survived intact. This is not the case. Ellen is not a true representation of femininity in the series. She is a rare example of gender conformity within the women of the fleet. There is, on closer inspection, a gender rebellion afoot.

Kara 'Starbuck' Thrace occupies the masculine sphere in a variety of ways. Time and time again we find Starbuck putting herself in dangerous situations not only for the good of mankind, but also to test the limits of her capabilities. Be it in the cockpit of an experimental spacecraft such as the Blackbird in 'Flight of the Phoenix' (2.09), or in preparing to assassinate Admiral Cain of Pegasus ('Resurrection Ship (Part Two)' 2.12), Starbuck's courage rapidly situates her as the female counterpoint to Apollo's daring bravado. Indeed if his early achievements in the cockpit can be read as symbolic of his innate masculinity, then what, we must wonder, do Starbuck's matching skills reveal about her?

Our attention is repeatedly drawn to Starbuck's mastery of the fighter ships, be it in piloting the unconventional Blackbird, flying the captured Cylon Raider in 'You Can't Go Home Again' (1.05), or even in knowing when to defer to her wingman in 'Scar' (2.15). Starbuck consistently overshadows the fleet's other pilots, mastering space in a way that perhaps only Apollo himself could aspire to. She becomes his mirror image; they are the fleet's most daring, talented pilots with only anatomical difference between them.

The consequences of this doubling effect for Starbuck's identity as a woman complicate our understanding of masculinity in *BSG*. Not only does Starbuck lay claim to Apollo's metaphorical phallus by asserting mastery over the spaceship, she directly situates herself in the realm of traditional masculine identity by mirroring his military prowess. If the role of the male in the series is to protect, then Starbuck's skills in a Viper attack ship show that the one most capable of filling this role, the ultimate in masculinity, is a woman. If Gaius' long, shiny hair feminizes his appearance, Starbuck's short, mannish hairstyle, coupled with her tough, muscled body and often shapeless military outfits not only place her within the traditional conception of masculinity, but actually confuse the boundary of what it is to be of a gender in the *BSG* universe at all.

This confusion is evident during the settlement of New Caprica that begins in 'Lay Down Your Burdens (Part Two)' (2.20), during which Starbuck is used to indicate the programme's approval of a form of womanhood that incorporates elements of normative masculinity. With the advent of a peaceful existence far from the Cylon threat, Starbuck, the bastion of the masculine female, loses her purpose. If there is no threat, there is no need to protect. If there is no need to protect, then masculinity in the sense championed by *Battlestar Galactica* begins to erode. Onboard Galactica, Apollo gains weight, his once muscled frame no longer the embodiment of masculine identity but rather a saggy reminder of compromise. Similarly Starbuck, so long androgynous of spirit, places herself resolutely in the female sphere by adopting a long, traditionally feminine hairstyle. Starbuck is no longer required to exist as a force to be taken seriously, and so is allowed to retire her strength and become, finally, a woman. The fact that this move is equated with weakness (it takes place under the regime of a certain President Baltar, after all) casts Starbuck's previous form, as the hybrid of female biology and masculine ideals, in a distinctly positive light. In *Battlestar Galactica* it seems impossible for an uncompromisingly feminine woman to hold the type of strength required to survive. Only in losing sight of the survival instinct, by lowering their defences to the eventual Cylon occupation, can femininity exist.

Indeed, it is telling that we only really see Starbuck completely at ease twice within the series. The first time is during this period of settlement on New Caprica. In 'Unfinished Business' (3.09), Apollo and Starbuck are seen in flashbacks to their time on this planet before the Cylons arrived. They get drunk together and make love outside amidst the natural world. Starbuck is relaxed and carefree, shouting her love for Apollo out into the night, not caring who hears her. This type of freedom, of course, comes at a heavy cost. The price that Starbuck and the crew pay for letting their hair down, literally in her case, is a long and painful occupation of their new world by the Cylons. To seek this type of happiness through letting one's guard down and allowing the indulgence of feminine ideals will, we are told, lead to disaster.

The second time that we see Starbuck in such a carefree mood it is not acquired by simply dropping her guard but by facing the problems that the universe throws at her and battling her way through them, and as such her freedom this time is not transitory. By the time that we see Starbuck standing on the surface of the new Earth in the series finale, at peace with the Cylons, Apollo and, crucially, herself, she has died, been reborn, learned about her past and her significance to the world and, most importantly, come to understand the meaning of her 'destiny' that has been discussed since 'Flesh and Bone' (1.08). With all of these tasks behind her, with nothing left to run from, Starbuck can finally claim: 'I am done here. I've completed my journey and it feels good'. Standing in her military uniform with her hair cut short, it is clear that Starbuck has not sacrificed her role as the hybrid of female form and masculine ideals that the series approved of. As unsatisfying as her final moments may be for the viewer, with her vanishing into thin air and leaving us to presume that she was literally an angel after all, the series rewards her for her unflinching adherence to masculine ideals by allowing her to remain happy and carefree and, presumably, to return to whatever version of heaven the *BSG* writers send her off to. It does seem clear that Starbuck is allowed to leave the programme in such high spirits because, unlike the last time she ceased to be at war, she has not succumbed to the temptation of femininity. Even the angels, we are told, want to be masculine.

The Fall of the Feminine

This is not, of course, to say that femininity, or at least the type of traditional female identity that the series uses Starbuck to denigrate, is not allowed to exist in the fleet at all. Laura Roslin, first president of the fleet, seemingly exudes it from every pore. She holds its traditional visual trappings (long hairstyle, gentle physical manner), but also embodies some of its more complex nuances. She allows herself to acknowledge her emotionality, particularly with regard to her lengthy battle with cancer, where her frailty is often on display, but also in her insistence on documenting the fleet's population throughout the early seasons, counting every life. This is a woman who embraces her humanity and is not afraid of allowing her emotions to guide her. We might well question how the series treats such a character, then, given its attitude towards even slight hints of supposed femininity in the men of the fleet.

When Roslin sends Starbuck in search of the Arrow of Apollo, a mythical object on a distant planet ('Kobol's Last Gleaming (Part One)' 1.12), it is only Roslin's faith, an intangible, ethereal and thus – within the logic of normative gender identities – feminine force, that guides her. Roslin is clearly a woman who embraces the impalpable and transitory with the same vigour that she engages the solid, material world. When the military, led by the strong, masculine Commander Adama, learns of her vision of the arrow, it collides with Roslin's faith, terminates her presidency and places her in a cell. Here the masculine and the feminine are diametrically opposed, encapsulated in the figures of Adama and Roslin, in the military and the mystical. In much the same way that Gaius' faith in the intangible Number Six leads him into conflict with the masculine world, Roslin's beliefs place her at odds with this brand of militarized manhood.

In much the same way that Baltar is eventually reconciled with normative masculinity through his embracing of the military and manual labour, Roslin's threatening femininity is in need of reconciliation with the dominant gender identities of the series. If this is a programme that champions masculinity, both in its male and female characters, then Roslin's uncompromising femininity is in need of taming.

If Roslin and Adama respectively represent the government and the military, femininity and masculinity, then the union of these ideas through the development of a relationship between these characters raises the interesting prospect of a uniting of the genders, a harmony that could resist the drive for masculinity. In Season Four, as Adama and Roslin find their way into each other's lives and beds, it seems, on the surface, that the programme's insistence on normative masculine identities might finally begin to ease.

This is, however, not the case. This was never a fair fight to begin with. While Adama remains calm and resolute as events reach their climax around him, Roslin's cancer returns, making her face her own mortality once more. Despondent after the discovery of the nuclear wasteland that was Earth, Roslin refuses her medication ('Sometimes a Great Notion' 4.11), precipitating her gradual decline towards the end of Season Four. By the time of the series finale, Roslin is very weak indeed and finally dies shortly after reaching our Earth. In the battle between unadulterated masculinity and femininity, the battlefield was not even. If Roslin and Adama's relationship represents the union between the two sides of the gender debate that rages through *Battlestar Galactica*, then the reality of the situation is not a peace but a gradual weakening and eventual subsuming of femininity beneath the weight of the masculinity that the series believes is necessary for the survival of the human race.

The Performance Challenge

What is troubling about this system of gender representation is that it prevents femininity from encompassing any strength or force whatsoever. If female characters behave in the ways that normative gender identities stipulate, then, like Ellen Tigh in the early series, they can only succeed on a purely social level and can never achieve on a larger scale. The only choice available is to discard any trace of femininity and to welcome the masculine invasion. Roslin may well have risen to the dizzy heights of presidency, but at what cost to her cherished (and female-coded) spirituality? Indeed, in a brutal but arguably necessary move during 'Resurrection Ship (Part One)' (2.11), Roslin advises Adama that the only way to handle Admiral Cain is by assassinating her. Roslin's humanity has fast evaporated in the face of what the series sees as real concerns. When dealing with spiritual matters it is acceptable for Roslin to embrace her femininity; when the fate of the fleet in involved, however, she must behave according to a more volatile, masculine code of conduct. While it must be conceded that the series does allow women the chance to break out of normative gender identities, it does not quite fulfil the promise of a gender-free existence. Though seemingly liberal, in so far as it allows women to behave in a masculine fashion, in reality the series enacts a restrictive construction of womanhood, enforcing masculinity rather than simply making it an available option.

This raises a further challenge in that it seeks to deny the existence of femininity as a possible mode of behaviour altogether. Though we have examined the consequences of this for the men of the fleet, the consequences for the women are no less serious. Once backed into this corner of gender performance, the only recourse available is to adopt masculine traits and to attempt to become normatively manly. This type of fluidity would not be a problem in a less restrictive world, but if it is enforced, as it is here, then it takes on a more sinister tone. If the men must try to be manlier, and the women must try to be men, then maleness becomes the ideal state and womanhood becomes obsolete. This becomes an even more serious threat when examined in conjunction with the biological implications of the Cylon resurrection technology.

The Biological Challenge

If this challenge to womanhood is launched in terms of gender performance, then a simultaneous assault is launched elsewhere in terms of biology. This is most clearly demonstrated if we consider Head Six's conversation with Gaius in the Opera House at the end of 'Kobol's Last Gleaming (Part Two)'. 'You are the guardian and protector of the new generation of God's children', she says, invoking the feminine spheres of motherhood and the ethereal. However, mixing this with the military idea of a 'guardian and protector' marks a clear trespass of the gender boundaries that the series imposes, polluting the masculine with the feminine.

Indeed, by casting Gaius of all people in the role of 'guardian and protector', Six further transgresses these boundaries. By taking Baltar, the icon of failed masculinity within the show, and calling him forth as a guardian and a military force, Six threatens the integrity of the programme's gender groupings. Baltar's angelic Six, and consequently the Cylons in general, can here be read as a site of gender confusion, as a point of collapse in the normative schemes the programme erects.

If, in the eyes of the series, the Cylons are gender abominations, challenges to the proper order, then new meanings can be read into the revelations made in 'Resurrection Ship (Part One)'. Here we discover that when a Cylon dies their consciousness is downloaded into an identical body. However, the download range for a humanoid Cylon is limited, and so a resurrection ship is necessary at certain strategic points. Onboard these vessels new, lifeless, humanoid Cylon bodies are housed, awaiting the consciousnesses of dead Cylon agents.

While this system works perfectly for the Cylons, for the humans it poses another threat to womanhood. During the events of 'The Captain's Hand', Laura Roslin declares abortion illegal in the fleet due to the need to repopulate the human race. This relegates women's bodies to a realm beyond their control, claiming them as the property of the state and, importantly, reducing them to a mere function of the reproductive system. The Cylons, however, take this logic a stage further and negate the need for reproduction at all. Whereas Roslin's law codifies the female body as purely a site of reproduction, the resurrection ship decodes it entirely, removing from it all function and, as such, necessity. If survival is the imperative, as Rosin decrees it is, then the resurrection ship, with its promise of ending death, is the ideal, and the female body, read exclusively as a site of reproduction, is obsolete. If the male body is understood through masculine ideals as a force of protection, the female body, deprived of reproduction and denied the right to protect unless it mimics the male, is left with nothing. As far as the logic of the series see it, it serves no military or biological function once Cylon technology is brought to bear and, in a fleet where survival is the imperative, it may as well not exist.[9]

This system is not without its complications. If the resurrection ship negates the need for pregnancy, then this is not only an attack on the female body, but on the male as well. If reproduction no longer relies on sexual intercourse then the male is as purposeless as the female in biological terms. The series' other reason for requiring men, the attempt to define the male as indispensable due to the need for protection, can also be collapsed, here by the figure of Starbuck, who takes on the men of the fleet at their own game and wins. If a man isn't needed for sexual reproduction, and a woman can fulfil his prescribed gender role, what is the point in men, after all? Indeed, if reproduction is outdated and both men and women can protect to an equal standard, is there a difference between the sexes at all? Is the series' instance on binary gender differentiation not responsible for its own destruction?

With all of these gender systems crumbling around us in the face of Cylon technology, the only recourse we have is to restore order, return to our appointed gender roles and destroy the resurrection ship, and later the resurrection hub, before it destroys us. It is little wonder that these ships become prime targets for the military in 'Resurrection Ship (Part Two)' and 'The Hub' (4.09). With that threat out of the way the series can carry on as before, pretending there is no problem in its view of gender roles. It seems that it is not just the survival of humanity that they are fighting for; it is to re-establish the security or our gender codes.

Battlestar and Us

At a time like this, the early twenty-first century, when Western society is undergoing such vast and unpredictable shifts in its construction and constitution, films such as the *X-Men* franchise (2000, 2003, 2006 and 2009) and programmes such as the relaunched *Doctor Who* (2005–) seem to call for us to move forward, embrace human values and champion tolerance in a brave new world. If we are to survive, they seem to say, then we need to be open to the possibility of change. *Battlestar Galactica* tells a different story, seeking to re-establish the dominance of traditional social norms, suppressing transformation and breeding intolerance. In the face of the threat of liberalism, *BSG* makes one last attempt at forcing us into prearranged categories.

This is, of course, not the whole story. There is another, more sympathetic, way to read the series. Look at the times in which we live in a different way and another narrative emerges. Entrenched in a seemingly endless ideological war and facing social, political and economic instability at home, contemporary American society certainly seems to resemble the fleet. Indeed, Ronald Moore, creator and executive producer of the show, has claimed that 'this was a chance to make a science fiction show that wasn't purely escapist, but actually dealt with the world that we live in'.[10] If the fleet is intended to mirror our own societies then the repressive gender roles found in its ranks should not be read as an attempt to enforce such oppression on us, or even as a positive representation of traditional values. Rather, the world of Galactica is a harsh critique of the society in which we live and the expectations we place on each other. If the restrictive systems of the fleet can essentially be reduced to the consequences of the need for protection in a time of war, then we must recognize that, during the original broadcast of the programme, we too were a society at war and, in the age of international terrorism, requiring protection. Whether *Battlestar Galactica* believes in the values it espouses or whether they are intended as a warning is a moot point; all the more pressing is the extent to which it can be said to mirror attitudes that have come to the fore in our own societies since 9/11, the Madrid and London bombings and the war in Iraq. A return to traditional values is upon us, seen in the re-election of George W. Bush in the United States in 2004, the deeply divided American electorate in the 2008 US election, the palpable shift to the right made by the European electorate in 2009 and the rise in popularity of the Conservative Party in the UK, not to mention the disturbing gains made by the British National Party. Conservatism and its repressive consequences are rising again in our own world, in our own military and civilian spaces, and if we want to know where this will take us we need look no further than our television screens; the fleet really could be the future.

Battlestar Galactica shows us the danger to social and personal liberty that is posed by living in a conflicted environment where peril lurks around every corner. The best science fiction shows us something of ourselves that we had not seen before; it is then our duty to use these insights to examine the way we live and act on what we find. If we do not, then the future we have seen, where men must be masculine, women have no function and the likes of me would simply not exist, may not be too far away. I may not belong on the Battlestar Galactica, but soon I may not belong here either.

Notes

1   This cycle of guilt and destruction is, eventually, broken, but Baltar has to wait for his redemption until the final moments of the final episode of the final season ('Daybreak (Part Two)' 4.20). The form that his salvation takes and the heavy price that he must pay to access it will be discussed later.

2   The Cylon model Six is tied early on to Baltar's guilt. By introducing us to Baltar and Caprica Six together at the start of the series the programme constructs a bond between them that predates the arrival of the viewer, suggesting an established relationship. When this Six betrays Baltar and uses the information he gave to her to bring about the downfall of the Colonies, this established bond suggests to the viewer that the manipulation of Baltar has been an ongoing Cylon project. He has, we must conclude, been a disreputable character since long before we were there to see it.

3   In fact, Head Six – the vision of Six in Baltar's mind – continues to do this throughout the series, even after Caprica Six and her

sisters have relented and joined the human cause. Consequently, every time the visionary Six uses her sexuality to manipulate Baltar, we are reminded of his mistake with Caprica Six back on the colonies. Baltar's guilt is thereby woven directly into the fabric of the programme, signified not just by his own actions but also by the very presence of this other major character.

4 It is worthy of note that this system relies on a binary model of gender and sex. This demonstrates another method the programme uses to reinforce normative ideologies of the body.

5 As an ironic side note, Jamie Bamber, who plays the overtly masculine Apollo, is also English. Perhaps it is only a particular type of Englishness, one that mirrors Baltar's type of masculinity, that is unacceptable. Or perhaps the fake American accent Bamber adopts covers all kinds of sins.

6 If the physical gives us clues to the psychological, then what happens to the mind when the body changes? There have been numerous internet discussions of the reason for Apollo's dramatic weight gain over the unseen year before 'Lay Down Your Burdens (Part Two)' (2.20). See 'Why the Lee/Apollo Fat Suit?' for some of the more common suggestions. In the model of understanding proposed here, however, where the male body becomes a symbol of the state of a character's relationship to normative masculinity, Apollo's weight gain renders him weak and, consequently, feminine just at the point where he is powerless in the face of the Cylon threat. In real terms his physical inactivity leads to his expanded girth, but a metaphorical system underpins this, enforcing punishment upon him for his inability to protect, to be a man.

7 The other men that find themselves in the strange position of believing themselves to be human before discovering their true Cylon nature also have their masculinity called into question. A discussion of Tigh's inability to attain a purely masculine identity, even before his revelation as a Cylon, is presented later in this chapter. Galen Tyrol, however, is a more complex creature. Both before and after his Cylon identity is revealed, he is sometimes allowed to be masculine, such as in his co-leadership of the resistance on New Caprica ('Occupation' 3.01) and in his immediate volunteering to take part in the seemingly suicidal rescue mission of Hera Agathon ('Daybreak (Part One)'

4.19), but is equally sometimes portrayed in a less than positive light, as in his involvement with a group who seek to execute those involved in the occupation of New Caprica, but who are shown to make mistakes in deciding on the guilt of the accused ('Collaborators' 3.05), or in his drunken tirade to William Adama in which he accuses his dead wife of having 'dull, vacant eyes' and a 'cabbage smell' ('Escape Velocity' 4.04). Tyrol, it seems, always was something of a mixed bag, given to traditionally masculine behaviours while also capable of some very questionable acts indeed. As such, the series did not need to make the concerted effort to distance him from normative masculinity that it did with Anders; Tryol never possessed it to begin with.

8   For one example of this see 'Battlestar: The Extinction of Gay.'

9   To be clear, I do not intend to argue that the women of the fleet are without purpose since this is demonstrably untrue. Starbuck, as just one example, is still an excellent pilot and a boon to the chances of humanity's survival. Rather, I am arguing that the resurrection ship has the potential to negate the need for the female body in much the same way as the mentality of the series has negated the need for femininity. They both still exist, but are rendered purposeless in this context.

10   In Wolverton.

Works Cited

'Battlestar: The Extinction of Gay.' Gay TV Blog. 12 May 2008. Gay.com. <http://tv.gay.com/2008/05/battlestar-the.html>.

'Why the Lee/Apollo Fat Suit?' Discussion thread. digitalspy.co.uk. <http://www.digitalspy.co.uk/forums/showthread.php?t= 463419>

Wolverton, Troy. 'Delve Into "Battlestar Galactica".' TheStreet.com. 5 April 2006. <http://www.thestreet.com/_tsclsii/funds/goodlife/ 10276628.html>.

Sci-Fi Ghettos

Battlestar Galactica and Genre Aesthetics

SÉRGIO DIAS BRANCO

'I was thinking, "I've got to get out of this sci-fi ghetto"', confessed Ronald D. Moore in an interview for *Rolling Stone* (in Edwards). The writer responsible for the development of *Battlestar Galactica* (2003–9) uttered these words for an article about the topicality of the series that incorporated contemporary and politically charged themes such as terrorism and torture. Some crucial information precedes Moore's sentence in the text. We are told that he worked for a decade on some of the incarnations of *Star Trek* and that with this new version of the cult show *Battlestar Galactica* (1978–9) he was hoping to create a political drama like *The West Wing* (1999–2006). That is, Moore is portrayed as an author of science fiction in contact with the classic and in search of the new. Commenting on the creative ideas that shaped the reimagining, he adds: 'I realized if you redo this today, people are going to bring with them memories and feelings about 9/11. And if you chose to embrace it, it was a chance to do an interesting science-fiction show that was also very relevant to our time' (in Edwards 2006).

Ron Moore is clearly referring to the conventions of science fiction. He is alluding to its imagined worlds, situations and beings, and referring to how remote they seem from our everyday life. This encompasses, not just its stories but also its appearance, not just the narrative aspects of the genre but also its aesthetic features. It is clear what Moore is referring to – but it is not easy to understand why. He surely knows that the notion that these characteristics hinder science fiction from reflecting current events and worries is uninformed. This genre has a rich tradition of addressing moral, political and social themes. Countless examples come to mind, but to limit our scope to television fiction, a drama such as *Babylon 5* (1994–8), with its interest in the efforts and complications of a peaceful co-existence between different creatures and cultures, is an eloquent example. Moore's statement can only be understood as an attempt to set the series apart from the other works of the genre: *BSG* would not be science fiction in the same way that HBO is not TV. In fact, the programme attracted a wider audience beyond sci-fi enthusiasts; at the same time it estranged some fans of the original show because of the changes introduced and the prominent gritty tone.

The idea of a sci-fi ghetto that *BSG* tried to escape from suggests a fruitful way of analysing the show. Genres, especially those that are popular simultaneously in television and film, are defined and definable through a repertoire of elements: characters, plot, setting, iconography and style. Since the focus of this chapter will be on aesthetics and not on narrative, the more relevant elements for the analysis of the series within the science fiction genre are its type and style of images. Arguably, the genre does not have a crystallized aesthetics, but there are aesthetic traits that are associated with it and that can be found in its popular manifestations. It is these traits that *BSG* presumably attempted to ignore.

First, the types of images will be discussed through the analysis of production design or simply design motifs. The discussion will centre specifically on the patterns of components designed and built during the development phase of production (costumes, sets, furniture and props). Such components may also be inserted after principal photography, in the case of computer-generated imagery (CGI). Analysing the design motifs in *BSG*, reveals elements that individualize the programme within the genre. Science fiction portrays an imagined tomorrow based on scientific and technological advances in which production design plays a fundamental part – the design of the show blends different and contrasting elements to present an imaginary yet recognizable future.

Second, the style of images will be addressed by paying attention to the particularities of the camerawork. The handheld, dynamic filming style of *BSG* has been both celebrated and criticized, but rarely examined in depth. The subtlety and variety of these stylistic features are often reduced to an active and trembling camera, yet it is more akin to an observant presence. Science fiction favours images that consistently balance the real and the unreal – and, although the series opts for an unconventional style within the genre, it similarly weighs the concrete against the imagined, the close against the distant.

Blended Design

Science fiction is sometimes identified by, or reduced to, particular iconographic elements – namely, creatures from outer space. Vivian Sobchack singled out instead the *look* of the genre and persuasively argued that what connects these works 'lies in the consistent and repetitive use not of *specific* images, but of *types* of images' (87, original emphasis). This visual typology mixes the unfamiliar and the familiar, the unknown and the known. It presents the strange as believable – leading Sobchack to conclude that science fictions strive 'primarily for our belief, not our suspension of disbelief – and this is what distinguishes them from fantasy' (88).

BSG may be likened to Joss Whedon's *Firefly* (2002–3), a series that openly blended old and new, western and sci-fi, and Eastern and Western cultures. Since its inception, the reimagined *BSG* also combined alien and well-known elements, presenting a world in which this blend created a calculated ambiguity. The

Cylons, machines that were once at war with their human creators, returned to annihilate humankind, forcing the survivors to flee to space. Cylons are now completely organic and indistinguishable from humans to the naked eye; only laboratory analysis can confirm their real identity. In the first scene, one of these humanoid Cylons walks into the Armistice Station after two mechanical, Cylon Centurions. The contrast is striking. Unlike the original series, where Centurions were actors in outfits, these robots were entirely created by computer. In this sense, CGI is truly a part of the design process, an aspect of the conceptualizing, planning and building stages. It can extend partial sets or insert virtual elements that seem to interact with the properly physical elements, as in this case. Moreover, the opening scene of the series demonstrates how expressive digital components can be, giving visual and kinetic expression to the differences between mechanical and organic entities, machines and living matter. The design of the new Centurions was not constrained by human physicality and motion, opening up the possibility of laying bare their mechanical composition and functioning. Contrastingly, the humanoid model takes the form of a tall blonde woman (Tricia Helfer), which we will later know as model Six, in its various incarnations. The human officer had been waiting for a Cylon representative for forty years, after the first war between Cylons and humans, and Six's presence is as unexpected as her appearance. Her tight red suit, with a long-sleeved coat and knee-length skirt, is at odds with the neutral dark colours of the space station. The series visually turns the imaginary into the real, robots into humans – which puts in doubt the assumption that Cylons are clearly and fundamentally different from humans.

Examples such as this show how intentionally designed *BSG* is. A look into the control room of Galactica reveals other facets of its design motifs. It became conventional in science fiction for commanding spaceships to have a centre of operations with a window looking out over the vastness of space. Think of the bridge in the USS Enterprise in *Star Trek* (1966–9), a television and film series that became a template for the genre in both media. Galactica is different. It has an intricate structure whose parts relate and function organically instead of merely hierarchically. The control room is embedded inside the ship instead of being on the leading edge of it (Hudolin par. 18). As seen, for instance, in 'You Can't Go Home Again' (1.05), the room is closed and angular. Its limits are well defined by subdued surfaces with, to all appearances, multiple layers of paint, conveying that this is an old warship that continues in operation after years of service and maintenance. Its spaces are clearly outlined by sharp corners and different floor heights. It is like an operating theatre with upper galleries from where people look down to Admiral William Adama (Edward James Olmos), who takes the role of teaching surgeon, always standing up, without a chair to rest, sometimes moving among the work stations (Hudolin par. 5). The set creates a central, lower space from where Adama usually speaks and gives orders and, at the same time, it allows him a mobility appropriate to his supervisory functions. The human proportion, logic and functionality of the design become apparent through the action and interaction of characters within the confines of the room.

Old objects dispersed all over the ship and particularly in this room also embody these qualities. Cases in point are the telephones from the 1940s that the military officers use to communicate, as originally used in warships (Hudolin par. 5). To talk, the officers have to come to the wall, pick up one of these bulky phones, and crank it. However, it would be hasty to interpret the presence of such objects as retro design. Devices such as these telephones are not meant to imitate styles from the past. They compose a world with a history, of which they are remains and evidence. That is why their existence is so thoroughly justified within the fiction. Adama participated in the first war against the Cylons and opted not to upgrade the ship and to continue to use outdated equipment that had proven reliable. Galactica was built in the beginning of the previous war. It is a veteran battlestar, the last of its kind still serving, and the only military vessel without integrated computer networks. Thanks to these unique characteristics, Galactica survives the attack that neutralizes the defence system of the Twelve Colonies and destroys them in the miniseries. This narrative justification indicates that these non-futuristic elements are to be taken not as imitating the past, but as coming from it. As Charles Shiro Tashiro recalls, 'Because the image of the future must rely on general, socially shared images in order to function, its appearance will inevitably be dated by the fashions and assumptions current during production' (10). The series makes this process of visual design manifest, giving it a narrative logic and justification: there is something from the past in its imagined future.

Private spaces follow a similar design pattern. Bill Adama's lodging is filled with homelike furniture and objects that make it habitable, even cosy. In 'You Can't Go Home Again', Admiral Adama and his son, Captain Leland Adama (Jamie Bamber), discuss the ongoing search for Starbuck (Katee Sackhoff) with President Laura Roslin (Mary McDonnell) and Executive Officer Saul Tigh (Michael Hogan). The walls have the same grey tone of the control room, but the lighting is now in warm browns and yellows instead of cold blues and greens. The oil painting revealed behind Roslin, the table lamps, the red rug, make up a personal and informal environment that is at variance with the straight, oblique and horizontal, lines of the architecture of the ship. This contrasts with the rooms of the Cylon basestar, first seen in 'Collaborators' (3.05). There the walls have an illuminated red band and bright circular lights, reminiscent of a Suprematist painting. The pure geometrical forms and the intense and diffused lighting imbue the space with an abstract quality. Unlike the chairs in Adama's lodging, the chaise-longue looks like a decorative object, something almost stripped of its utility and positioned to be admired.

Other identifiable objects become at times a focus of attention. Tashiro posits that 'objects exist independently of a story. In this state they have their own string of associations. Once placed in a narrative, objects and spaces acquire meaning specific to the film' (9). Commander Adama builds and paints a miniature boat in his cabin throughout the first and second seasons. It is a large model of a sailing vessel, square-rigged, and with several decks; but it is not a warship, because it lacks any openings for cannons. Using a warship would have reduced it to a small-scale replica of Galactica, the battleship that Adama commands. The miniature is crucial for itself, as a unique object, and not for its figurative and general meaning. Specifically, it is crucial because of the actions that Adama has to carry out to create it. This is readily confirmed when the context in which modelling appears in the series is taken into account. In 'Litmus' (1.06), Adama is cutting and perfecting small pieces for the model while reprimanding Chief Tyrol (Aaron Douglas). Tyrol had abandoned his post, causing a serious breach of security. One of his subordinates directly took the blame and was consequently imprisoned. In this scene, Tyrol tries to persuade Adama to release the detainee, but the reply that he gets is that he gave a poor example of leadership and organization. Adama's work on the model, on the other hand, is patient and meticulous – it underlines his entitlement, stemming from his commitment and not simply from his rank, to call attention to Tyrol's carelessness.

The construction of large models of sailing vessels is not exactly a hobby for Adama. He may do it for pleasure, but from what is shown, he does not do it in his leisure time. In 'Home (Part One)' (2.06), Adama confides in Lieutenant Anastasia 'Dee' Dualla (Kandyse McClure) about his son and Roslin and a recent shooting incident, while painting the boat. The fleet of refugees had been divided into two factions: one led by Roslin, the other by Adama. Dualla reminds him that parents, children and friends are separated. Adama attempts to dismiss her, but she insists that it is time to heal the wounds. This heated discussion happens while Adama is finally finishing the model with paint. He sustains his attention to the totality of the work at hand, handling the paintbrush with a relaxed assurance – showing the kind of overall understanding that he is currently lacking as a leader.

The blend of disparate features and components is customary in the science fiction genre. In *BSG*, design motifs have a distinctly expressive purpose. The physical appearance of Cylon models, the location and configuration of the control room and its telephones, the furnishings of Adama's lodging, the decoration of the Cylon basestar, the miniature boat that he constructs – all these are aspects and elements that are contrasting and unexpected. The design visual tone of the series – its character – is based on a mix that expresses and fosters ambivalence, mixed feelings, contradictory ideas about technology and humanity, the old and the new.

Present, Observant Camera

In a recent essay, Kevin McNeilly comments on the mobile, handheld camerawork of *BSG* as a hallmark of its visual style. It is worth quoting most of his paragraph because there is very little written on this subject:

> The series eschews a stable perspective, preferring the feel of embedded points of view, and the textures of improvisational immediacy and documentary presence that a handheld camera offers. We're reminded in every scene that perspective is contingent and temporary, that someone is taking these pictures, making these images. The aperture constantly jingles, drifts, redirects its attention, pulls, and readjusts its focus . . . The point however is not to expose the viewers' capacity to be duped by illusion . . . Rather, the documentary textures of *BSG*'s visuals serve as reminders of a corporeal, human materiality, that informs the whole aesthetic of the program. The handheld, quasi-documentary camera introduces into the screen-image material traces of hands and eyes — two key tropes, the tactile and the visual, that pervade nearly every episode.
> (McNeilly 186)

These are suggestive words. McNeilly is onto something here. Yet he does not develop it in detail since his essay has a different focus: how the audience is audio-visually confronted with the difficulty of experiencing and addressing human duress and ruin.

The writer cautiously avoids calling the camerawork documentary, instead he uses the term *quasi-documentary*. It is wise not to claim that the camera is seemingly documentary simply because its unstable perspective and improvisational feel make it feel that way. Documentary filmmaking allows many different styles of direction and therefore of camerawork – recall the patient and long takes of Frederick Wiseman's documentaries, for example. In *BSG*, the camera is seemingly documentary because of the way it is placed in relation to the fiction, standing both inside and outside the fictional world as something present and observant.

The first scene of the miniseries, already described and analysed, closes with the Armistice Station being blown up into pieces as the initial act of war from the Cylons. One piece of debris hits the camera and causes it to shift, abruptly, revealing its material existence in the fictional universe of the series. As long as technical differences are unable to supplant perceptual differences, our relationship with photographic images will be different to that with digital imagery. Even when the textures and lighting of the latter give an impression of reality, their elements lack the sense of weight and mass that we instinctively recognize in the former. This gap is crucial to understand the role of the collision that makes the virtual camera move. We can see it as providing proof for the presence of the camera there, at that moment, through the physical interaction that is shown on screen. Only this kind of evidence can give additional grounds for the belief that something real, not simulated, was there in front of the camera.

In *BSG*, the camera does not just jingle, drift and reframe. Sometimes it follows a more fluid scheme. In 'A Disquiet Follows My Soul' (4.12), the sick and frail Roslin trots along the vast corridors of Galactica. She turns a corner and the camera accompanies her movement, avoiding obstacles and people, first from the front and then from the back, until she comes across Adama. This is a moment that brings to mind the much longer take that unfolds during the opening credits of the miniseries. For more than three minutes, the camera tracks various characters, making a diverse record of what is happening on the day that Galactica, now a relic of the First Cylon War, is to be decommissioned as a warship and converted into a museum. From the jogging Starbuck, the camera moves to an attentive group of reporters who are learning about the history of the ship; then to Adama as he crosses Starbuck's path, talks to three mechanics and proceeds to the control room; then to Lieutenant Felix Gaeta (Alessandro Juliani), who leaves the room with paperwork; then to the drunk Tigh whom Gaeta runs into; and finally the camera returns to the group of reporters in the guided tour. Similar to the nervous yet intensely directed viewpoint that prevails throughout the series, the use of the Steadicam in these two scenes underlines the unimportance of what lies beyond the frame. Of course, it does not erase the awareness that there are things off screen, occasionally glimpsed, but this awareness is downplayed through visual focalization. Usually, nothing in the shots points to the off-screen space in any salient way. The images are centripetal instead of centrifugal, they point towards the interior instead of the exterior.

This reading is confirmed when we look at the two opposite end of the scale that visually structure the series; the screen is filled either with extreme close-ups or with very wide shots. Tightly concentrating on details and settling on partial views – such as the twirling knife in the telefilm 'Razor' (4.00) – directs our attention to something limited and small, detached from its surroundings. At the other end of the spectrum, presenting events with multiple points of interest – such as the space battle in 'Resurrection Ship (Part Two)' (2.12) with the curved firings from the Cylon ships – cues the audience to make spatial sense of the sequence within the screen. It is obvious that the range of stylistic choices of the show, from short to long takes, from close to distant views, from tentative to fluid movements, has different narrative and expressive functions. The dynamism of the direction consists of precisely this openness, in which the positions and behaviour of the camera respond to the specificity of the scenes. These stylistic choices have something else in common, something more essential. The images that result from them tend to point inwards and not outwards, as if the camera is permanently observing; not merely capturing the action, but tentatively or confidently noticing and registering what is significant.

This present and observant camera may seem very unlike the discreet position that cameras often adopt in science fiction, yet the role it plays is not. Sobchack explains that these plain camera angles give the same vantage point for humans and non-humans, giving a balanced, symmetrical attention to both real and imaginary (144). The camera of *BSG* emphatically creates a similar balance. It seems to approach what it is filming in an unplanned, immediate way, as though participating in and even being surprised by the events that it is capturing. The rough, vivid visual textures of the series enhance the feeling of factuality and objectivity that the loose framing fosters. Such feeling is, at the same time, balanced by the subjectivity of the camera, guiding our attention to quickly fading details and stressing the predominance of the on-screen space.

Space Oddities

The series finale aired in March 2009 on the Sci-Fi Channel. In the following month, Ron Moore appeared in 'A Space Oddity' (9.20), an episode of *CSI: Crime Scene Investigation* (2000–) that parodies and examines fan culture as well as the scholarly interest in popular culture. The involvement of Bradley Thompson and David Weddle in both *BSG* and *CSI* as writers and producers facilitated the participation of actors from *BSG*. In the episode, *Astro Quest Redux*, a dark and dramatic new version of the dearly loved *Astro Quest*, is presented at a fan convention. Kate Vernon (who starred in *BSG* as Ellen Tigh) is Dr Penelope Russell, a cultural studies scholar. Grace Park (who played the various Number Eights, including Boomer and Athena) and Rekha Sharma (who was Tory Foster, Laura Roslin's chief of staff) can be spotted in the middle of the crown during the presentation of the reimagined version of *Astro Quest*; so can Moore. The parallel is evident. Even though it is more similar to the original *Star Trek*, *Astro Quest* stands for the old *Battlestar Galactica* and *Redux* for the reimagined *BSG*. When Moore, playing an angry fan, gets up and shouts 'You suck!', he is re-enacting his own history from the opposite side. The scene may consequently be construed as mocking the inhabitants of the sci-fi ghetto that Moore desperately wanted to get out of. The passionate admirers of Glen A. Larson's series were vocal about their dislike of the remake right from the first contact, when it was presented at the San Diego Comic-Con in 2003. This deserves some comment, given the relationship between the aesthetic and narrative conventions of the genre and how they are valued or devalued.

It is possible that this strict rejection by some fans of the original has less to do with the genre and more to do with the cultural understanding of the genre – or, more precisely, with the lack thereof. Sci-fi lovers who are not insular are eager to connect the past, the present and the future. This is what *BSG* did when, in the opening scene, the armistice officer reviews a document with specifications for an old Cylon Centurion model from the previous series. The museum in *Galactica*'s starboard landing bay displays a copy of the same droid and also a Cylon baseship from the first war. There are several nods like these that those acquainted with the original series easily notice. Creating a narrative continuity between the two shows was a way of reclaiming the important role that recollection plays in the genre; we cannot imagine the future without knowing the past.

The new viewers whom Moore wanted to attract and who have only discovered how rich and engaging sci-fi can be with *BSG* lack a sense of memory of the genre. The fans who dismissed it as a fashionable misreading of the original that disregarded genre conventions, take genre as having a normative rather than descriptive function. The thematic wealth and the stylistic richness of the series are complementary. The show is not a rupture, either from the thematics of the genre, or from its aesthetics. It explores a central preoccupation of the genre: the dramas of the limits of the human and of the limitations of humanity. What was disappointing about the show's conclusion was exactly how it abandoned the intimate drama of the characters, and thus what resonantly embodied its themes, for a cautionary tale.

As a cult genre, science fiction creates its own ghetto, but one quite different from that which Moore suggests. Some works of science fiction, like J. J. Abrams's *Star Trek* (2009), may be popular, may be liked, but only some members of the audience understand them as additions to the history of the genre. This makes those people a somehow isolated group, uninterested as they are in the transient box-office numbers. For this immense minority – always keen to become larger – the measure of success of such a work is its pertinence and permanence in the popular imagination. They see it as a means of making sense of the world through the powers of creativity, connecting people in a projection of the future that can illuminate the present. There is a distinction to be made here. Undoubtedly, some aficionados think that their knowledge of trivia separates them from the rest, in an elitist and exclusive way. By contrast, genuine affection for popular art in general, and sci-fi in particular, is ideologically open and inclusive.

My analysis of the design motifs and camerawork of the series has shown that its visual style does not break away from the aesthetics of the genre and instead finds inventive forms of continuing it. The way the series deals with the aftermath of 9/11 is similar to how films such as *On the Beach* (1959) tackled the fear of a nuclear holocaust after the Second World War.

It is one of the achievements of the show that it did not reject the rich tradition to which it belongs, based on a conception of the genre as an isolated category or an artistic ghetto. Instead, *BSG* interacts with the history of the genre, carries it on, or better yet, freshly reaffirms it with vigour. Despite Ron Moore's confused words quoted at the beginning of his chapter, his other statements make it clear that he did not want to create a non-genre science fiction work that merely used the trappings of the genre for action adventures. His show is genre science fiction because it reflects on current affairs and approaches ontological questions about humanity that are not bound to an era. Far from being a series that rejects the conventions of the genre, *BSG* enacts a return to the essence of sci-fi, acknowledging its place within it. How appropriate, then, that this strategy mirrors its storyline: the plight of humans and Cylons while trying to find meaning and coherence in the present through a grasp of the past. The truth is that new creative contexts give rise to original science fictions, but all of this has happened before, and all of this will happen again. We can only hope.[1]

Note

1   I am grateful to Professor Murray Smith (University of Kent) and Dr Steven Peacock (University of Hertfordshire) for their insightful comments on sections of this chapter.

Works Cited

Edwards, Gavin. 'Intergalactic Terror.' *Rolling Stone*. 27 Jan 2006. <http://www.rollingstone.com/news/story/9183391/intergalactic_terror>.

Hudolin, Richard. 'Interview.' Future-Past.com. 2003. <http://future-past.com/interview/richardhudolin.php>.

McNeilly, Kevin. '"This Might Be Hard for You to Watch": Salvage Humanity in "Final Cut".' *Cylons in America: Critical Studies in 'Battlestar Galactica'*. Ed. Tiffany Potter and C. W. Marshall. New York: Continuum, 2008. 185–97.

Sobchack, Vivian. *Screening Space: The American Science Fiction Film* [1980]. 2nd edn. Piscataway, NJ: Rutgers University Press, 1997.

Tashiro, Charles Shiro. *Pretty Pictures: Production Design and the History Film*. Austin: University of Texas Press, 1998.

The Luxury of Being Simply Human

Unwritten and Rewritten Queer Histories in *Battlestar Galactica*

KAREN K. BURROWS

When *Battlestar Galactica* debuted on the Sci-Fi channel in the USA in December 2003, critics and viewers alike agreed that it was a smart, well-written science fiction drama that both embraced and transcended the trappings of its genre. The series has since revealed itself to be concerned with the post-apocalyptic fate of a fictional Earth, yet has managed to engage its characters and its viewers in debates more germane to our Earth. The plot has dealt at various points with hot-button issues such as conventions for the treatments of prisoners of war, the abortion debate, suicide bombers, occupying forces, fixed elections, the right to refuse medical treatment for religious reasons, the stem cell debate and more[1] – all straight from contemporary, particularly American, headlines. *Battlestar Galactica* has always been about 'the pressure of making genuine choices in real, and often horrific situations' (Ryan, 'Answers to Your "Razor" Questions'). The show typically refrains from direct commentary on the real-world treatment of the issues: though the leftist leanings of the (film) crew are evident, no moral or ethical line is drawn in any of the above examples. The characters are forced to muddle through as best they can and the audience is caught up in the uncertainty and is meant to question their own knee-jerk prejudices. Despite this demonstrated ability to deal sensitively with hot issues, which clearly shows the effort the creative team applies to understanding the effects their show has on its audience, in one area they have conspicuously failed to present a neutral, or even a balanced, representation. The portrayal of queerness on *Battlestar Galactica* has been entirely negative. Queer characters appear rarely; when they do, they are written out of the human history to which Galactica's crew is heir.

The first character on *Battlestar Galactica* who was allowed to be unambiguously queer was only canonically established as a lesbian retroactively and posthumously. Admiral Helena Cain[2] (Michelle Forbes) was introduced in the middle of the show's second season, in the episode 'Pegasus' (2.10). She came in as an outsider: on a show about the crew of the good ship Galactica she arrived on the newer, stronger, better Pegasus and disturbed the chain of military command as well as the established relationships between the inhabitants of the Colonial Fleet. She lasted three episodes before being murdered in 'Resurrection Ship, Part Two' (2.12). Nearly two years later, however, in November 2007, Cain returned in the made-for-TV movie *Battlestar Galactica: Razor*.[3] Her lesbianism is revealed in the movie, but only in flashbacks; her story is a tragic one, representative of the worst stereotypes of queerness.

Battlestar Galactica is a show in which questions of appearance are consistently important, particularly in regards to how one's appearance reflects – or conceals – one's essential truth. The discovery that the mechanical Cylons who destroyed the human Colonies and continue to attack the fleet 'look like us now' ('33' 1.01) – that 'monsters' may look 'human' – is constantly foregrounded in the plot. A character's appearance can thus be seen as an important part of her creation and portrayal. Cain's character design sets her apart from the other characters, particularly the other female characters, from the moment she first steps on screen, and consistently emphasizes her differences. Her entrance is bookended by reminders of the defining traits of (arguably) the two major human female characters in the show:

Kara 'Starbuck' Thrace (Katee Sackhoff) and President Laura
Roslin (Mary McDonnell). Kara arrives late, her dress uniform
dishevelled, suggesting her independence and disdain for the
trappings of appearance. Laura, when her fitness for her office is
subtly questioned, refuses to take offence and assumes the role
of mediator. Between these two portrayals of what femininity
looks like in the man's world of the fleet, Admiral Helena Cain is
first introduced.

Several aspects of Cain's character are apparent from this
first scene. Most immediately striking is her youth: when she
greets Commander Adama (Edward James Olmos), who was
formerly the senior officer of the fleet but whom she outranks,
she is clearly much younger than he is.[4] She is described as
'a very young officer on a very fast track. Very smart, very
tough. The fleet promoted her to rear admiral over half of the
commanders on the list' ('Pegasus') – including, clearly, Adama
himself. Everything about her is exacting: her ramrod-straight
hair, the crispness of her uniform, the precision of her salutes.
With her first words, she assumes a position of command and
uses it to permit the crew of Galactica 'back to the Colonial Fleet',
suggesting that her presence is the legitimizing force in creating
the fleet itself. Even her greeting emphasizes her dominance: she
does not merely clasp hands with Adama, but manipulates the
grip so her hand is on top. To an audience well-versed in science
fiction, her appearance is reminiscent of the ill-fated Number
One (Majel Barrett) from the original 'Star Trek' pilot, who:

> possesses the stoic nature of Mr Spock, but without the alien
> ancestry that would explain her emotional repression. The
> implication is that a normal woman could never have attained
> such a high rank [without] having totally repressed all emotions
> and much of [her] 'femininity' in order to function within a male-
> centred workplace.   (Tulloch and Jenkins 198)

For attentive readers, Cain is already positioned as abnormal.
Her apparent heartlessness is shown not only in her inability

to understand or acknowledge the interpersonal, non-military relationships between the Galactica crew, but also in the tales told of her ruthless command style and her disaffection for the importance of family relationships. Most important to the plot, however, is the revelation of her treatment of her Cylon prisoner of war, a model Six whose name is Gina.[5]

Before this arc, the Number Six models[6] were portrayed as infiltrators into human society who used their sexuality to deceive the men in their lives into allowing the destruction of humanity. The copy known as Six professed to love Gaius Baltar (James Callis), sacrificed herself to save him and appears to him as Head Six, an hallucination or projection of some sort throughout the series. In the episode 'Pegasus', through Six and Baltar's horrified gazes, the audience discovers that under Cain's command, the Gina copy has been tortured, raped, starved, and chained in a cell. Cain's interaction with Gina is always violent, humiliating, and dehumanizing: she kicks and spits on the prostrate Gina and pronounces judgement on the 'thing' from a towering position of extreme authority over her. Baltar and Head Six are always present for these outbursts: the emphasis on their relationship, placed against the passion of Cain's hatred, suggests but never confirms that Cain might be reacting to a betrayal more personal than simply that of commanding officer by crewmember.

Cain's final (chronological) scene continues to play with this possibility. After a successful mission, she retires to her quarters and, in the first sign of weakness – or humanity – she has shown, discards her jacket and gun belt in order to ease her aching neck and back muscles. Turning, vulnerable, she is confronted by Gina, who has escaped with Baltar's help and is now holding Cain at gunpoint. 'Do you know how to beg, Admiral?' she asks bitterly, referencing Cain's earlier description of Baltar coaxing Gina to eat as similar to getting a dog to roll over or beg. 'Frak you', Cain replies. 'You're not my type', Gina retorts. ('Resurrection Ship (Part Two)' 2.12). The camera closes in on Cain's face as her prideful façade crumbles to reveal fear and pain, just before Gina fires.

At the end of this three-episode arc, then, Cain's sexuality has been strongly hinted at but not confirmed, enabling 'the text's silences about [the] character's sexuality or motives [to] be filled with homosexual desire ... since such desire must often go unspoken' (Tulloch and Jenkins 259). Such unspoken desires, however, typically 'cohere around a particular character, who appears to embody the richest potential for queer visibility, who builds upon the iconography and stereotypes of queer identity' (259). While Cain's self-confidence and the visible tension she enjoys with other female characters suggest at her queerness, the other stereotypes that she embodies are more troubling. Simultaneously, she has been portrayed as violent, extremely masculine and emotionally distant, placed in opposition to the two parent figures of the audience-friendly Galactica crew, and entangled in an intense battle for the loyalty of the young, nubile Kara Thrace. Any one of these aspects of her personality would be offensive enough on its own: taken together, the list above reads as though Moore has read too many of Freud's, or perhaps Havelock Ellis', outdated theories.

The stereotyping continues in Cain's next appearance, the tie-in comic book by Brandon Jerwa, *Battlestar Galactica: Pegasus*, released in October 2007, which flashes back to one of Pegasus' pre-series missions. The comic allows a greater glimpse into Cain's past, particularly through partial views of two letters she composes over the course of the story – letters she apparently cannot face writing without the aid of a stiff drink. Close examination of the visible text of the letters reveal that they are addressed to her dead father, once a colonel in the fleet, and the phrases that can be read include telling statements such as 'I apologise for my gender', 'know you had hope [sic] for a son', 'you always said I didn't have what it takes' and similar sentences (Jerwa 3). By situating Cain's feelings of inadequacy in a war story bookended by letters to her father, the comic brings to mind Ahmed's reading of Freud: 'Freud's case of homosexuality in a woman should be read as a family case, as being about the demand that the daughter return family love by reproducing the line of the father,' carrying on 'the family name' (94). Although no overt reference to her sexuality is made, Cain's self-constructed hyper-masculinity is foregrounded through scenes of her lifting weights, suggesting that her lesbianism is the result of 'the disappointment of not being the object of men's desire' (94), whether that desire is sexual or paternal. In this context, the comic also introduces Cain's drive to be recognized and remembered, with her declaration that 'the rest of [the non-martyred soldiers] are left to *earn* our place in history. We have to die on our feet before we can lay claim to *immortality*' (Jerwa 27). The question of (human) history and Cain's right to history as a queer woman is woven throughout the rest of her story. The comic closes with Cain's final letter to her father, in which she asserts that although he never believed in her, she now stands as the 'defender of the human race' and will not fail in 'her finest hour' (31). The letter leaves readers with the certainty that Cain's absent father and her thirst to revenge herself against the Cylons are intertwined as the defining aspects of her adult personality.

Cain is marked bodily as an inheritor of the masculiniszed violence of military history by both her continuing allegiance to her dead father and also her appearance, in tune with a military ethos that, while present, has always been largely a background force on Galactica. This institutional alignment informs Cain's interactions with the young women who fall under her direct command: Kara Thrace, in the 'Pegasus'–'Resurrection Ship' (2.10–12) arc, and Kendra Shaw (Stephanie Jacobsen), in 'Razor'. Both characters are marked by Cain's attention to them: they are the inheritors of Cain's history, her concept of the perfect officer, someone who knows that 'we have to leave people behind so that we can go on . . . so that we can continue to fight' ('Razor').

Kara, whose period under Cain's influence is shorter than Kendra's, is perhaps the less changed, yet her speech at Cain's funeral service indicates the rapidity with which her loyalty – previously given to Adama in the heterosexual association of filial love due a father from his daughter – has come to be aligned with the charismatic Cain, through a shared desire to undergo missions that the Adama–Roslin leadership alliance deemed impossible. Their likeness becomes a major point of identification for Kara, positioning her in readiness to receive the inheritance of Cain's teachings (see Ahmed 125). In becoming Kara's mentor, Cain sets herself against Adama's patriarchial rule and, in tandem, the matriarchial force that Roslin wields as president. Cain's opposition to the 'familial', and her abstraction of Kara from that family, suggests the tension inherent in queerness and its relation to the traditional family. In fact Cain disrupts literal families, reassigning not only Kara[7] but also Adama's son Lee from their positions on Adama's ship to her own, where Kara is taken into Cain's confidence and earns compliments such as 'I have a lot of faith in you', and 'I am so very proud of you', with astonishing rapidity. Though her loyalty is never truly tested, Kara eulogizes Cain with more feeling than longstanding members of the Pegasus crew, and with knowledge that goes beyond that which Adama has apparently contextualized:

> When I think about what she went through after the attack – one ship, no help, no hope . . . she didn't give up. She acted. She did what she thought had to be done, and the Pegasus survived. It might be hard to admit, or hard to hear, but I think we were safer with her than we are without.   ('Resurrection Ship (Part Two)')

Kara benefits from her time under Cain not only by virtue of being promoted, but also by gaining a new perspective on her existence within the fleet's organization.

Kendra's identification as Cain's protégé is a longer and more complex process, yet also notably rapid. Her first conversation with Cain establishes that her mother is dead,[8] a fact with which Cain is distinctly unimpressed, emphasizing her disdain for the trappings of 'family'. Nevertheless, when Pegasus comes under enemy fire minutes later, Cain takes Kendra literally in hand, lifting her off the floor and guiding her back to her station. Kendra's desire to impress Cain is immediately apparent in her dedication to the post-attack repairs as well as a stammering conversation about how much she has already changed under Cain's guidance:

> Kendra: Sir. I'm sorry. I'm sorry about the way I behaved when the nukes hit. I was scared.
> Cain: You're not afraid any more, are you, Lieutenant?
> Kendra: No, sir.
> Cain: Good. You hold on to that anger and you keep it close. It'll stop you being afraid the next time.   ('Razor')

Kendra's attachment to Cain is more than familial, however, as shown by her ability to discern the truth of Cain's relationship with Gina as well as her apparent fascination with discussing as many details of said relationship as Gina is willing to divulge:

> Gina: To satisfy your curiosity, we met a few months ago when I presented the plans for the retrofit. We spent a lot of time together working out the details and I guess one thing led to the other. You seem so surprised.
> Kendra: It's just that Cain seems so self-sufficient.
> Gina: She has needs, just like the rest of us. No one can survive entirely on their own. Trust me, Lieutenant, in the end we're all just human.   ('Razor')

Indeed, Kendra and Cain are further paralleled through Gina. After she learns that Cain and Gina are lovers, Kendra's attitude towards Gina changes markedly. Where previously she interacted with Gina only within the bounds of military protocol, she becomes far more willing to bend those boundaries: she easily reveals her access codes, which eventually allow Gina to hack into the Pegasus computers.

The discovery of their mutual betrayal seems to push Cain to bind Kendra more closely to her. She chooses to impart to Kendra the basis of her life philosophy, suggesting that she is aware of Kendra's similarity to her as well as her desire to please:

We have to do things we never thought we were capable of, if only to show the enemy our will. Setting aside our natural instincts . . . when you can be this, for as long as you have to be, then you're a razor. This war is forcing us all to become razors. If we don't, we don't survive. And then we don't have the luxury of being simply human again.   ('Razor')

Whether Cain is suggesting that their inherent ability to 'be a razor' makes them something more than human or something less, she is certainly marking them as a breed apart.

After Cain's death, her history seems to be written by Kara in the form of her eulogy. Kendra, however, inherits that history, in the Marxist sense, which Ahmed further expands: 'history is a gift given that, when given, is received . . . Reception is not about choice . . . we convert what we receive into possessions' (125–6). Kendra comes into possession not only of Cain's 'legacy', as described in 'Razor', but also of its physical representative, her razor. She initially suffers for this development: unwilling to reassign her loyalty to subsequent superior officers, she is demoted until Pegasus comes under the command of Lee Adama. Lee, who is Commander Adama's son and thus heir to both the heterosexual order and Galactica's status as normative, verbally acknowledges Kendra as representative of Cain's command. He goes so far as to describe her as 'carrying a torch for Cain' ('Razor'), a phrase that typically suggests the desire for a sexual relationship. Once her position as Cain's inheritor is made clear, Kendra is able to continue her successful military career as Lee's second-in-command, though she and Kara are often portrayed as self-destructive and irrationally at odds – each still perhaps jealous of the importance the other held for Cain.[9] Eventually, however, Kendra's affiliation with Cain forces her into the position of outsider, and she inevitably sacrifices herself for the good of her crew, a move of which Cain would have approved.

Before 'Razor' was broadcast, Cain was still a fairly one-dimensional character: she had been coded queer but not textually confirmed as such. Part of the aim of the movie was to flesh out her background, to contextualize her actions within the boundaries of her own history (Ryan, 'Answers to Your "Razor" Questions'). The story is situated firmly in the pre-marked universe of Galactica, however: each of Cain's actions parallel those taken by Adama in a similar situation, ensuring that she is always read against his pre-established correctness. Despite the fact that Cain outranks Adama, his are the choices that the audience is meant to identify with and judge her by. Her fitness for command, and by extension her femininity, are consistently compared to his seemingly logical choices.

Like Adama, Cain is caught unaware by the outbreak of war, with a ship not at full capacity. Their subsequent challenges are nigh-identical: both are forced into ordering the death of civilians for what they perceive as the good of the crew; both place their trust in and are personally betrayed by a Cylon agent, whom they imprison and who is mistreated by their crew; both mislead their crew, manipulating emotions to ensure morale remains high. When Adama takes these actions, they become the focal point for the show's trademark analysis of moral dilemmas. He is never explicitly stated to have made the right choice under difficult circumstances, but he is shown to have logically reached and rationalized his decision. Cain's actions, however, are portrayed as irrational, ill-considered and often emotional, leaving the impression that her emotions and instincts are 'wrong' and often get her in trouble. Even Michelle Forbes sees this essential divide between Cain's and Adama's command styles and thus their selves: 'The questions [Adama] has had to face – ethical dilemmas, life and death questions. He's just made them from a more human place. He hasn't lost his sense of humanity and compassion and he's constantly questioning that' (in Ryan, '"Battlestar Galactica: Razor" Cuts to the Heart').

Cain's lesbianism is revealed in the midst of this series of implied judgements upon her very humanity. The moments of revelation are both mediated through the eyes of Cain's assistant, Kendra. The first is a matter of Cain's unwontedly giggly response to the pressure of Gina's hand on her shoulder, the second the coy comment from Gina that she thought they'd been 'so discreet'. In a show that consistently earns its mature rating for sexual content with its heterosexual couples[10] – including, among others, Six and Baltar, who had sex on screen three times in the miniseries alone – this is already a strong statement about the suitability of lesbianism. Gina's statement that her relationship with Cain is a reflection of how 'we're all just human' appears to be an attempt to soften the negativity, yet the audience knows the 'woman' making the declaration is actually a genocidal machine, rendering it ineffective and underscoring the association of lesbianism with violence, cruelty and inhumanity.

Ultimately, the relationship is one the audience already knows won't have a happy ending: it leads to Gina being raped at the order of her one-time lover, tortured into taking Cain's life, and doing so with a final refutation that their attraction was in any way mutual.[11] The single suggestion that the relationship may be as important as its heterosexual counterpart, which is typified by Six's constant declarations of her love for Baltar, comes when Gina is first revealed to be a Cylon. Upon being discovered, she kills three crewmembers, wrestles a gun from one and takes aim at Cain. She hesitates before firing, however, just long enough for Kendra to knock her unconscious. The hesitation is clearly meant to convey that the depth of her feelings for Cain override even her survival programming (Ryan, 'Answers to Your "Razor" Questions'); nevertheless, the moment is not enough to balance the negative representations of lesbianism in the rest of the series.

Indeed, Gina's apparently selfless moment earns her, not the death she had expected,[12] but a berth in Cain's brig and a chance for Cain to repay her for her betrayal. Cain's treatment of Gina is problematic on several levels. It reinforces the concept that Cain makes her decisions emotionally and that those emotions instinctively lead her into bad choices. It also emphasizes the suggestion that she is unfit for command, given her inability to treat a prisoner of war humanely.[13] The most distressing aspect of the relationship, however, is the implication that lesbianism and violence are inescapably related. By structuring the most visible queer relationship on his show around a lead-up of torture and rape and a climax of murder, Moore ensures that queer sexuality is represented as unhealthy. Forbes states that she played the revelation of Gina's duplicity as pivotal to Cain's character and her command:

> It was a massive betrayal. This woman is rarely vulnerable with anyone. She doesn't allow herself that. For her to have taken that step [and become Gina's lover] and been so ultimately betrayed, it did her head in, it did her heart in. She became very misguided at that time.
>
> (Forbes, in Ryan, '"Battlestar Galactica: Razor" Cuts to the Heart')

Although Forbes maintains that 'there's nothing that [Cain] did that some world leader has not done' (in Ryan, '"Battlestar Galactica: Razor" Cuts to the Heart'), series co-creator David Eick believes that Cain's initial appearance presented her as 'someone [to whom] human rights were utterly meaningless in the face of war [and who] epitomized a lot of what was going on in the culture [in America post 9/11]' (in Solove). Cain's methods inevitably reflect the cruel, unusual and degrading forms of torture used at Guantanamo Bay by the American military, which were in the news as her introductory episodes were aired. This reflection and the creators' admissions of their aims suggest that they intended to position her as a monster against whom the righteous characters could set themselves, and that they thought portraying her as queer would assist in that character development. By making Gina both Cain's lover and her target, the show ensures that her sexuality cannot be unwound from the violence of her command style.

The broadcast version of 'Razor' aired in the USA on 24 November 2007. A little over three weeks later, an 'unrated, extended edition' was released on DVD, incorporating approximately sixteen minutes of additional footage. Among the new material are further flashbacks to Cain's childhood, which is presented as extremely traumatic and reveals her to have lost her family in a Cylon raid of which she was the sole survivor. 'That trauma at that young age is what shaped her. As a child, on her own, she had to find a way to survive and that was by hardening herself . . . And if that hadn't happened, who's to say [who Cain would have become]?' Michelle Forbes says in describing Cain's motivations (in Ryan, '"Battlestar Galactica: Razor" Cuts to the Heart'). By tying this backstory to the revelation of Cain's lesbianism, Moore hints towards at least an association, if not a causal relationship, between the two facts: she survived by 'hardening' herself – against pain, but also, the relation implies, against a normal sexuality. Additionally, he brings to mind Havelock Ellis' theory that 'some event, or special environment, in early life had more or less influence in turning the sexual instinct into homosexual channels' (108), which suggests queerness as a negative consequence of traumatic events.

One of the most important factors in the portrayal of Cain's lesbianism is the timeline of the plot revelations. Due to the nature of science fiction storytelling as well as the methods Moore chose to employ, Cain's story is not told in a straightforward manner. The audience first meets her during the last week of her life, in the 'Pegasus'–'Resurrection Ship' arc of December 2005–January 2006. Although we learn much about her, she dies before any context can truly be established. She returns first in the *Battlestar Galactica: Pegasus* tie-in comic in October 2007, in which a small bit of her military backstory is established and her relationship with her family is referred to. In November 2007 'Razor' airs: the queerness that was previously subtextual is canonically confirmed, which in turn provides context for her original appearance. And finally, in December 2007, the unrated, extended edition of 'Razor' is released on DVD, containing flashbacks to Cain's youth that are clearly meant to further contextualize her choices and actions as an adult. Quite aside from the storytelling technique, what is intriguing about the series of events as played out in the story's timeline versus their appearance in real time is the manipulation of information.

Exactly what is revealed exactly when says more about the importance of its previous concealment than does its position in the story.

Cain's initial appearance, as stated earlier, is so brief that it cannot be contextualized. This fact is even flagged in the text, during discussion of the tales of her command circulating between the crews:

> Adama: Context matters.
>
> Tigh: Context? That woman shot an officer right in front of the crew.
>
> Adama: We shot down an entire civilian transport with over a thousand people on board. It says so right there. *[pointing to logbook]*
>
> Tigh: That was completely different . . .
>
> Adama: Which is why I hope the admiral reads the complete log and understands the context.
>
> Tigh: We should ask Admiral Cain for her logs. Just so we can put her in context.
>
> Adama: Wouldn't that be nice.   ('Pegasus')

While she is in command, before she is confirmed as queer, Cain's history exists and is accepted, but is inaccessible to the other officers. Regardless, the impression she leaves both on the crew and on the audience is of a woman unfit for command, where megalomania and thirst for revenge eclipse any humanity she might once have possessed. Official promotional materials even describe Cain as a war criminal.[14] This, then, is the woman we see in the comic book, drinking hard liquor and lifting weights in her attempts to dull the pain revealed in the letters she writes – but does not send – to her dead father, letters in which she continues to apologize for not being strong enough, not being male. And the comic serves as a promotional item for the broadcast version of 'Razor'.

The broadcast version of the movie was essentially a promotional item in itself for the unrated, extended edition. Leading up to the broadcast, there was an awareness that anything might be expanded on, that the movie, meant to illuminate Cain's past, would still be keeping its own secrets. And the very concept of promoting the DVD release as not just 'extended', but also 'unrated', carried certain connotations: the additional material, it suggested, could be risqué, daring, could cause the already mature-rated show to be seen in a different light. And if the broadcast version confirmed Cain's queerness, as was generally known it would before it aired, then what more might surface in an unrated edition?

In fairness, the broadcast version of 'Razor' introduced facts about Cain other than her queerness and her propensity for mentoring young and intense female officers. It deliberately humanized her, or at least attempted to do so. It also contextualized, though did not seek to excuse, her treatment of Gina in 'Pegasus'. Nevertheless, whatever else it did was coloured by its confirmation of her intimate relationship with Gina, which is lent undue weight by the fact that it was concealed in the first place. 'Razor' revealed the depth of the personal betrayal that Cain seeks to revenge on Gina: another layer of humiliation was added to the bodily degradations Gina suffers because she was Cain's lover, creating an understanding of the violation that Cain felt and sought to redress, and that negativity became characteristic of the entire relationship.

Given that the broadcast version contained revelations of such importance to both the plotline and the emotional weight of the show, the DVD version was highly anticipated for what it would reveal further. Its contents gained a certain importance ahead of time by being held back so that their release might become an event. In terms of the storytelling, most of the new details revealed are to do with the development of the Cylons, which are important plot elements; in terms of their emotional weight, they are revealed as part of the details of Cain's childhood, which gives them an entirely different focus. It also further emphasizes the thematic and causal link between her childhood trauma and her adult sexuality, given the way both are treated as 'big reveals'.

Interestingly, this process of extra-textual revelation seems to parallel the plotline that queries the importance of, particularly textual, history. The show presents Cain's story through textual history, oral history and physical history – the ship's logs, the tales that circulate and the razor that represents her philosophy. The razor, which passes from Cain to Kendra and then from Kendra to Kara, is an unspoken legacy, but confers no official status on its recipients; their experiences cannot be represented (see Castle). Similarly, the oral histories, while taken into consideration, are given less importance than the history recorded into the ship's logs. Such history provides context for both Cain and Adama: it legitimizes, immortalizes, their actions and their choices. By the end of 'Razor', however, control of that history has shifted: where Cain was originally the ultimate authority, having to scrutinize Adama's logs as part of her duties as commanding officer, now Adama and Lee are in command. They pass final judgement through that medium:

> Adama: I've been going through Cain's logs, and from a tactical perspective it's hard to find fault in anything that she did, or that Kendra did.
>
> Lee: They butchered innocent civilians, Dad. Come on, how can you ignore that?
>
> Adama: I know that I didn't have to face any of the situations that she did. I had the president in my face, arguing for the survival of the civilian fleet. I had Colonel Tigh keeping me honest, balancing my morality and my tactics, and I had you. Now, you don't have any children, so you might not understand this, but you see yourself reflected in their eyes. And there are some things I thought of doing with this fleet, but I stopped myself because I knew I'd have to face you the following day.
>
> Lee: If you hadn't been in CIC, I would have ordered that strike. Kara would be dead. So would the rest of the team.
>
> Adama: You did nothing wrong. Neither did I. We both made decisions that we had to to accomplish our missions.
>
> Lee: Yeah. Cain. Kendra. Were they wrong?

Adama: If I believed in the gods, I'd say they'd be judged by a
          higher power.
Lee: But since you don't believe?
Adama: Then history will have to make its judgements. And since
          history's first draft will be written in our logs . . .
Lee: Well then, I guess I've got some writing to do.   ('Razor')

This exchange emphasizes their family relationship: Adama
weighs his son as the most important factor in his ability to remain
'human', immediately bringing to mind Cain's lack of family
and indeed her seeming opposition to family relationships. Not
only is history required to be overseen by an ultimate authority,
but at the end of Cain's storyline the authority is entirely male,
heterosexual and patriarchial; it is explicitly portrayed in the text
as a replacement for godly judgement. Cain was ultimately in
opposition to all of these normative organizations, yet they end
up in control of her desire for immortality in the pages of history.
Indeed, her access to that history at all is removed, suggesting
that she does not meet the requirements set out for humanity.
Cain, Gina and Kendra – all the women who showed evidence
of queerness – are dead by the end of the plotline, either by
their own hands or by their lover's. Only Kara remains, uneasily
balanced between her own ambitions and the familiarity of her
relationships with Lee and Adama, walking the tightrope of Cain's
razor. 'Not a lot to show for a life, huh?' she asks in contemplation
of the razor ('Razor'), and in the normative judgement scale, it
certainly isn't. Nevertheless, at the end of the same conversation
Kara absents herself from Lee's command. 'I have a destiny', she
insists. Given the inability of the show to handle the strength of
queer women elsewhere in its history, the end still raises hopes
that Kara's destiny will be one she can herself write.

Ultimately, Kara's rejection of heterosexual bliss with Lee
gestures towards but refuses to define clearly her status as queer.
This cannot redeem the show's treatment of queerness overall,
nor can it suggest why the topic was treated so differently from
other controversial subjects. Moore has all but admitted that the

move was partially intended to 'cause a stir' among the fanboy base, characterizing the 'lesbian angle' as 'fresh territory' more than a textual necessity (Alexandria). Even the later conciliatory move of queering main character Felix Gaeta (Alessandro Juliani) emphasizes the association of queerness with criminality. Gaeta's relationship with Louis Hoshi (Brad Dryborough) is revealed outside the televised canon, in webisodes released in December 2008 and January 2009, and comes to an end within them so as not to impinge on the series itself. Shortly after the revelation and destruction of the relationship, Gaeta conspires to mutiny and takes over command of Galactica. He is ultimately condemned and executed by Adama for his presumption, thus removing any queer influence on shipboard history and reinstating the heterosexual hierarchy ('Blood on the Scales' 4.14). By writing queerness as a monstrosity, an abnormality, an opposition to the historical order within the storyline, Moore gives it a lesser status.

The wider implications of this treatment extend beyond the fictional universe and speak to the perception of queerness as a plotline to begin with. Where the other contemporary social issues dealt with in *Battlestar Galactica* embodied confrontation narratives both within and without the text, forcing both characters and audience members to (attempt to) come to grips with them, the question of queerness is addressed only extra-textually. Within the story, the existence of Cain's relationship with Gina is not questioned; it is the audience who are manipulated into a prejudice towards queerness. 'Razor' writer Michael Taylor admits he is 'not sure why our characters are seemingly more enlightened in [their view of queer relationships] when in every other way they're just as flawed as we are. We've certainly explored themes of both bigotry and class conflict' (in Lo). Taylor's logic is faulty, however: the characters are not 'more enlightened' at all, but are simply not allowed the luxury of a reaction. By ignoring the necessity of addressing queer issues within the text when other social issues have received thoughtful treatment, *Battlestar Galactica* inadvertently but firmly concludes that there are no moral quagmires around the consideration of queerness: its negative portrayal is a foregone conclusion, which speaks sadly to its perceived status as an acceptable plotline in the wider entertainment industry.

Notes

1   In the episodes 'Flesh and Bone' (1.08), 'The Captain's Hand' (2.17), 'Precipice' (3.02), 'Occupation' (3.01), 'Lay Down Your Burdens (Part Two)' (2.20), 'The Woman King' (3.14) and 'Epiphanies' (2.13) respectively.

2   The name 'Cain' is borrowed from the original *Battlestar Galactica* series and thus not a commentary on Cain herself.

3   Hereafter 'Razor', which is included in the episode guide at the end of this book as episode 4.00.

4   At the time of filming, Michelle Forbes was thirty-nine and Edward James Olmos was fifty-eight.

5   Gina's name is not revealed until the last of Cain's three episodes, but I use her name throughout to differentiate from the other Six copy crucial to the arc.

6   All played by Tricia Helfer (in various wigs).

7   Who is, after all, 'like a daughter' to Adama – and only avoided becoming his daughter-in-law because of Zak's death.

8   No mention is made of her father, who is thus conspicuous by his absence.

9   In 'Razor', their mutual dislike is reduced to the level of a titillating catfight by Adama's comment that he'd 'like to sell tickets to that dance', or would pay to see the two of them face off physically.

10   Rated in the UK 15, Canada 14+, USA TV-14.

11   Her parting words to Cain: 'You're not my type'.

12   In 'Resurrection Ship, (Part Two)' Gina declares that she expected to die and be reborn when she completed her mission, but the torture has demoralized her so that she only wants to die without subsequent rebirth.

13   It's worth noting that Cain and the Pegasus crew are vilified for abusing their Cylon prisoner, whereas the member of the Galactica crew who kills *their* Cylon prisoner is given a laughable reprimand

and seen as a hero by the rest of the crew and, by extension, the audience.

14 'What the Frak is Going On – Three Seasons in Eight Minutes', promotional video <http://www.scifi.com/battlestar>.

Works Cited

Ahmed, Sara. *Queer Phenomenology: Orientations, Objects, Others*. Durham, NC: Duke University Press, 2006.

Alexandria, Michelle. 'BSG's Ron Moore Speaks!' Eclipsemagazine.com. 2007. <http://eclipsemagazine.com/2007/11/30/bsgs-ron-moore -speaks-we-discuss-the-battlestar-galactica-crappy-video-games- itunes-razor-strike-dvds-and-more/>.

Castle, Terry. *The Apparitional Lesbian*. New York: Columbia University Press, 1993.

Ellis, Havelock. *Sexual Inversion*. New York: Arno Press, 1975.

Jerwa, Brandon. *Battlestar Galactica: Pegasus*. New Jersey: Dynamite Entertainment, 2007.

Lo, Malinda. 'Tricia Helfer and Michael Taylor on "Razor".' Afterellen. com. 2007. <http://www.afterellen.com/TV/2007/11/razor -triciahelfer-michaeltaylor>.

Ryan, Maureen. 'Answers to Your "Razor" Questions and Clues About "Battlestar Galactica's" Final Season.' Blog. *Chicago Tribune*. 2007. <http://featuresblogs.chicagotribune.com/entertainment_ tv/2007/11/answers-to-your.html>.

—— '"Battlestar Galactica: Razor" Cuts to the Heart of the Matter.' Blog. *Chicago Tribune*. 2007. <http://featuresblogs.chicagotribune. com/entertainment_tv/2007/ 11/battlestar-ga-1.html>.

Solove, Daniel. 'Battlestar Galactica Interview Transcript.' Concurring Opinions. 2007. <http://www.concurringopinions. com/archives/2008/03/battlestar_gala_4.html>.

Tulloch, John and Henry Jenkins. *Science Fiction Audiences: Watching Doctor Who and Star Trek*. London: Routledge, 1995.

Interrogating Galactica
An Interview with Jane Espenson

JENNIFER STOY AND ROZ KAVENEY

Jennifer Stoy and Roz Kaveney: What did/do the writers know about the arc? When did they know it? In interviews, Ron Moore has stated that he radically re-envisioned the ending of the show during the writers' strike – to what extent did this get discussed and what implications did it have for people's plans for their episodes?

Jane Espenson: He did. On the day after the strike ended we met at Ron's house and discussed his ideas for a different approach to the second half of the season. We threw away a couple of outlines as a result, I believe. I don't recall us actually throwing away any drafts – It seems to me that they hadn't been written yet. If a draft was thrown away, I'm sure the writer who wrote it remembers that pretty clearly, of course.

JS&RK: How do episodes get broken at *BSG* compared to elsewhere?

JE: The process was more bottom-up than on a lot of shows – the stories were driven by Ron, but there was a great deal of inspiration coming from the room as a whole. As individual writers, we would even be able to improvise during the script-writing process, adding moments and even changing the story in some major ways. Ron was incredibly open to this kind of fluid process.

JS&RK: The pacing, rather than the elements of the plot, has often been a weak point of *BSG* – for example, the 'quadrangle' of Lee/Kara/Sam/Dee – that is often shored up with finales. Are there reasons this happens?

JE: I'm not sure what you're referring to. Do you mean Lee/ Kara/Zak – that was more central to the finale.

JS&RK: Relatedly, how did the cost of the show affect what story got told when, and what showed up in the series, e.g. Centurions?

JE: Every time a Centurion is in frame, it's a special effects shot. Even if it's just standing there. And, of course, all the space battle stuff was expensive – even just using the full view of the hangar deck required a green screen. So, yes, sometimes you wouldn't be able to afford something you really wanted, some great sequence. But that kind of thing is rarely crucial to a story – the characters are – so it never led to our having to change the stories we wanted to tell. And our effects team was amazing at delivering well beyond what we would think possible. The webisodes were originally designed to use lower-quality visual effects than the show as a whole . . . but the money was found and now they look gorgeous.

JS&RK: What did you think was the worst misfire, and what turned out better than you expected?

JE: 'The Hub' (4.09) probably fills both categories for me. The episode underwent a lot of changes in editing – a big reordering of scenes to make the story more linear, easier to follow. But the finished product works so well that what could've been a misfire turned into something that was much better than I expected. I now count that episode as my favourite of the ones I wrote.

JS&RK: Who are some characters you wish you could have focused on more?

JE: Oh, gosh – Hoshi and Seelix and Racetrack and Paula
and Billy – I never got to write for Billy . . . there are
so many, I could just keep listing them. So many great
characters.

JS&RK: How did you balance the various concerns of your
viewers? There seems to be a large contingent that
would criticize you about action and other 'fanboy'
stereotype concerns vs. people who would call the series
woman-hating and 'sketchy' about gay representation.

JE: I think it's dangerous to write scripts to order. You can't
try to write to what the viewers are asking for – you'll
end up resolving all the conflicts, for one thing, and
for another, you won't be using your own instincts. A
writer has to find the thing in the story that interests
them and trust that there are others out there who will
be interested too. If you're writing to satisfy someone
else's instincts, you're bound to miss the mark. But
you still have to write with sensitivity and conscience.
I certainly hope we did that. I felt that the *BSG* universe
had amazing women characters and presented a much
more gender- and orientation-balanced world than most
shows. It's always possible to do better and I hope to
continue to be given chances to do better. I'm stunned
that anyone would call the show 'woman-hating.'

JS&RK: How did some of the casting of extras come about? I
remember an incident at San Diego Comic-Con when
Ron got asked about all the black Gemenese, followed
by Gemenese being the religious maniacs . . .

JE: I have no idea how extras were cast or placed into shots.
It certainly had nothing to do with anyone's vision for the
Colonies – the divisions between Colonies are designed
to be entirely cultural, not racial. That's explicit.

JS&RK: Parenthood and parent–child relationships are a major
theme of the show. What motivated the show to have

so many major characters to be obsessed with parenthood, even the ones who aren't parents? There seem to be some very problematic moments, such as Caprica Six and Saul's baby, or Laura's relationship with Hera, which is never fully explained . . .

JE: The show's most central premise is about whether or not humanity survives. A certain concern with reproduction comes along with that unavoidably. Once the Cylons were also given an interest in reproduction, it was destined to be a big part of the show. I never saw Laura's relationship with Hera as having anything to do with a concern about parenthood – the idea is startling to me – I saw it entirely as a concern with the survival of mankind.

JS&RK: Did the show's bible ever spell out systematically what the Colonies and the Cylons actually believe? The show had two flavours of monotheism, a polytheist mainstream and a solid minority of agnostics among both humans and Cylons – are you happy that consistency was maintained on this?

JE: I don't recall the show's bible going into great detail about the beliefs on the Colonies, but I think we can take the beliefs that we've seen in the fleet as a good reflection of what they left back home. This is something we're going to explore in a major way in *Caprica*, and I'm very happy to have the groundwork that *BSG* has done already in place.

JS&RK: The show sometimes added important details of people's pasts at a late stage, particularly in the finale. Was it always planned, for example, that Baltar would have a working-class agricultural background? Did the show's bible really did spell out Roslin's dead-by-drunk-driver family, why they never let that play in before now? Where did that come from so late in the game?

JE: Oh yes, the show bible totally covered the tragic accident in Roslin's family. The bible had lots and lots of backstory on various characters – what their parents did for a living, things like that. Some of it had been rendered incorrect or obsolete, so it wasn't something we regularly drew on as an authority, but it definitely reflected Ron's thoughts on the characters in an early stage of the process, and we did turn to it when we were thinking of the backstory elements for the finale. Baltar's working-class background is one of those things that was not in the bible, I believe. I think that was discovered along the way.

JS&RK: What is/was going on with Kara and Baltar's mystic abilities? At times it seemed that they shared the Cylon's ability to 'project', which in Hera is an indication of her half-breed status and in Roslin is presumably a consequence of Hera's blood.

JE: *BSG* takes place in a universe in which there are ineffable forces at work. Sometimes a character (i.e. Head Six) seems to be a manifestation of that force. Sometimes a character seems to be influenced by that force. Sometimes the status of a character is left to the audience to interpret.

JS&RK: Was the presence in the show of two Daniels (plus one in Caprica), always going to be just a coincidence? And why 'All Along the Watchtower'?

JE: Why not 'All Along the Watchtower'? If there's an ageless song in the ether, it seems like a good candidate. And Daniel – well, first off, there weren't two Daniels on *BSG*, unless you count Bulldog, whom I think was named Daniel. But we'd have to know more about what was going on when the first Cylon children of the Final Five were being named to know whether or not that model was connected to any other character. That was never covered in *BSG*.

JS&RK: How much have the mysteries been deferred to *Caprica* or *The Plan*? And why is that? Or is 'God did it' a default explanation which we should use to iron out difficulties?

JE: I would say that *Caprica* and *The Plan* fill in gaps, rather than that they solve mysteries.

JS&RK: We need to ask about *The Plan* without having seen it. What should we be asking?

JE: Great question. You should ask about Dean Stockwell's performance, which is amazing. We are so very fortunate to have him. And Eddie's [Edward James Olmos] directing, which was a delight to behold – I got to watch him work with actors during casting sessions – got to see him teaching acting, which was a revelation. And *The Plan* itself – it's so much fun – it is a revisiting of some events you thought you know everything about.

JS&RK: What is the status re the show's canon of deleted scenes such as Adama's first meeting with Tigh, and the webisodes?

JE: I don't know. I assume these are the sorts of things that go on DVDs, but I don't have specific info on that. I certainly would love to see the 'sodes released as part of the second-half-of Season Four DVD and I've sort of been assuming that would happen.

Thanks to Jane Espenson for answering our questions.

Jane Espenson is one of the most respected scriptwriters and showrunners in Hollywood

On the End, Decline and Fall of Television Shows

ROZ KAVENEY

Most television dramas exist along a spectrum between those which, like David Lynch's *Twin Peaks*, are total serials, to the extent of being nearly impenetrable to new viewers who have not been there from the beginning, and those which, like the various shows in the *CSI* franchise, are largely standalone to the extent that it will only be some way into an episode that one might work out from which season it came by the current state of play in the interpersonal relationships among the forensic teams. Networks anxious about syndication possibilities prefer the latter – an audience that has learned to appreciate the long duration of television box-sets is drawn to the enhanced possibilities of the former.

In *From Alien to the Matrix* (2005), I argued that among the pleasures of significant works of culture, including popular culture, is revisiting in retrospect: 'that the pleasures of the best of these films are not merely those of surprise and exhilaration, but are also that different exhilaration which comes from going around the track a second time and a third' (1) I also argued that all such works have to be read, particularly reread, as provisional, contingent, collective compromises, as thick texts that we read in awareness of the processes that produced them. This is, perhaps, particularly necessary when considering television shows or runs of comics that are serials, produced across time, in changing economic and cultural circumstances. However great the allowances made for those circumstances, if we are going to look at shows, or runs, as autonomous whole artistic enterprises rather than merely judge them episode by episode or issue by issue, we have to expect a certain conscientiousness on the part of creators, a consistent vision. (In Chapter 4 of *Superheroes!*, for example, I discussed how such a consistent vision is one of the pleasures of Grant Morrison's run on *New X-men*.)

Many – one might argue all – television shows are inevitably compromises between the vision of the creator and the demands of the network. It is regularly complained about when shows that were clearly envisaged as having a story arc have a high level of standalone episodes imposed on them – Joss Whedon's show *Dollhouse* (2009–) is a case in point here. The first version of *Battlestar Galactica* was primarily a series of standalone episodes with certain givens that were from time to time complicated or set aside. The reimagined show struck a conscious balance between its overall narrative, ideational and character arcs, and standalone episodes that portrayed the economic and political arrangements of Galactica and its accompanying fleet, or which took its central characters off on brief-lived adventures. It is primarily a serial, one whose standalones are never subjected to a reset button, and sometimes turn out to have more consequences than might have been imagined on first viewing.

There is an implied narrative contract between the show-runners of serial dramas with a strong arc and their audience – a contract that has only in part to do with the proportion of standalone material that sometimes is there to relax the narrative drive of the overall arc, but often serves to slacken tension and diffuse the strength of the narrative. One of the strongest points in that contract is that, at the end of the show, the audience do not feel cheated, that the narrative tension from season to season will have a cathartic pay-off. This chapter will argue that *Battlestar Galactica* fell short in this respect and that its doing so revealed some fundamental weaknesses in its central givens. Specifically, the show-runners were sometimes clumsy with their own continuity, revealing mysteries that were given inadequate solutions, forgetting plot strands altogether, involving the show in radical internal contradictions and opting for lazy mechanisms to get themselves out of writing quandaries to which there were more intelligent solutions. If the standalone episodes never have a reset button, the show does something worse from time to time – it undoes clearly established bits of plot in favour of resolving inconsistencies – the parentage and thus nature of the boy Nicky Tyrol is a case in point.

In an interview with the *Chicago Tribune* Moore addresses this issue:

> We're starting to sort of resolve some of the plot threads and provide answers to things and one of the questions was, 'Is Hera the only hybrid, the only Cylon-human child, or not?' If Nicky was a Cylon-human child, what does that mean? Now there's two of them. It was important to the mythology of the show that only Hera be the only one. We had always sort of said that. . . .
>
> Yeah, we had to retrofit that. We knew that was going to be a problem back when we decided that Tyrol was a Cylon. We said, 'OK, how are we going to deal with that?' And [someone] said, 'Well, maybe at some point we just find out Tyrol's not the father.' And we all kind of laughed. And then we said, 'Actually, that's a very elegant solution to it.' We just say, 'Tyrol's not the father,' and we move on. And that's kind of how the show is. We take these gambles, then we take time to make sure it fits in with what we've got. Or we try to at least address it and make it fit into what we've got, so the mosaic is still consistent.
>
> (Moore, as quoted in Ryan)

It is significant that he regards it as 'elegant' to refit a female character, Cally, whose obsessive love for Tyrol has been one of the show's most consistent emotional currents, as a promiscuous deceiver.

Often, the vicissitudes of television dictate that shows do not get a satisfactory ending, of course – shows die before their time or have artistic compromise forced on them by the network or other circumstances such as Hollywood strikes. We experience this as loss, as the breaking-off of a relationship that was good but ended before its time; this is perhaps one reason why *Angel* (1999–2004) is remembered with rather less nostalgia than *Buffy the Vampire Slayer* (1997–2003), since one show lasted out a natural length – some would say outstayed its welcome a little – and the other had to end on a note of ambiguity rather than completion. *Battlestar Galactica* does not have this excuse.

By contrast, one need only consider the particular satisfaction that comes from a show whose end is entirely a fit with its beginning and its middle. *Six Feet Under* (2001–5) is perhaps an even better example of this than such much-admired shows as *The Sopranos* (1999–2007) and *The Wire* (2002–8), simply because as a show about a family of undertakers it was obliged to have a finale that dealt comprehensively in last things. Some episodes previously, the show's protagonist, Nathan Fisher, had had an aneurism and died and the last episodes showed his wife, mother, brother and sister coping with this. Every death in the show's five seasons has been the occasion for a moment of calm summation when we see the name and dates of the Fishers' clients; Nathan's death is no exception. In the final episode, as his sister Claire drives across country to her destiny as an artist in New York, we see the deaths (and occasionally the marriages) of the characters we have watched for five years, and one after another we see their names and dates, culminating in the death of Claire at an advanced age full of artistic honours (*Six Feet Under*, 'Everyone's Waiting' 5.12). This perfect sense of rounded conclusion is, I would argue, part of the artistic point of television shows and is one of the reasons why we love them.

When a show's conclusion falsifies much of what has gone before, we feel that contract has been broken and betrayed. What, say, was the point of watching the progressive redemption of Irena in J. J. Abrams' *Alias* (2001–6) if at the end she simply and uncomplicatedly dies as a villain? What was the point of the endlessly multipled mysteries of the anachronistic discoveries and inventions of the Renaissance sage Rambaldi if at the end we were to be given nothing convincing by way of solution to those mysteries?

Falling out of love is a process of retrospective disillusion – if the beloved did that, how can they ever have been the person you thought they were? It becomes hard to remember the good times you had together, hard to remember the fascination, easy to construct a version of the past in which you always had your doubts. And, in the case of a television show such as *Battlestar Galactica*, this is more reasonable a process than it often is when dealing with actual people. If the illusion of unity and conclusion is broken, we decide that the show's reality was always a set of artistic compromises, a piece of shoddy carpentry put together in a hurry and for commercial gain.

The eventual set of bad choices that produced *BSG*'s three-part show finale – 'Islanded in a Stream of Stars' (4.18) and 'Daybreak (Part One/Two)' (4.19/4.20) – are both logical outcomes of things that were wrong with the show from the start and decisions that might not have been taken, had things gone otherwise. The show was affected by the writers' strike, though not as disastrously as many others; *Nip/Tuck* (2003–), for example, suffered some substandard scripts and dodgy plot turns, almost certainly because of haste to get scripts shot before the strike.[1]

The alternative ending considered by Ron Moore prior to the strike, in which Ellen Tigh's bad choices led to catastrophe for everybody is hardly an improvement, and points to the ways in which *BSG* was so often a show in which women were punished for sins that men could commit with impunity.[2] He describes the alternative ending thus:

> There was a different ending that we had, it was all about Ellen aboard the Colony. She was sort of turned by Cavil, because she found out that Tigh had impregnated Caprica Six, and that deeply embittered her. And she sort of became dedicated to the idea of destroying Galactica and the fleet out of revenge. And [she and Cavil] got Hera, and then the final confrontation became very personalized between Tigh versus Ellen, and should they forgive.
> (quoted in Woerner)

The original Glen A. Larson show, of which Ron Moore's was a reimagining, was soaked in Christian, specifically Mormon, mythology; as Tony Keene has pointed out, the new show had religion in its DNA, and what's bred in the bone will out in the blood, as they say. Even in the first episode, Six lectured Baltar about the love of a monotheist's God for both the victims and perpetrators of universal genocide and it never occurred to me that we were supposed to take what she said at face value – it seemed the set-up for narrative irony rather than revelation.

Like many viewers, I assumed that the show was going to deconstruct the religious faiths of its humans and humanoid Cylons, that we were going to learn some ultimate truths, and that they would be the sort of ultimate truths appropriate to the decorum of science fiction, which is a literature of reason and not of faith. Almost to the end, this was a sustainable view – after all, when Baltar announced that the Starbuck who had returned from the dead was an angel, and that the visions of Six which had led him through power politics to antinomian religion were another such, we could assume that he was making a mistake, reasonable enough in a man of faith, but that we would learn that his Head Six, and Six's Head Baltar, were rationally explicable in science fictional terms. Most of the points necessary to some non-supernatural explanation were, at various points, thoroughly established – as late as her kidnapping by Boomer in 'Someone to Watch Over Me' (4.17) it is established that Hera can enter the Cylon virtuality, and both Baltar and Starbuck are shown as entering a dream state that in his case at least is clearly established as being the Cylon virtuality. If Hera's ability to enter that virtuality derives, as it is clearly stated it does, from her dual nature, a logical inference would be that those who can do so in some measure share that nature. But, no, at the end of things, in 'Daybreak (Part Two)', Six and Baltar meet their Head Baltar and their Head Six and we are told, yes, these are messengers of the Will of God, and Starbuck realizes that she has been sent back from the dead for a purpose and her work here is done.

Up to this point, the show has been finely balanced in its portrayal of the two religions: the monotheism of the Cylons that has led them to the arrogance of genocide, and the polytheism of the humans, which so often sends them off on quixotic – though often successful – missions that have the character of pilgrimages. We have always seen that there is much to be said for both sides, that these are religions that could equally well both be true or both false. Baltar's cult, which adapts its creator's need to feel comfortable with his sins to the needs of a larger group, draws on Cylon belief, but is more sophisticated in its theology than we ever see theirs being. Roslin's visions, which are so important to the show's portrayal of her as prophet as well as politician, clearly draw from the polytheist tradition in which she was reared. For the show suddenly and arbitrarily to opt for one side in this debate, and thereby junk everything we have seen as positive about the other, is to break faith with an ambiguity that was far more interesting than this final resolution.

There are also inconsistencies here – after all, much of what has got the human fleet to this point has been prophecies in accordance with the mythology and practices of the human religion: the Arrow of Apollo, the Temple of Jupiter, the visions of an opera house consistent with sketches of it in a mystical manuscript. We are shown, in the finale, that Roslin's repeated vision of chasing the child Hera through an opera house with Caprica Six and Athena was, all along, a foreshadowing of a chase through the corridors of the Galactica; in which case, why were the visions earlier shown to be taking place in an opera house that existed once and had left a record in Elosha's mystic manuscript? If the faith that has guided and sustained Laura Roslin is a lie, where does that leave our respect for her? It reduces her from a brave visionary to a pathetic figure who has been deluded all along.

Science fiction is a genre in which problems, once they have been rightly understood, have rational solutions, solutions that are at once a way of ending one story and the start of some slingshot sequel; this is one of the principal sources of science fiction's capacity for the sublime. We reason our way out of imminent death and come out of danger and look out at the stars. This is the promise – some, like Geoff Ryman and the other members of the Mundane Manifesto group would say the dangerous and the fallacious promise – that science fiction offers. To say at the end of the story, *oh well, it's God, innit*, is fundamentally to betray the protocol of the genre– God is the end of conversation and reason rather than their beginning.

God does not have to make sense; he is the ineffable. This means that, in a story, even a story as complex and fascinating as *Battlestar Galactica* had become right up to that moment, he is bad writing and worse plotting. Starbuck dies and is brought back to life to lead people to Earth – God did it; Starbuck was taught by her father to vamp a tune which is also the tune which awoke the Penultimate Four–- this was a divine plan, and God loves Bob Dylan songs; Laura Roslin has fatal cancer briefly alleviated by the blood of a half-human, half-Cylon child – this is God's way of giving her visions of an opera house that will ensure that she protects that child. Starbuck's death, her loss of her father, Roslin's agonizing illness and death – these are all God's Rube Goldberg machine for getting the child Hera born and shipped to Earth. The fact that God could have saved everyone a lot of trouble, and us hours of ultimately disappointing viewing, by simply telling Helo and some random Eight, to make love and get in a spaceship, is irrelevant, because he moves in mysterious ways, which is very handy for Ron Moore and his writing staff if they have an off day.

Nor is all this theodicizing – the creation of theodicies – the only problem with the *BSG* finale. There were the various flashbacks that rewrote the pasts of the characters so as to make their eventual fates more logically palatable – which would have been tolerable had we known all this from an early stage but is less so when it gets made up at the last minute. In an earlier episode, Roslin saw, in a drug dream, that her family waiting for her on the other side of a river across which she is being ferried – here we learn that she lost her sisters, father and her sister's unborn child, in a single car crash, so that her death is a reunion with those she lost, a reunion she once sought by wandering into the middle of a municipal pond. This is noxious sentimentality that cheapens our love of the tough-minded president who kept humanity alive at awful cost.

Similarly, we learn that Lee and Starbuck almost had drunken sex while her fiancé, his brother, lay in a drunken stupor – it is all right that they be denied a happy ending because they are flawed people who behaved in an inappropriate way. Earlier, and at a moment when it affected Chief Tyrol's passionate hatred of him, we learned that Baltar was a working-class scholarship boy; here we learn that he disrespected his farmer father and Six, before wiping out the human race including his father, taught him valuable lessons about how to behave.

All of this would be bad enough in all conscience as a way of reinventing characters we have got to know over four years and who are not easily reduced to these simple formulae. In fact, though, these revisions have a palpable design on us, and that design is to make us swallow one of the daftest plot conclusions in the history of genre. The human fleet gets at last to our Earth in its distant past, and Lee suddenly suggests that everyone throw their ships into the sun, set the Cylon Centurions free to seek their destiny, and abandon technology to live simple lives among the pre-linguistic hominids they find there. When Romo Lampkin announces that 'people are suprisingly amenable to Lee's suggestion', you know that they and the show are doing something staggeringly stupid – let's abandon medicine and live short unhappy lives in the cold. At some level, the writers knew this was daft, or they would not have had one of the show's more sensible characters carry out damage control like this. All this effort to get Hera to Earth to become the Mitochondrial Eve, and she will die in her late teens.

And Baltar, that wonderful complex intellect, and Six, that deadly courtesan, what of them? Well, it is the will of God that they be humbled, that they become the farmers that Baltar should always have been; all that fancy education and carefully acquired social grace is less important in the end than the farming that was in his blood from the beginning. He wins Caprica Six back simply by acting in a manly fashion and taking a gun into his hands, and then they farm – this is of a piece with the engrained American populism that distrusts fancy people with no relish for violence. It is no coincidence that James Callis played Baltar in his own, very English, accent.

A show that has, all along, played with the romance of vast machines – and the heroism of human beings pitted against titanic pieces of metal – suddenly becomes an unconvincing hymn to the simple life and to the casting aside of technology, and medicine, and culture, to wander through an uncluttered paradisical wilderness and die there. This decision is sold to us by the most dishonest of visual rhetorics: where almost every other episode has been set in dimly lit rooms and exteriors under skies that are overcast, the Earth of 'Daybreak' is as sunny, brightly coloured and full of wildlife as New Caprica or Kobol were barren and gloomy. This is effective, but it is also a cheap trick.[3]

Of course, not everything in 'Daybreak' was dross. The end of the first part, where Bill Adama asks people to join Galactica on its last doomed mission, is an effective piece of rabble-rousing, and the space battles early in the two-parter are wonderfully pyrotechnic even if they do not make especial military sense. Both sides pull rabbits out of hats – the ability of the brain-damaged Sam Anders to act as the equivalent of a Hybrid – but the show manages moments of that attractive ingenuity that we describe as cool – Galactica's Centurions being distinguished with a red sash, for example.

All the fighting hand to hand ends up being peculiarly pointless, though, because the Galactica crew end up fighting just far enough into the Cylon base to be *given* the child by Sharon – who has stolen her, again – and then discover that, meanwhile, Cavil's Cylons have fought their way onto the bridge of Galactica and are waiting for them. And then, and only then, Ellen makes Cavil an offer of what he has wanted in the first place: access to the cloning and downloading technologies that created the

Cylons in the first place. It is not only God who goes about things in a bizarre way. Ellen could have made such an offer by radio the moment they got to the black hole before fighting a colossal battle – but where's the fun in that?

The plot then starts depending on weird givens: the technology turns out to have been distributed between the minds of the Final Five for safe-keeping – for a very odd value of safe-keeping – and they have to link their minds in order to access it. Only this leads to Tyrol's finding out that Tory killed Cally, and he kills Tory in revenge, instantly, so that the secret is lost forever. And everyone stands by while he strangles her, with no idea of why he is doing it. And Tory is seen as deserving death, whereas Tyrol, who killed a random Eight to enable Sharon's escape with Hera, is later congratulated by the Tighs on being her executioner. Given that Tory kills Cally to protect the secret identity of the Four, thus saving the life of Cally's son whom his mother is clearly planning to take with her, and facilitating a suicide on which Cally seemed already set, it is hard to answer those critics who suggest that Tory's killing is just another rehearsal of the tired trope of the Tragic Mulatta (see Raimon).

And Cavil, whom the show had gradually made responsible for almost everything, the rebellious creation who had destroyed humanity out of Oedipal resentment, and killed and mind-wiped the Five, and made his amnesiac creator his whore, what happens to this Dark Lord when he realizes his plans are all undone? Why, he suddenly shoots himself in the head, saving everyone else the trouble. This was, we are told, a piece of improvisation by Dean Stockwell – if so, it was a piece of improvisation from which he should have been restrained, because it makes a sudden opportunistic nonsense of his character.

I could elaborate dodgy plot points for pages, but the issue is ultimately this: the finale of *Battlestar Galactica* contains a lot of material that is staggeringly ill-judged as well as concluding with revelations that are a cheat, and an epilogue that is trite and nonsensical. If the whole point of everything that has happened is to ensure that we are descended from Cylons as well as humans, then God has pretty much failed if the end result is that toy robots are a sign that we are about to undergo our own apocalypse. There was so much to love in *Battlestar Galactica* – the sarcastic bad-assery of Starbuck, the quiet sweet-natured fury of Felix Gaeta, the sardonic grumpiness of Dr Cottle, a myriad of interesting doomed characters such as Billy and Kat – and in the end everything is reduced to the staggering cliché that the point of all these travels and deaths is to become our ancestors, a plot twist that was only unforeseeable from the beginning because it is a cliché so total and shop-worn that no one seriously thought writers as talented as Moore, Eick and Jane Espenson could come out with it.[4]

Much of what precedes it, especially in the second half of Season Four but to some degree earlier, is also misconceived and inconsistent. Other chapters in this book also point to some of these weaknesses, as well as to the series' many strengths, and this account does not in any case aspire to be complete or definitive. It will, however, point to some of the areas in which the sexual politics of the show, which had at times seemed admirable, start to fall apart as part of this general process of intellectual collapse.

Battlestar Galactica was always a show about Laura Roslin as well as Bill Adama; I have written elsewhere in this collection about the show's portrayal of Adama as the admirable military man, admirable because in some ways so deeply ordinary. Roslin is a schoolteacher turned politician turned prophet – she is almost by definition extraordinary, and we assume from an early stage that she is destined to die before reaching the Promised Land. This is a mythic structure so embedded in the foundational myths of Western culture that it was an extraordinarily risky strategy – but not thereby necessarily a mistake – for the show to raise the possibility that she is not the only doomed leader.

Starbuck has her mystic destiny and is able to lead humanity to the end of its journey, or possibly to their end if the Hybrid in 'Razor' (4.00) is to be believed, precisely because she has had a Gandalf-like death and resurrection. The Cylon leader Natalie is shot – oddly without consequences – by Athena as a result of misunderstanding, and dies, but has brought the Cylon rebels to their destiny, which is to join the fleet of the humans they had tried to wipe out. Nonetheless, when Laura Roslin announces in the course of Baltar's trial ('Crossroads (Part One)' 3.19) that her cancer has returned, we assume that she has become the doomed leader yet again, and so, to some degree, she proves to be. She sees the human race to both the radioactive version and the shiny new version, and then dies quietly and without fuss.

The trouble with this is that the process of dying gives Mary McDonnell less and less to do except portray a slow death, and this is something which inevitably produces diminishing returns the longer it goes on. She does a wonderful job of it in 'Faith' (4.06), where she has an encounter with a one-off character, played by Nana Visitor (who had worked with Ron Moore on *Deep Space Nine*). There is a problem with this episode, though, which is that, placed where it is, it feels like a standalone, intended to demonstrate the quality of McDonnell as an actress, rather than an entirely convincing moment in the arc of Laura Roslin's dying.

Subsequent to this, after all, we have in 'The Hub' (4.09) the culmination of her suspicions of Baltar. Roslin, who has spent some three and a half seasons suspecting Baltar of involvement in the destruction of humanity, gets final and definitive proof of his responsibility, if not of his guilt, and realizes that she cannot justify letting him die, after all. This is an impressive moment – one of the central moments of the show in some ways – and it comes, in part, from her visions of the dead priestess Elosha. As with so much in Roslin that is admirable, it derives from her faith; as I have remarked above, to discount the tenets of that faith and to endorse the monotheism of the Cylons and Baltar as a resolution of the show's plot, is retrospectively to weaken such moments both in terms of plot logic and in terms of our respect for the characters involved in them. Her wisdom in this act of forgiveness derives in part from a vision of her own imminent death, of course, but it is not, it has to be noted, in any sense a true prophetic dream. Roslin's eventual death has only Adama in attendance and takes place on Earth rather than in an almost empty Galactica, with several people at her bedside. It is a false dream that leads to right action, and as such needs more glossing than it gets in the show.

Laura Roslin has a last finest hour during the mutiny, in 'Blood on the Scales' (4.14) when she addresses the fleet from the Cylon basestar where she has taken refuge and makes it clear that the seizure of power by Gaeta and Zarek is an illegality that will be resisted. She and Adama are both at their best in the fight back against the coup – not least because their love for each other and their sense of duty are for once entirely unified. Adama is told that Roslin is dead and does not despair; she makes it clear to the plotters that she will fight them to the last: 'I will end you', she says. Television space opera has a small pantheon of completely impressive female characters – *Babylon 5*'s Delenn and Ivanovna, *Farscape*'s Aeryn Sun – and Roslin when in this mode, or judging Baltar, is entirely worthy to be in their company; it is a shame that, given how little she had to do in the remaining six episodes, Laura Roslin did not die at the height of her powers.

To feel that the Roslin of the last episodes is a waste, one does not have to believe – as both my colleague Jennifer Stoy and I have been to some degree inclined to – that for much of the show's run, it was intended that Laura Roslin rather than Ellen Tigh would be revealed as the unknowing last Cylon. One of the problems with the decision to, instead, show her as a woman dying and running out of energy as she dies is that, however plausible this artistic decision is in terms of strict realism, it is something that the show should, in strict realism, have done two seasons earlier. Instead, Laura Roslin was saved, by Baltar, with a concoction of Cylon-human hybrid blood; it is, to put it mildly, implausible that at no point during her relapse was this panacea tried again, and yet it is not, nor is any explanation given, even in terms of outrageous technobabble, as to why it would not work. Not only is this careless plotting, but – given the emphasis of the later episodes of the show on the virtues of hybridity – it is

peculiar that that this original foreshadowing of the possibility
of hybridity being a good thing is entirely neglected

The show is radically undecided about this issue of hybridity,
in the end. On the one hand, we get such powerful images as
the patching of Galactica with Cylon resin and the placing in
the shrine to dead pilots images of the Cylons who had died
in the raid on the hub. On the other, we have the revision of
where things had stood earlier so that Hera is the only viable
hybrid. Nicky is revealed not to have been Tyrol's son, which
retrospectively makes Cally's obsessional love for her husband
and suicidal impulses when she discovers he is a Cylon more than
a little odd, if she was sleeping with another man and fathered
that man's child on Tyrol. Even more bizarrely, the hybrid child
conceived by the two kinds of humanoid Cylon, Saul Tigh and
Caprica Six, miscarries when Ellen Tigh returns and is angry that
her widower slept with another woman. The child literally dies
in the womb because its father stops loving its mother; this is
magical thinking. Given this, it has to be assumed that there will
be no hybrids other than Hera, that her combination of human
and Cylon blood will feed into future humanity, but that every
Cylon apart from Athena – all of the Sixes and all the other
Eights, and Leobens – will die childless on Earth. They gave up
their immortality to die sterile, a terrible human tragedy that is
presented to us as if it were a happy ending.

For much of the show's length it offered fascinating and
admirable female role models, but in the last ten episodes almost
all of those characters are diminished, not only Laura Roslin.
We have already seen Athena murder the Cylon leader Natalie
over a misunderstanding of her intentions in respect of Hera; we
now see her vengefully kill Boomer, her more than sister, at a
point when the endlessly wind-changing Boomer has repented
yet again and returned the child she stole. It is not clear,
either, whether Athena kills her for her many betrayals, or for
kidnapping her child in the first place, or simply because Boomer
seduced Helo after knocking Athena on the head and stuffing
her in a cupboard to watch. Dee despairs and kills herself; Tory

is throttled; D'Anna maroons herself on the radioactive Earth. I have already mentioned how Caprica Six dwindles into a wife. The second half of the last season of *Battlestar Galactica* is not a safe place for women characters, and particularly not for women of colour.

The one exception to all of this is Ellen Tigh, who is revealed in 'No Exit' (4.15) to have been the brilliant Cylon scientist who created resurrection technology and the skin jobs and was betrayed by her own creation, Cavil.[5] At the moment when Kate Vernon wakes in a resurrection vat as the Ellen we have known – she sees a Centurion and panics, and then shakes her head and comes to the remembrance of the deeper richer person she has been in the past and now is again, while still being the Ellen we have known – we see a wonderful performance that sells material that is a deal less convincing.

The backstory we get is, after all, not especially clear as a key to the show's mythology. Ellen and the other four of the Final Five are the only survivors of a world full of skin job Cylons who were destroyed in an atomic war at a point when she had just invented resurrection. They downloaded into new bodies on a ship in which they travelled at sub-light speeds to the Twelve Colonies, where they found a human–Cylon war already underway and mediated its end by promising the Centurions a new generation of skin jobs. One of these, Cavil, the first, resented that he was not a machine with machine senses and murdered his parents, downloading them into bodies on the Twelve Colonies without their memories, in the hope that, after the genocide he planned, and which they would survive through resurrection, they would accept that he was right. It is hard to say which character comes out of this looking dafter, Cavil or Ellen.[6]

Wonderful as Vernon's performance in 'No Exit' is, the show generally thereafter forgets that she is this cold and unsympathetic intellect and reverts her to being the same Albee-esque bitch queen that she had been in the first two seasons. We are supposed to see the love she shares with Saul Tigh as eternal, but it is distinctly toxic as well; she is vicious to Caprica Six, whom

Saul loved when he had every reason to believe Ellen dead and gone, at the expense of the hybrid embryo that by uniting the skin jobs with their creators might have offered her entire species a future. Some of the time Ellen Tigh is supposed to be the mother of her race and sometimes she is a petty vindictive housewife; the combination makes her quite remarkably unsympathetic to an extent that one has to attribute to misogyny. This is what happens when women get power, we are being told – they use it badly, unlike men.

The portrayal of Ellen as the creator of the Cylons is an unresolved paradox and as such only one aspect of an even larger unresolved paradox at the heart of the show. Constantly, both humans and Cylons refer to the skin jobs as machines, as programmed, as either inferior or superior because they are not human. Yet they are flesh and blood, and bleed and feel pain; even their vaunts of superiority rapidly segue, in the hands of Cavil, into annoyance about not being perfect with infrared senses that sounds humanly petulant. It is far from clear, come to that, that the 'machine' Cylons – the Raider Scar who seeks vengeance, the other Raiders who refuse to fire on the awakened Four – are machines in the sense of only being their programmes; can a machine feel an emotion and, if so, can it be held to be a machine? When that 'machine' is made of flesh and blood – as even the 'machine' Cylons appear to be in part as we see in 'You Can't Go Home Again' (1.05) – in what possible sense does this war of human and machine make sense? The Cylons believe themselves to be cold rational machines, but they are under just as much of a misapprehension as are the humans when they call the Cylons toasters. It may be that *Caprica* will resolve this paradox; as it is, we are left with a profound sense that both the Creator, and the creators, of these characters has left them fairly thoroughly in an existential lurch.

And yet, and yet … if we did not care so much about the characters in whom Ron Moore and his team made us invest so heavily for four years, it would be impossible to be so infuriated by the missteps of the show's final phase. If *Battlestar Galactica*, in the last analysis, stumbles, it is because it was a show that – in its handling of politics, religion and the influence of character on both – gave us reason to judge it by the highest of standards. It was a television science fiction show that demanded to be taken as seriously as any other drama to a degree that even its best predecessors had never quite done; it gave itself a misson statement of refusing the comfortable cheesy clichés in which even the best sci-fi shows had indulged – the semi-parodic aliens of *Farscape*, the mysticism of *Babylon 5*.[7] *Battlestar Galactica* set a high standard to beat – and then fell short of it itself. There is a sadness in this ultimate failure that comes from the magnificence of much of the show's achievement.

Notes

1   In 'Candy Richards' (*Nip/Tuck* 5.12) for example, Eden shoots Julia, faking a suicide attempt, and the investigating police officers fail to take routine swabs for gunpowder residue.

2   See for example the interview with him (Woerner).

3   We see sunlight in the flashback to the Final Five's last day on their original planet – it is not clear whether this is intended to indicate that it is the future of our Earth, or whether it is simply something else that was not thought through properly.

4   This plot is known mockingly, in sci-fi critical circles, as the Shaggy God story – the term was coined by Brian Aldiss in 1965 in *New Worlds* magazine. It is standardly listed as a cliché to be avoided in, for example, Shiner Sterling.

5   The episode's title, and the way that for much of its length it takes place in a room, with Ellen, Cavil and Boomer bitching at each other, is presumably a reference to Jean-Paul Sartre's play *Huis Clos* (1944), which is often translated thus, but I don't feel that the insight that Hell is Other People is especially relevant here.

6   It may, of course, be that the upcoming *Battlestar Galactica – The Plan* or the *Caprica* prequel series will make all of this clearer and more palatable; it is clear, though, that as a series *Battlestar Galactica* ends up looking oddly incoherent, and perhaps more so after all this explanation.

7   See for example, Sergio Dias Branco's chapter in the present volume, for the way its design avoids the clichés of genre television and film as well as Ron Moore's professed desire to 'get out of this sci-fi ghetto'.

Works Cited

Kaveney, Roz. *From Alien to the Matrix*. London: I.B.Tauris, 2005.

—— *Superheroes!* London: I.B.Tauris, 2008

Raimon, Eva Allegra. *The 'Tragic Mulatta' Revisited*. New Brunswick, NJ: Rutgers University Press, 2004.

Ryan, Maureen. '"Battlestar Galactica's" Ron Moore discusses "A Disquiet Follows My Soul."' *Chicago Tribune*. 23 Jan 2009. <http://featuresblogs.chicagotribune.com/entertainment_tv/2009/01/battlestar-galactica-ron-moore-disquiet-follows-my-soul.html #more>.

Shiner, Lewis and Bruce Sterling. 'Turkey City Lexicon – A Primer for SF Workshops'. Updated edn. 2009. <http://www.sfwa.org/2009/06/turkey-city-lexicon-a-primer-for-sf-workshiops/>.

Woerner, Meredith. 'The Battlestar Galactica Finale You Didn't See'. io9. 23 Mar 2009. <http://io9.com/5180872/the-battlestar-galactica-finale-you-didnt-see>

Appendix
Battlestar Galactica Episode Guide

Editor's Note: The nature of *Battlestar Galactica* complicates episode guides – the reimagined series began life as a miniseries, the television show itself contains seventy-three standard American television episodes, then there is also a television movie that counted as part of Season Four, three sets of 'webisodes', and an upcoming, second television movie. Everything except the television movie *The Plan* will be included in this guide. Webisodes will be placed in between the seasons where they aired, though this does not always conform to the chronology of the series.

Further, the multiple names used by characters and the multiple versions of Cylon models are nearly as confusing as a Russian novel. To prevent confusion, certain characters will be referred to by the following names:

Kara Thrace = Starbuck
Lee 'Apollo' Adama = Lee
Karl 'Helo' Agathon = Helo
The Six that appears to Baltar only = Head Six
The 'Baltar' that appears to Caprica = Head Baltar
The Six in a sexual relationship with Baltar before the attacks = Caprica Six
The Eight in a sexual relationship with Helo and is Hera Agathon's mother = Athena
The Eight in a relationship with Chief Galen Tyrol = Boomer
William Adama = Adama
Chief Galen Tyrol = Tyrol

Miniseries

The miniseries introduces us to the Twelve Colonies of Kobol, after a war between the Colonials (human) and the Cylons, intelligent robots developed by the humans to make life easier. The Cylons rebelled and went to war. The miniseries starts forty years later, when humanoid-looking Cylons appear and perpetrate nuclear attacks on the humans, killing all but about forty thousand humans. The only remaining military vessel is the ageing battlestar Galactica, commanded by Commander William Adama. Battlestars carry Vipers, smaller ships that attack targets: Adama's best pilot is a young woman named Kara Thrace, but known by her call sign 'Starbuck'. The ship also includes Raptors, a form of space helicopter. The most prominent Raptor pilot is another young woman, Sharon Valerii, also known as 'Boomer'. Because Galactica is being decommissioned and turned into a space museum, Adama's estranged son Lee has been sent to the ceremony, which is also attended by the minister of education, Laura Roslin. The attacks happen shortly after the ceremony. Roslin is elevated to the presidency after her ship is saved by Lee; the two of them gather a civilian fleet of survivors. Adama encounters the pair and is conflicted about whether to protect the fleet and accept Roslin as the top authority or to go on the attack against the Cylons. While Adama decides, all the humans go to Ragnarok anchorage and find a strange man named Leoben Conroy there. Adama realizes after Leoben attacks him that Leoben is a Cylon and Cylons can now look like humans. He also realizes that Roslin is right and humanity cannot attack the Cylons; they must flee. They make an agreement and at a group ceremony for the dead, Adama lies to the gathering and tells them that he knows the way to Earth, a planet of legend in Colonial mythology.

Also during the miniseries, Dr Gaius Baltar discovers his lover, a beautiful blonde woman, is a Cylon and that she has been using him to get access to security codes that the Cylons used to disable the fleet defences. He survives the initial attacks thanks to her and runs across Boomer and her co-pilot Helo on Caprica as their Raptor removes the last survivors from the planet. Helo gives up his seat for Baltar, who is returned to the fleet. Baltar tells everyone he is able to detect Cylons and identifies a man named Aaron Doral as a Cylon simply to take suspicion off himself. However, and strangely, Doral is indeed a Cylon. We also discover that Boomer is a Cylon, unbeknownst to her and anyone else, and that there are only twelve Cylon models.

Season One

'33' (1.01) The Colonial Fleet suffers the effects of extreme sleep deprivation as the Cylons attack them every thirty-three minutes, requiring constant faster-than-light (FTL) 'jumps'. Boomer continues her relationship with Chief Tyrol. Head Six insists God has a plan for Baltar, who is now constantly having hallucinations of her both on and off his former home on Caprica. On Roslin's orders, Lee destroys a civilian ship, which may contain evidence of Baltar's involvement in the attacks, because it is the way that the Cylons are tracking the fleet. On Caprica, Helo is on the run from Cylons when he is reunited with a woman he believes is Boomer, but is a different Number Eight whom we will later know as Athena.

'Water' (1.02) Boomer finds herself alone in an arms locker with no idea where she is or how she got there. She is soaking wet and near a container with missing bombs. She only tells Tyrol about it. Not long after, an explosion destroying Galactica's water tanks put the entire fleet in danger of destruction. Tigh's alcoholism is established. Baltar and Kara meet and flirt, while Helo and Athena stay on the run on Caprica. Adama informs top leadership (Roslin, Tigh, Lee and Baltar) that there is a Cylon on Galactica. Lee anguishes over the destruction of the civilian ship before helping Roslin and Adama establish more cordial relations during Roslin's first official visit to Galactica since their original agreement. Boomer finds a planet with water after a long search and coming out of a fugue state where it is implied she may blow herself and her Raptor up. Roslin establishes Lee as her special liaison to the military.

'Bastille Day' (1.03) The Colonial Fleet needs people to mine the ice on the planet from 1.02. They offer the work to a ship of convicts, who are led by revolutionary/terrorist Tom Zarek. Zarek takes control of the ship and hostages – Lee, Specialist Cally, Petty Officer Dualla (Dee) and Billy Keikeya, the president's aide, who are there negotiating. Baltar continues work on a Cylon detector he has basically made up. Tigh and Starbuck continue to clash. On Caprica, Helo and Athena try to find other humans. A Six and a Five discuss the couple's trek, suggesting that Athena is a Cylon agent. Lee negotiates a solution with Zarek – sovereignty for the prison ship and democratic elections in exchange for the ship's labour, preventing a bloodbath by a team of Galactica marines desired by Zarek. Roslin tells Lee she has cancer.

'Act of Contrition' (1.04) After an accident kills many of Galactica's pilots, Adama demands that Starbuck train new ones while a military investigator looks at the incident. Training the pilots triggers Starbuck's memories of Zak Adama, whom she allowed to pass Basic Flight even though he was not qualified – an incident that led to Zak's death. Adama learns of this and coldly rejects Starbuck. Guilt-stricken, Starbuck and her new pilots get into a battle with eight Cylon Raiders and she crashes her Viper on a desolate planet.

'You Can't Go Home Again' (1.05) The Adama men go to extraordinary lengths to rescue Starbuck; these actions are eventually shut down by Roslin as a waste of resources and a risk to the fleet. Starbuck finds a crashed Cylon Raider and discovers how to fly it while nursing a broken leg. Athena is 'kidnapped' by Centurions to further the Cylon plan for Helo and Athena.

'Litmus' (1.06) A Five perpetrates a suicide bombing on Galactica, partially facilitated by Boomer and Tyrol's ongoing romantic liaison. The incident forces Roslin and Adama to admit that Cylons can look like humans now and to create an independent military tribunal, led by a Sergeant Hadrian. Hadrian becomes obsessed with Tyrol's actions, causing many of his deck crew to commit perjury to save him. Adama is forced to shut down the tribunal, observing that it has become a witch-hunt, and to reprimand Tyrol for his actions, causing Tyrol to end his relationship with Boomer. Back on Caprica, Athena and the other Cylons observe Helo, revealing the test is to see if Helo is in love with Athena and if he will try to rescue her. When he does, Athena is beaten to prepare for her reunion with Helo.

'Six Degrees of Separation' (1.07) A Six calling herself Shelley Godfrey appears on Galactica with falsified evidence of Baltar's very real involvement in the attacks. Baltar desperately tries to 'prove' his innocence by appealing to any and all authorities, and is finally induced to pray by Head Six to save himself. At this point, Godfrey mysteriously disappears, the evidence is proved false, and Baltar is exonerated. Roslin's cancer treatment causes her to collapse. Boomer reacts strangely to the Cylon Raider. On Caprica, Helo and Athena have sex.

'Flesh and Bone' (1.08) Leoben Conroy appears in the fleet, claiming that there is a nuclear warhead hidden among them, set to go off. Roslin orders Starbuck to interrogate the Cylon to discover the location of the warhead. Starbuck tortures the prisoner and wrestles with that emotionally as Leoben plays mind games with her. Roslin begins to have strange visions. Leoben is finally executed on Roslin's orders, but not before he suggests to her that Adama is a Cylon.

'Tigh Me Up, Tigh Me Down' (1.09) Tigh is reunited with his wife Ellen, who immediately ruffles feathers among Galactica's command with her outré ways. Roslin suspects Adama of being a Cylon, and demands that Baltar test him with his new Cylon detector. Meanwhile, Adama wants Ellen tested as a Cylon as well. During all of this infighting, Baltar actually discovers that Boomer is a Cylon but keeps it from her at the suggestion of Head Six. In a possible plot hole, Ellen is tested for Cylonity and Baltar tells the others that the test is negative.

'The Hand of God' (1.10) With fuel running low in the fleet, the Colonials must attack a planet currently held by Cylons to get tylium to create fuel. Starbuck, Lee and Tigh create a plan to take the planet from the Cylons; using a variation on the 'Trojan horse' – a squadron of Vipers led by Lee takes the fuel planet and destroys the Cylon base. Roslin and Baltar both continue to have strange visions and both are certain that they are divinely inspired, though it remains unclear whether they are right. Helo discovers that Cylons look like humans now, while Athena is unusually nauseous.

'Colonial Day' (1.11) The Colonial Fleet has a political summit at the hitherto unmentioned luxury ship, Cloud Nine. Zarek, who has become the voting representative from the former planet Sagittaron, outmanoeuvres Roslin by declaring that she needs a vice-president and humbly suggests himself for the duty. Roslin, dubious of Zarek's motives, eventually chooses Baltar as her candidate and wins the election. Head Six begins to suggest parenthood to a rattled Baltar. On Caprica, Helo discovers that Athena is a Cylon and is not Boomer, as he previously believed.

'Kobol's Last Gleaming (Part One)' (1.12) Boomer and her co-pilot, Crashdown, discover the legendary planet of Kobol, where all human (and Cylon) civilization began; however, so have the Cylons. Roslin and Adama come into conflict, because Roslin's scriptures tell her that by going to the Tomb of Athena on Kobol with the Arrow of Apollo (which is on Caprica), they will find the way to Earth. She thus wants to use the captured Cylon Raider to go back to Caprica and retrieve the arrow. Adama wants to use the Raider to land a bomb on the Cylon basestar and blow up the Cylons. Things become more critical when a team of engineers and Baltar are stranded on Kobol with Cylons surrounding them. Roslin eventually convinces Starbuck to go to Caprica for the arrow, much to Adama's dismay. In less crucial subplots, Boomer tries to commit suicide because she's fairly certain she's a Cylon, Baltar and Starbuck have semi-disastrous sex, and Athena attempts a reconciliation with Helo.

'Kobol's Last Gleaming (Part Two)' (1.13) The team stranded on Kobol must find places to hide from the Cylons. During this period, Baltar has a vision of Head Six and an Opera House – and finally a child, 'the shape of things to come'. Athena tells Helo that she is pregnant with the first half-human, half-Cylon child, which reconciles them. Starbuck returns to Caprica, and fights and kills a Six to retrieve the Arrow of Apollo before discovering Helo and Athena. The discovery that Athena/Boomer is a Cylon distresses Starbuck. Back in the fleet, Adama and Roslin get into a tense standoff as he demands her resignation and she refuses. This standoff is not helped when Lee refuses to arrest Roslin. When Roslin then surrenders, Tigh arrests both of them. Boomer is sent to the Cylon basestar on Kobol and destroys it, but not before discovering that she's a Cylon. When she returns to Galactica, she shoots Adama twice, ending the season.

Season Two

'Scattered' (2.01) Tigh must guide Galactica through twin crises: Adama being shot and being separated from the rest of the fleet due to a mistaken FTL jump. Shaken, he remembers how he and Adama rejoined the fleet after the First Cylon War and finally agrees to Gaeta's plan of using networked computers, which allows Centurions to get onto the Galactica, even as it serves to reunite Galactica with the fleet. On Kobol, there is a command conflict brewing between Tyrol, Baltar and Crashdown as Crashdown, the least experienced of them, is the one technically in charge. Crashdown's leadership leads to the death of another engineer on Kobol as Cally and Tyrol retrieve a medical kit from the crash site to save a critically injured crewmate, Socinus. On Caprica, Athena steals Starbuck's Raider, much to the dismay of Helo and Starbuck, who must continue on foot to find a way off-planet.

'Valley of Darkness' (2.02) Centurions get aboard the Galactica and the remnants of the Cylon virus cause ship performance problems. In the ensuing chaos, Roslin has to escape the brig to flee Cylons, and Lee and a group of pilots have to fight against the Centurions. Lee eventually kills the last Centurion and Roslin narrowly escapes death at their hands. Helo and Starbuck hide out in her old apartment, pondering a way off-planet. On Kobol, Baltar continues to have visions and is slowly being converted to Head Six's ideas. Despite his heroic actions, Tyrol must euthanize his crewmate Socinus, further increasing the tension among the Kobol survivors.

'Fragged' (2.03) The Quorum of Twelve arrive on Galactica, demanding to see Roslin. Roslin is deteriorating rapidly due to a lack of her cancer medicine, and when Ellen discovers this, she goads Tigh into having the Quorum see Roslin, believing this will discredit the president. However, Roslin outmanoeuvres Tigh and declares to the Quorum that she believes herself to be a prophesied leader with a plan to get them to Earth. In retaliation, Tigh declares martial law. On Kobol, Crashdown becomes erratic as a result of post-traumatic stress, and the others are at increasing risk because of his plans to dismantle a weapon to improve their chances for rescue. Baltar finally kills Crashdown in front of the others, just before they are rescued, to Head Six's approval.

'Resistance' (2.04) On Caprica, Helo and Starbuck meet the human resistance, led by sports superstar Samuel T. Anders. Starbuck immediately falls for Anders. Back on Galactica, Roslin and Lee decide martial law is a step too far, especially when Tigh's marines kill civilians. Lee makes a deal with Zarek with the assistance of some Galactica officers and gets himself and Roslin off Galactica. Tyrol, accused of being a Cylon again, is thrown in the brig with Boomer. Despite appearances, he is devastated when Cally kills Boomer at Baltar's instigation.

'The Farm' (2.05) Starbuck gets shot in a Cylon raid, taken to a hospital, and meets a 'doctor' named Simon who steals her ovary and plays mind games with her. Unsurprisingly, he is a Cylon implicated in a breeding farm where the Cylons are using human women to try to create Cylon-human hybrids. Starbuck destroys the farm and as she escapes, the resistance and Athena appear, saving her. Athena, Helo and Starbuck return to the fleet; Anders is left behind. On Galactica, Adama has returned to command and is trying to hunt down Roslin and Lee. Roslin, meanwhile, convinces a third of the fleet to go with her to Kobol to await Starbuck, splitting humanity.

'Home (Part One)' (2.06) Starbuck returns to Kobol with the arrow – and Helo and Athena. Roslin, while pleased about the arrow, is none too pleased about Athena, until Athena says she can help them find the tomb. A small group then goes down to the planet's surface: a land mine kills Roslin's priestess friend and Cylons attack them, though Lee and Starbuck fight the Cylons off. Back on Galactica, Adama considers abandoning Roslin's third of the fleet until Dee chides him about dereliction of duty. Head Six suggests to Baltar he might not be human, which upsets him.

'Home (Part Two)' (2.07) On Kobol, Roslin's group struggles along until intercepted by Adama and a group that agrees to help them. Zarek's underling, part of Roslin's Kobol group, arms Athena, who then dramatically explains to Adama that she is not the same as Boomer, before killing Zarek's underling. Adama, Roslin, Starbuck and Lee enter the Tomb of Athena, which shows them a star map to Earth. At this point, Adama and

Roslin are reconciled and the fleet continues on its way to Earth. Baltar, having discovered there is no Cylon chip in his head, is nonetheless shaken to discover Athena's pregnancy, which comes uncomfortably close to Head Six's prophecies.

'Final Cut' (2.08) Outlaw journalist D'Anna Biers angers Adama after her documentary about the riot in 2.04. Roslin convinces Adama to give Biers unlimited access to Galactica to make another piece about the military serving there. While this is going on, the head of the military group responsible for the riot stalks Tigh and Ellen, and Tigh eventually talks the young man down after the man kidnaps and menaces Ellen. Biers makes a positive documentary that pleases Adama and Roslin, but there is a twist: she is a Cylon and has transmitted footage of a pregnant Athena back to the Cylons.

'Flight of the Phoenix' (2.09) Chief Tyrol is running out of material to repair new Vipers with, so decides to make a new type of ship. Everyone is resistant to his plan at first, but slowly begins to help, culminating in the 'blackbird', a stealth ship that cannot be detected. Roslin's cancer is reaching terminal stages. Meanwhile, a Cylon virus infects the ship's systems and requires the help of Athena to stop it as well as give the fleet an upper hand in a battle against the Cylons.

'Pegasus' (2.10) *[The episode reviewed is the 'extended' version on the Season Two DVDs, not the aired episode. Very little is different plot-wise; character scenes are extended.]* Another battlestar, Pegasus, discovers the fleet. Pegasus is commanded by Admiral Helena Cain, who takes control of both ships as a senior military officer. She then explains to Adama and Roslin that a Cylon fleet has been following Galactica the entire time and she is attempting to deal serious military blows to the Cylons, a plan that pleases many soldiers on Galactica. However, Cain's ruthless behaviour towards civilians and vicious treatment of Cylons – particularly a Six, Gina, who has been repeatedly raped – leads to discontent, culminating in a disagreement with Cain declaring Helo and Tyrol guilty of murder. The two battlestars are ready to attack each other over this matter as the episode ends.

'Resurrection Ship (Part One)' (2.11) Starbuck averts the confrontation between battlestars twice over – first by discovering that the mystery ship Cain has been tracking is a 'resurrection ship' where dead Cylons regenerate, and second, by assisting Lee in disseminating this news, causing Cain and Adama to cease fire. Impressed, Cain promotes Starbuck and a wary alliance to destroy the resurrection ship is formed with Adama. However, it is clear that the alliance between Cain and Adama/Roslin will not survive much beyond that. Roslin and Cain both decide that someone must die, leaving Adama in the middle. Adama wrestles against the cold-blooded murder of Cain, even as evidence of Cain's barbaric behaviour mounts. Finally, he orders Starbuck to assassinate Cain, as Cain orders her first officer to do the same to Adama after the resurrection ship is destroyed. Meanwhile, Baltar's interest in the badly traumatized Gina increases.

'Resurrection Ship (Part Two)' (2.12) The united battlestars attack and destroy the Cylon resurrection ship. Lee barely survives the mission and the blackbird ship is destroyed. Baltar 'breaks up' with Head Six due to his obsessive interest in Gina. After the attack ends, both Adama and Cain back off their previous murderous intentions towards the other. However, Cain finds Gina waiting in her quarters. Gina kills Cain with a gun given to her by Baltar as he helps her escape. A now-dying Roslin promotes Adama to admiral of the fleet after Cain's funeral.

'Epiphanies' (2.13) As Roslin's cancer is about to kill her, she flashes back to just before the attacks, revealing that she was the lover of former President Adar, and that she had seen Baltar with Caprica Six after receiving her cancer diagnosis. Baltar saves Roslin's life with blood cells from Athena's foetus – ironically, because one of Roslin's last decisions is whether or not to abort the hybrid foetus. This act is doubly ironic because Roslin informs Baltar that she doesn't think he's mature enough to be president in a traditional letter given to one president by the outgoing one. Roslin also manages to outmanoeuvre a peacenik civilian group (partially run by Gina as a front) sabotaging ammunition, a sign of her return to power.

'Black Market' (2.14) A disaffected Lee is investigating the murder of Commander Fiske of Pegasus. We discover that Lee is depressed because of his dead, possibly pregnant girlfriend who died on Caprica in the attacks, and that he is handling his depression by going to a prostitute on Cloud Nine. The prostitute has a young daughter whom Lee has helped with medicine. In Lee's investigation, he discovers and then kills the head of the fleet black market, who has been helped by Zarek.

'Scar' (2.15) Starbuck is disaffected and drinking heavily because she cannot rescue Anders from Caprica. Her irresponsible behaviour causes tension, particularly with the pilot Kat, who had been Starbuck's temporary replacement while Starbuck was on Pegasus. The two pilots are also in competition to kill 'Scar', a Cylon who has been mercilessly killing pilots protecting a mining operation. Kat actually kills Scar, but Starbuck steals her moment of glory by commemorating the many dead pilots who gave their lives to protect the fleet.

'Sacrifice' (2.16) A hostage situation involving Lee, Dee, Billy and Ellen Tigh arises on Cloud Nine when a civilian mourning her husband demands Athena so that she can kill the Cylon. Adama refuses to negotiate, and most attempts to outplay the civilian group fail, including a particularly feckless attempt by Starbuck. Billy is killed and Lee is wounded in the action that finally kills the civilian woman and most of her group, and we discover that Dee and Lee are romantically involved.

'**The Captain's Hand**' **(2.17)** Two Vipers go missing from Pegasus, and Adama sends Lee to figure out their fate. When the stubbornness of the current commander of Pegasus gets the commander and several soldiers killed, Adama makes Lee the commander of Pegasus. Meanwhile, a pregnant young woman from a repressive Colonial culture sets off a firestorm surrounding abortion, forcing Roslin to outlaw the procedure (after the young woman gets one). Roslin also manages to offend Baltar, causing him to run against her for president, with the help of Zarek.

'**Downloaded**' **(2.18)** We follow Boomer's experiences on Caprica after her resurrection following the events of 2.04. Boomer and Baltar's lover Six – now known as Caprica Six – start a political movement declaring that the genocidal attacks on humans were wrong after they have saved Anders' life from D'Anna Biers on Caprica. On Galactica, Athena has her baby and Roslin steals it, ordering Dr Cottle to tell Athena the child is dead while giving it to a young woman named Maya to look after.

'**Lay Down Your Burdens (Part One)**' **(2.19)** Roslin looks guaranteed to win the presidential election until the discovery of a marginally habitable planet in a nebula that could hide humanity from Cylon detection. At the behest of Head Six and Zarek, Baltar declares that if he wins the election, they'll settle on the planet, an act that turns the electoral tides in his favour. Meanwhile, Starbuck finally gets her wish and is allowed to return to Caprica to rescue Anders and the resistance, which she does. Tyrol is slowly deteriorating mentally and is counselled by a nihilistic priest named Brother Cavil.

'**Lay Down Your Burdens (Part Two)**' **(2.20)** Starbuck returns home with Anders and another Brother Cavil, revealing Cavil as a Cylon. Both Cavils are executed. Roslin loses the election and decides to fix the vote with the help of Tigh, Dee and her aide, Tory. Adama discovers her deception, prevents it, and Baltar is elected president. The fleet settles on the planet, named 'New Caprica', and ekes out a miserable existence, especially after Gina destroys Cloud Nine and her chances of resurrection with a nuclear explosion. Ironically, this explosion leads the Cylons to New Caprica eighteen months later, where they easily defeat the planet-bound population, which includes Baltar, the Tighs, Starbuck, Roslin and Tyrol, while the battlestars and a few other ships, led by the Adamas, jump away.

Season Three

'The Resistance' (W01–10) *[These are ten webisodes, played on scifi.com, that link Seasons Two and Three. They are also included on the Season Three DVDs.]* Tigh and Tyrol attempt to recruit new resistance members while also hiding a weapons cache in a temple. The Cylons attack the temple in an attempt to find them, killing the wife of the potential recruit named Duck. The event causes Jammer, a former deck hand and member of the resistance, to defect to the New Caprican police force. Duck also joins the police – as a double agent.

'Occupation' (3.01) The show resumes 134 days after Baltar's surrender to the Cylons, and everyone remaining on New Caprica is miserable. Tigh loses an eye and has been imprisoned, released only because Ellen is having an affair with Cavil and funnelling information to the Cylons. Starbuck has been imprisoned by Leoben, who returns, no matter how many times she kills him, and declares that he will help her find her destiny. Tyrol and Anders plot violent attacks on Cylons; Tory and Roslin do behind-the-scenes work for the resistance. Baltar, though reunited with Caprica Six, remains a virtual prisoner among the Cylons. The human insurgency gets more violent, leading to a suicide bombing at the graduation of the secret police. The Cylons are divided about how to handle the human insurgency; the Adamas are divided on whether they can retrieve the population of New

Caprica. A small glimmer of hope appears, however, when the resistance and Adama's people make contact.

'Precipice' (3.02) In response to the suicide bombing, the Cylons imprison many people, including Roslin and Cally. Baltar attempts to get Roslin to help him decry insurgent violence, but she refuses. The Cylons eventually force Baltar to sign an extermination order condemning many people – including Roslin and Zarek – to death. Starbuck remains trapped with Leoben, who claims that they have a daughter, whom he leaves with Starbuck. Meanwhile, the resistance coordinates efforts with Galactica. Galactica is still unsure of how to retrieve the New Caprican population and Lee is dubious that it is possible. Finally, Athena, who has joined the crew of Galactica, is dropped with the insurgents on New Caprica, who come under attack.

'Exodus (Part One)' (3.03) In a slight rewind, Tyrol and Tigh learn about the extermination order and rally the resistance to save the people about to be shot. Anders and Athena survive the Cylon raid and realize that Ellen is a collaborator. D'Anna Biers has strange dreams and upon consulting a human oracle, discovers that Athena's daughter is alive. She then tells Athena of this when Athena crosses her path on a mission to retrieve launch keys for the resistance. Galactica and the resistance are now in the final stages of countdown to the evacuation – which nobody might survive.

'Exodus (Part Two)' (3.04) Lee saves the day and allows the evacuation of New Caprica by destroying Pegasus. Tigh poisons Ellen for collaborating. Starbuck is saved by Anders and discovers the child Leoben gave her is not actually her daughter. During the battle, Hera's foster mother is killed and Hera is rescued by D'Anna. Baltar is taken along with Caprica Six and the other Cylons.

'Collaborators' (3.05) A group of former resistance leaders known as the 'Circle' are investigating and executing collaborators thanks to an ex officio order given by Zarek during his brief presidency before he returns power to Roslin in a complicated parliamentary manoeuvre. Gaeta is nearly executed by this group before it is revealed that he was the inside man in Baltar's government for the resistance. Roslin, displeased by the precedent, grants all of humanity a blanket pardon for New Caprica. Baltar is trapped on the Cylon basestar, dependent on Caprica Six – who is not happy with him – for survival.

'Torn' (3.06) Starbuck and Tigh continue on a nihilistic downward spiral, splitting the crew on Galactica and causing Adama to issue an ultimatum – shape up or leave the service. Starbuck comes back to work, but Tigh does not. On the basestar, Baltar discovers the Hybrid – a humanoid being that controls each Cylon ship and who babbles gibberish that might be important. He also learns that the seven known Cylon models are significantly different from the other five, who are not on basestars. Both Cylons and Colonials continue on the path for Earth, heading for a particular nebula. However, Cylons get fatally ill when approaching the nebula and Baltar must investigate the deaths, all while worrying that he is also a Cylon.

'A Measure of Salvation' (3.07) D'Anna tortures Baltar for information about the virus on the nebula. With the help of Head Six, Baltar survives the torture and forms a strange connection to D'Anna. Meanwhile, the Colonials discover the Cylon-killing virus and decide to use it on the Cylons. They also discover, via Cylon contact, that Baltar is alive. Helo, however, decides that their plan is wrong and prevents the biological warfare.

'Hero' (3.08) An old comrade and pilot of Adama's called Bulldog returns to the fleet from Cylon imprisonment, surprised at Adama's demotion. It's revealed that during his time on the battlestar Valkyrie, Adama was sent to play a game of chicken at the Cylon armistice line and left Bulldog behind – beyond the line. These events, a year before the attacks, may have convinced the Cylons that the Colonials were ready to attack. Bulldog finally attacks Adama, who is saved by Tigh, who then returns to duty. Adama must further be recognized for forty-five years of military service by Roslin, who informs him that his flaws will be ignored for the greater good. On the basestar, D'Anna is having strange dreams and sharing Baltar with Caprica Six.

'Unfinished Business' (3.09) The episode transitions between no-holds-barred boxing matches on Galactica and flashbacks to a ground-breaking celebration on New Caprica. We discover Starbuck and Lee had sex, professed love . . . and then Starbuck chose to marry Anders instead. Roslin and Adama spent significant time together discussing the future that same night, causing Adama to let Tyrol and Cally resign from Galactica. In the present, Starbuck and Anders maintain a sexual relationship, though Starbuck and Lee also have a strange connection. Adama finally gives a speech that declares that they need to get professional again and stop pining for New Caprica.

'The Passage' (3.10) With food supplies running low, the fleet's only way forward is through a radiation-heavy sector of space. The Viper pilots are forced to shepherd near-empty ships at great personal risk and do so. Kat dies of radiation after heroic efforts that are inspired by trying to prove to Starbuck that she can overcome her past as a petty smuggler. On the basestar, D'Anna and Baltar are increasingly obsessed with the vision D'Anna saw after dying and before resurrection.

'The Eye of Jupiter' (3.11) Tyrol finds a strange ancient temple on the planet where the fleet is harvesting food. It may contain the legendary Eye of Jupiter, further directions to Earth. The Cylons intersect with the fleet not long after its discovery and Baltar and a Cylon delegation come to Galactica, demanding the Eye. When the Colonials refuse to give it to them (not that they have it), the Cylons send the Centurions to the planet's surface. Boomer informs Athena that Hera is alive and ill; Helo and Adama also learn of the news and are appalled. But before this new information can be processed, a very unlikely supernova threatens both fleets.

'Rapture' (3.12) While the Cylons debate whether to attack the humans, D'Anna ignores the consensus and takes herself and Baltar to the temple, where D'Anna sees a vision of the Final Five Cylons before being permanently boxed by the other Cylons. Baltar, meanwhile, is picked up by the humans and put in jail. Tyrol continues trying to decipher the message in the temple and partially succeeds. Starbuck, we discover, has been drawing pictures of the Eye of Jupiter since childhood, but the significance of this is unclear. Meanwhile, Anders and Lee quarrel over saving Starbuck from danger; despite currently having an affair with Starbuck, Lee sends his wife Dee to rescue her. Dee and Starbuck rescue each other and return to Galactica. Helo shoots Athena so that she can resurrect on the basestar and rescue Hera, which she does with the assistance of Caprica Six. Caprica Six and Athena return to Galactica, where Caprica Six is immediately arrested as both fleets continue on the way to Earth.

'Taking a Break From All Your Worries' (3.13) Despite the food shortages, the Colonials still have the resources and will to create 'Joe's Bar' in a secret location on Galactica. Lee and Tyrol have been spending a great deal of time at the bar, alienating their wives. An extremely angry Roslin decides to drug and torture Baltar to get as much intelligence about his actions during the occupation of New Caprica and while he was among the Cylons. Baltar is more worried that he's a Cylon, until Gaeta stabs him with a pen, an act that Baltar narrowly survives. Starbuck's art may hint at a larger destiny for her.

'The Woman King' (3.14) Helo discovers that a doctor who has been working among the Gemenese, a religious fundamentalist minority, has been giving them substandard medical care because of his prejudices, thanks to a woman named King who alerts him to the problem though she is not believed by the upper echelons of Galactica.

'A Day in the Life' (3.15) Adama hallucinates his dead alcoholic wife, Carol Ann, speaking to him on their wedding anniversary. He admits to her that he is strongly attracted to Roslin, but will not undertake a relationship with her for ethical reasons. Lee also tells his father that Carol Ann was an abusive drunk and that the dissolution of the marriage was not entirely Adama's fault. Tyrol and Cally get stuck on the wrong side of an airlock and nearly die except for a daring rescue; they reconcile after previous marital problems. Roslin also suggests Lee should be in charge of starting a trial or tribunal to handle Baltar's fate.

'Dirty Hands' (3.16) Civilian labour on the fuel ship is on strike because their conditions are shockingly unsafe and there is child labour, strongly suggesting the end of any social mobility. Tyrol, having seen these conditions after being sent to end the strike by Adama and Roslin, expands the strike to a general one. The strike is short lived and Adama threatens Cally's life, but Tyrol does win some minor concessions from Roslin for the workers. Baltar has also become an unlikely hero of the working class, thanks to his clandestine book, *My Triumphs, My Mistakes*.

'Maelstrom' (3.17) Starbuck, who has been on a downward spiral since her imprisonment by Leoben on New Caprica, begins hallucinating to the point of nervous breakdown. The subjects of her hallucinations are her harsh mother, who died alone of cancer after abusing Starbuck while telling her she had a special destiny, and also Leoben. At the end of the episode, Starbuck chases a phantom Cylon Raider into a space maelstrom (which looks very like her previous art) and disappears, causing everyone to assume her dead.

'The Son Also Rises' (3.18) Baltar gets a new lawyer, Romo Lampkin. Lampkin convinces Lee to assist him and Baltar in the name of justice, which Lampkin does not feel is being met by Roslin and Adama, causing Lee to leave military service. Meanwhile, Lee continues to mourn Starbuck, as does Anders, who breaks his leg doing so.

'Crossroads (Part One)' (3.19) While Baltar's trial begins well for the prosecution, Lampkin quickly convinces Caprica Six not to testify against Baltar, and Lee scores when cross-examining Roslin by getting her to admit she's using chamalla again. Roslin tells the court that her cancer has returned. She also has a vision of herself and Athena chasing after Hera in the opera house previously seen by Baltar in 1.13; Athena has the same vision. Tigh, Tyrol, Anders and Tory hear odd music that no one else can hear in the ship and begin acting strangely.

'Crossroads (Part Two)' (3.20) Baltar is found not guilty, thanks to Adama's deciding vote, and is spirited away by a group of women who believe in his message. Athena, Caprica Six and Roslin consult on their shared visions. The Cylons attack the fleet and, during this attack, we discover Tigh, Tyrol, Anders and Tory are Cylons. Also during the attack, Starbuck appears in her Viper and tells Lee she has been to Earth and will take them all there.

Season Four

'Razor Flashbacks' (RF) *[These webisodes were shown before the premiere of the television movie 'Razor' (4.00) on scifi.com.]* These focus on Adama's youth as 'Husker'. On the last day of the First Cylon War, his girlfriend is disfigured by a Cylon attack, the battlestar he flies for is under attack, and Husker chases Cylons down to a planet. He discovers Cylons are experimenting on humans and sees in a vision an elderly male Hybrid telling him that all this has happened before and all this will happen again. The narrative ends with the war.

'Razor' (4.00) *[A two hour television movie, may also be considered 4.01 and 4.02 in terms of production number.]* Razor has four main narrative tracks. There is the track that covers Pegasus from the attacks until Cain's death at the hands of Gina, which reveals that Gina and Cain were romantically involved. This storyline is largely from the point of view of Kendra Shaw, a young officer who is involved with the shooting of civilians on Scylla and is trusted by Cain. In another narrative track, set between 2.17 and 2.18, Shaw is appointed Lee's executive officer and sacrifices her life to rescue people from a basestar. In this same basestar, she hears a cryptic prophecy about how Starbuck will 'lead them to their end'. In two more historical narrative lines, we find Cain's family died on the last day of the first war, and that Adama discovered that Cylons were experimenting on humans, leading to the creation of Cylon-human hybrids.

'He That Believeth in Me' (4.01) Starbuck is back with directions to Earth. Roslin is certain that Starbuck's a Cylon and that this is a trap. Starbuck is shocked that she's been gone for months, not six hours, and has picked up the ability to feel if they are going in the right or wrong direction, which of course opposes Roslin's directions. Anders interacts with a Cylon Raider, stopping the battle in progress. This, plus other dilemmas, are on the minds of the four secret Cylons. The remaining five Cylons are also on the mind of Roslin, who demands answers from Caprica Six and does not get them. Baltar, meanwhile, has found a home among a number of beautiful women who venerate him as a prophet. The episode ends with a faceoff: Starbuck is aiming a gun at Roslin, demanding that they follow *her* path to Earth.

'Six of One' (4.02) Starbuck and Roslin's armed faceoff ends with Starbuck in the brig and Adama torn: he cannot bear either woman to be angry at him. In the end, the main fleet stays on

Roslin's course, while Starbuck and a crew of Galactica stalwarts go on a reconnaissance mission using Starbuck's directions. The four secret Cylons send Tory to seduce Baltar to get more information about the final Cylon; he knows nothing, but Tory has an affair with him anyway. Baltar also finally sees Head Baltar, a version of himself Caprica Six has seen before. In the Cylon fleet, civil war is brewing. The Sixes, Eights and Leobens want to unbox D'Anna and find out about the Final Five, while also making mechanical Cylons autonomous again. The Cavils, Fours and Fives disagree and win because Boomer turns on the other Eights. The leader of the Sixes finds this unbearable and kills everyone in the conference room and makes Centurions autonomous again.

'The Ties That Bind' (4.03) Cavil, in light of last episode's massacre, sets a trap for the Cylons opposed to him, agreeing to unbox D'Anna only to slaughter the opposed Cylons too far from resurrection to regenerated. We also discover that Cavil and Boomer are involved. On Galactica, Cally is slowly going insane from insomnia and depression when she discovers Tyrol and the other three are Cylons. She plans to commit suicide with her toddler son, but Tory intercepts her, retrieves the child, and kills Cally by sending her out of an airlock. Meanwhile, Zarek is attempting to use Lee, the new delegate from Caprica, to oppose Roslin's executive overreach, with mixed results. Starbuck and her group, which includes Gaeta, Helo, Anders and Athena, continue to search for Earth as more and more of the crew feel Starbuck is out of her mind.

'Escape Velocity' (4.04) When interrogating Caprica Six in the brig, Tigh begins seeing Ellen, and has sex with Caprica-as-Ellen. Cally's death hits Tyrol hard, finally causing Adama to demote him. Tory is still spending time with Baltar and his nascent cult; however, Baltar's followers are in danger, thanks to anti-Baltar thugs. Roslin tries to use this as an attempt to cut Baltar's power base apart, but Lee resists this, declaring it is a danger to freedom of association. Baltar, aware of his advantage, begins preaching to a wider audience, declaring they are all perfect and God loves them as they are.

'The Road Less Traveled' (4.05) Starbuck's ship discovers the remnants of the anti-Cavil Cylons, who are in desperate need of assistance. Among them is Leoben, who immediately isolates himself with Starbuck to find answers. This galvanizes an already dangerous situation, as most of her crew thinks she has no idea where Earth is – and especially annoys Anders, who is already worried because of Starbuck's anti-Cylon tendencies. Baltar's following continues to grow, and Baltar attempts to find a high-profile convert in the form of Tyrol. Tyrol, who continues to be very angry about Cally's death and his Cylonity, refuses loudly; however, Baltar offers comfort later privately, and Tyrol accepts this.

'Faith' (4.06) Anders quickly ends the anti-Starbuck mutiny and in the chaos Gaeta is shot in a way that forces amputation of his leg. Starbuck decides to go to the Cylon ship alone to test if the offer is a trap. It isn't, but Starbuck also encounters the Hybrid, who reiterates that Starbuck will lead them 'to their end' and that D'Anna will be able to identify the Final Five, causing Starbuck to make temporary alliance with the rebel Cylons. Back in the fleet, Roslin gets cancer treatment and meets a dying woman who believes in Baltar's theology, which shakes Roslin's faith to an extent.

'Guess What's Coming to Dinner' (4.07) While the Colonial Fleet is divided over the idea of allying with Cylons, Roslin and Adama both see the benefits of uniting to find Earth as well as identifying the remaining Cylons in the fleet and agree to help get D'Anna back. The deal is sweetened when the Six in charge offers Roslin a chance to take out the 'hub' and end Cylon resurrection. The four Cylons in the fleet are less pleased, as they are unsure they want to join the Cylons. In his radio broadcasts Baltar tells the entire fleet that Roslin is having shared visions with Cylons; Hera is also beginning to share in the visions. The visions include many images of Six, which upsets Athena and causes her to kill the leader Six in a hallway, when Hera crosses her path. Finally, Roslin finds Baltar and takes him and pilots to the basestar to talk to the Hybrid; when they do, the Hybrid immediately jumps away with both of them aboard.

'Sine Qua Non' (4.08) The fleet is dealing with the double shock of Athena's assassination of the Six and Roslin and Baltar being kidnapped by the Cylon basestar. Zarek attempts to take over, but with Adama refusing to deal with Zarek, Lee and Romo Lampkin intervene. The political manoeuvring ends with Lee as acting president. Meanwhile, tensions grow between Adama and Tigh, as Adama is angry at Tigh for impregnating Caprica Six, and Tigh is angry at Adama for not admitting that he is angry at Roslin for leaving without him *again*. Adama finally admits that his personal feelings for Roslin outweigh his interest in keeping the fleet safe, and takes a Raptor to wait for Roslin while leaving Tigh in charge of Galactica.

'The Hub' (4.09) While Adama waits for Roslin, Roslin begins seeing her dead friend, the priestess Elosha, during FTL jumps. Elosha explains that Roslin needs to find love to be a better leader, and this theory is put to the test when Baltar is serisously wounded and admits he is responsible for the Colonial genocide. Roslin almost lets him bleed out, but changes her mind. Everyone involved blows up the resurrection hub, ending the practice of Cylon resurrection, and they unbox D'Anna, who is the only member of her model left. D'Anna also explains that the fifth of the Final Five is not with the fleet, but she knows who the other four are. The basestar returns to the waiting Raptor, and Roslin tells Adama she loves him.

'Revelations' (4.10) A standoff situation develops when the basestar returns to the fleet: if the secret four do not return to the basestar, D'Anna will begin executing hostages. The four, who are unsure if they want to return to the Cylons, do not know what to do – Tory sneaks aboard, pleased to be a Cylon, Tigh admits he's a Cylon, and the other two are also revealed, ending the hostage situation only because they help Starbuck discover the coordinates to Earth in her Viper. Most of the fleet, human and Cylon, are also shocked about Caprica Six's pregnancy, but this pales in comparison to the shock they find when they reach Earth – a nuclear wasteland.

'The Face of the Enemy' [*This, the third and last set of* Battlestar Galactica *webisodes, aired in the lengthy hiatus between the first and second half of Season Four.*]

'Sometimes a Great Notion' (4.11) Earth's desolation and the revelation that it was the Cylon home planet rocks the fleet. The four Cylons have flashbacks to their lives there, culminating in Tigh realizing that his wife Ellen is the final Cylon. The Colonials are more distressed: Roslin burns her scriptures and withdraws from human interaction and Dee commits suicide. D'Anna decides to remain on Earth. Starbuck and Leoben discover the wreck of Starbuck's Viper from the events in 3.17, as well as her body, leading to the question: who or what is Starbuck?

'A Disquiet Follows My Soul' (4.12) The only people even moderately happy after the loss of Earth are Caprica and Tigh, who are delighted about their unborn child's development; their happiness alienates Gaeta. Roslin continues her withdrawal, ends her cancer treatment, and starts having an affair with Adama. Tyrol discovers his wife had an affair and his son is not his. Meanwhile, Zarek is making the Cylon–Colonial alliance extremely difficult via political game-playing. Adama finally has him arrested and bluffs, informing Zarek he has proof of Zarek's treason about a missing ship. Zarek seems to fold, but instead contacts Gaeta and begins plotting mutiny.

'The Oath' (4.13) Zarek and Gaeta execute their plans for mutiny and uprising. The Cylons on Galactica are detained and beaten while Gaeta sabotages Adama and Tigh's attempts to control the fledgling uprising. Starbuck and Lee, who are aware of Zarek's treachery, begin a counter-resistance on Galactica, rescuing Roslin from Adama's quarters. Roslin must retake power upon hearing of Adama's peril. Once Adama becomes aware of Gaeta's treachery, Gaeta takes over the bridge and demands Adama's resignation and arrest. Adama and Tigh manage to escape Gaeta's jailors and reunite with Lee, Starbuck and Roslin. While Roslin and Baltar escape Galactica for the basestar, Adama and Tigh are left behind to fight against those who have taken over Galactica.

'Blood on the Scales' (4.14) The Cylons are unnerved by the civilian uprising and consider leaving the fleet. Roslin deters them from this and effectively demands control of the basestar while giving Adama time to retake Galactica. Baltar, also on the basestar, admits he dislikes his followers, but that he must return to them because they are his responsibility. Adama, recaptured by Gaeta's forces, is given a secret show trial by Zarek, disgusting Lampkin, who is Adama's lawyer. Zarek also kills the civilian Quorum of Twelve when they oppose him. Sentenced to execution, Adama and Tigh are not shot, thanks to Lee and Starbuck, who have spent most of the episode liberating the Cylons in detention. Anders, however, is critically wounded during the Cylon escape. Meanwhile, Tyrol gets control of the ship away from Gaeta, allowing Adama to retake Galactica and preventing Roslin from attacking the fleet with the basestar, which she strongly considers doing when she is told Adama is dead. Once order is restored, Zarek and Gaeta are executed.

'No Exit' (4.15) Ellen Tigh's life post-resurrection, stuck on a basestar with Boomer and Cavil, is retold to us and we discover that after the resurrection hub is destroyed, Cavil is so desperate he threatens to experiment on Ellen to get the information from her. Boomer prevents this by helping Ellen escape and return to the fleet. Back in the fleet, Anders' head injury has caused him to remember their past lives on Earth, that downloading came from Kobol, and that Cylons can reproduce biologically. This takes a toll on him and he is permanently brain damaged at the end of the episode. Roslin and Lee reformulate the nature of democratic representation in the fleet, and Roslin puts Lee in charge. Adama must use Cylon technology to keep Galactica flying, much to his chagrin.

'Deadlock' (4.16) While various Cylon allies try to repair Galactica and tensions between the crews remain high, Ellen Tigh returns and the Final Five Cylons must decide whether or not to stay with the fleet or return to the Cylons and abandon humanity. Boomer has also returned and reconnects with Tyrol. Ellen's return causes Caprica Six to miscarry after a fight between Tigh and Ellen causes Ellen to declare that Tigh's real love is Adama. Baltar returns to his followers and tries to help the general public against violent civilian gangs hoarding food.

'Someone to Watch Over Me' (4.17) While hanging out with a mysterious piano player, Starbuck remembers a strange tune from her youth that is also known by Hera Agathon that may have something to do with Starbuck's mission. The Cylons in the fleet wish to execute Boomer for war crimes; Tyrol does not agree with this and helps her escape. Unfortunately, Boomer has been the inside man for Cavil the whole time and, while escaping, she kidnaps Hera after throwing Athena in a closet and causing even more damage to Galactica.

'Islanded in a Stream of Stars' (4.18) Ellen explains that Cavil will take Hera to the 'Colony' to experiment on and the humans must decide whether to rescue the child or not. The four have hooked Anders into Galactica as a sort of Hybrid, which nobody else knew, causing fluctuations. Starbuck discovers that she definitely found her own dead body on Earth, and Baltar reveals that to the rest of the fleet. Baltar also meets Caprica Six again. At Roslin's urging, Adama decides to abandon Galactica.

'Daybreak (Part One)' (4.19) As the fleet strips down Galactica, Adama discovers that Anders can find the 'Colony' and decides Galactica's last mission will be to rescue Hera – an all-volunteer mission that includes a very ill Roslin, Baltar, and the Final Five Cylons. We also learn a great deal about the main characters' pasts, split over this episode and the next: Roslin's father and sisters were killed in a drink-driving accident and she got into politics only after that, Starbuck and Lee nearly had sex the first time they met (while Starbuck was still with Zak), and Adama refuses a civilian job because it feels dirty. Caprica met Baltar's father, and found the man a good retirement home, starting their love affair.

'Daybreak (Part Two)' (4.20) Adama's volunteer crew goes to the 'Colony'. Hera is rescued by Boomer, who turns the child over to Athena and is shot dead for it. In the next skirmish, Caprica and Baltar rescue Hera while Athena and Roslin follow close behind, fulfilling the opera house vision. After a bloody battle in Galactica CIC, Cavil says that the fighting can stop if the Final Five will restore resurrection. Ellen agrees, but in the doing, Tyrol discovers Tory killed Cally. He then kills Tory, destroying that chance and reviving the battle. Cavil's forces are wiped out by accident and by the Galactica crew, and when Adama desperately orders Starbuck to escape the black hole that the colony is located above, she types in notes from the song and finds a habitable planet that is apparently 'our' Earth. The fleet decides to scrap all of the starships and Anders guides them into the sun. Roslin dies, and Starbuck was apparently an angel sent to guide humanity to Earth. Caprica and Baltar reunite, as do Athena, Helo and Hera. Hera is apparently 'Mitochondrial Eve,' and the ancestor of all living people, which Ron Moore reads as Head Six and Head Baltar look on and comment, implying our technocratic culture may lead to another 'cycle'.

Index

Characters

The main entries for characters are under the name by which they are usually referred.

Creators and Actors

Subjects